We the People

IN THE SERIES

Critical Perspectives on the Past

EDITED BY

Susan Porter Benson, Stephen Brier, and Roy Rosenzweig

We the People

Voices and Images of the New Nation

*Alfred F. Young and Terry J. Fife
with Mary E. Janzen*

Temple University Press
Philadelphia

Temple University Press, Philadelphia 19122
Copyright © 1993 by Temple University
All rights reserved
Published 1993
Printed in Canada

Library of Congress Cataloging-in-Publication Data

Young, Alfred Fabian, 1925–
    We the people : voices and images of the new
    nation / Alfred F. Young and Terry J. Fife ; with
    Mary E. Janzen.
        p.   cm. — (Critical perspectives on the past)
    Includes bibliographical references and index.
    ISBN 0-87722-937-6. — ISBN 0-87722-938-4 (pbk.)
    1. United States—History—Revolution, 1775–1783.
2. United States—History—1783–1815. I. Fife, Terry J.,
1954– . II. Janzen, Mary E., 1943– . III. Title.
IV. Series.
E208.Y68   1992
973.3—dc20   92-1596

This book is based on the Chicago Historical

Society's permanent exhibition *We the People:*

Creating a New Nation, 1765–1820.

THE COLOR REPRODUCTIONS IN THIS BOOK

ARE MADE POSSIBLE BY A GRANT FROM THE

ILLINOIS HUMANITIES COUNCIL, the National

Endowment for the Humanities, and the

Illinois General Assembly.

Contents

INTRODUCTION

Remembering the American Revolution

The Tree of Liberty

The Tree of Liberty that a New England militiaman carved on his powder horn in 1776 was the most common symbol of the ideals of the American Revolution. It was a symbol of defiance of arbitrary authority and of the rights of people to be ruled by representatives of their own choice and to be protected in their natural rights.

Beginning in 1765, Bostonians designated a giant elm on the main road into town as their Tree of Liberty and conducted demonstrations there resisting British measures. Town after town all over the colonies either set aside a Tree of Liberty or erected a giant Liberty Pole. The tradition reached back centuries in England and Europe to celebrations centered on the maypole and May tree.

In 1775 Thomas Paine published a poem set to music that declared that the Goddess of Liberty had planted the Liberty Tree in America and as a result:

> The fame of its fruit drew the nations around,
> To seek out this peaceable shore.
> Unmindful of names or distinctions they came,
> For freemen like brothers agree;
> With one spirit endured, they one friendship pursued,
> And their temple was Liberty Tree.

Powder horn made by
James Pike, 1776

LIBERTY } PRO
TREE. } DE

In 1809 John Adams wrote two letters to a political friend about the attitudes of Americans to their history. His thoughts still ring true. Adams was alarmed at "a very extraordinary and unaccountable Inattention in our countrymen to the History of their own country." The country's "original Historians" of colonial times were "very much neglected," their books unavailable. Patriots like Samuel Adams and John Hancock, who had played a major role in the making of the Revolution, were "almost buried in oblivion," and the histories that were appearing were "Romances." In a second letter Adams lamented that "the History of our country is getting full of Falsehoods," especially because it was partisan history based on tales spread by his own political enemies.[1]

Adams's litany of complaints—public indifference to American history, once-famous leaders now forgotten, romantic history, partisan history, history "full of Falsehoods"—could have been compiled in almost any generation. That these complaints were written within only one generation of the Revolution suggests how soon after the Revolution Americans turned history into legend and myth. In the creating of a nation there was a need to glorify the past, create heroes, and find symbols that would bind the new nation together. Furthermore, as the historian Michael Kammen has pointed out, the Revolution had liberated Americans from the past and denied them their colonial heritage. In welcoming whatever was new, in prizing change over tradition, Americans had turned away from history in general.[2]

This process may help explain why present-day Americans find the era of the Revolution so inaccessible. The history of this period is obscured by hero worship and sacred symbols; even the legends that attempt to humanize godlike figures make them too good to believe. It is hard to see past the legends, to separate myth from reality, or to challenge the sacred. Consequently, many people are put off by the too-perfect founding fathers, and, as a result, turn away from American history altogether.

This is not a book about John Adams, but it is a book that we hope would have won his grudging approval. It is based on a museum exhibition and includes many of the documents and objects that were part of Adams's own life: the first printing of the Declaration of Independence, which he helped draft; a map of 1783 showing the boundaries of the United States, which he fought for as American peace commissioner; the elegant suits he likely wore as foreign minister, vice-president, and president; the oil portrait painted of him in old age. This book also includes his letter about the fate of American history. All of these he would have liked; they granted him the recognition that eluded him in his lifetime and ever since as one of the least remembered founding fathers.

[1] John Adams to Joseph Ward, June 6, 1809, and August 31, 1809, Joseph Ward Papers, Chicago Historical Society.
[2] Michael Kammen, *A Season of Youth: The American Revolution in the Historical Imagination* (Boston, 1979; New York, 1978), chap. 1.

Other items in the book he would fume over: Thomas Paine's pamphlet of 1776, *Common Sense*, whose message of independence Adams applauded but whose egalitarian spirit encouraging disrespect for "persons of authority" he deplored; the drawing of Matthew Lyon, a feisty Irish-born Jeffersonian congressman from Vermont found guilty under the Sedition Law of 1798 for criticizing President Adams for his "unbounded thirst for ridiculous pomp"; and the poems by Mercy Otis Warren, who in her history of the American Revolution criticized Adams for his lapses from true republicanism. But we think that Adams, a crusty, crotchety conservative who never toed any party's line, would have granted that even such opponents should also be rescued from oblivion.

This book is an effort to answer Adams's objections to the history of his own day and of our own. It is an attempt to win the attention of Americans to the history of an era on which recent scholarship has given new perspectives, an era that has been made more exciting and more interesting than ever before. It is, we hope, a book free from the romance and falsehoods of history that Adams detested. Above all it is an attempt to rescue from oblivion not only the extraordinary leaders of the Revolution but also the ordinary men and women who played so vital a part in the events of the day.

I t is remarkable how certain images dominate the vision of the revolutionary era, intimidating even the most knowledgeable Americans. These images adorn the classroom walls of our elementary schools, appear as symbols of the Revolution on television, and are exploited by advertisers and politicians. They include patriotic paintings, sacred documents, and children's stories. Scholars have analyzed and criticized them at length, but they persist.

Mention the American Revolution, and two paintings come to mind: John Trumbull's *The Declaration of Independence, 4 July, 1776* and Emanuel Leutze's *Washington Crossing the Delaware*. Reproduced in countless engravings, lithographs, and television images, they dominate the imagery of the Revolution.

Most people assume that Trumbull's painting depicts the signing of the Declaration; actually it shows the Continental Congress receiving the draft of the Declaration from the drafting committee. The delegates, gentlemen dressed in the aristocratic clothes of their class, sit or stand, self-conscious of their historic role, harmonious in their unity.

Leutze's version of George Washington crossing the Delaware River depicts a heroic commander-in-chief on the way to his surprise attack on Hessian troops at Trenton, New

George Washington Chops Down the Cherry Tree, Crosses the Delaware, and Wins the Revolution

*The Declaration of
Independence, 4 July,
1776*, oil painting by
John Trumbull, 1816.
Copyright, Yale
University Art Gallery

Jersey, on Christmas night 1776. Washington stands upright, a soldier holds the American flag, some men row, some pole the boat across a river strewn with ice floes.

The sacred documents of the Revolution, the Declaration of Independence and the Constitution, are as formidable. When we think of them, we envision the engrossed (handwritten) versions on parchment signed by the founders, the Declaration with John Hancock's over-large signature heading the rest. These now-faded versions are at the National Archives in Washington, D.C., where they are kept in a fireproof, bombproof vault and displayed in a glass case filled with helium to preserve them from further deterioration. They are so familiar through facsimile reproductions that it never occurs to us that these preserved versions are not the historic printed documents that were seen and read and passed from hand to hand by Americans in 1776 and 1787; they are, instead, the "official," formal copies that were stored away in govern-

Washington Crossing the Delaware, engraving by John Chester Buttre, after an oil painting by Emanuel Leutze, 1851

THE LIFE
OF
GEORGE WASHINGTON;
WITH
CURIOUS ANECDOTES,
EQUALLY HONOURABLE TO HIMSELF,
AND
EXEMPLARY TO HIS YOUNG COUNTRYMEN,

A life how useful to his country led !
How loved ! while living !—how revered ! now dead !
Lisp ! lisp ! his name, ye children yet unborn !
And with like deeds your own great names adorn.

Twenty-third Edition greatly improved.

EMBELLISHED WITH EIGHT ENGRAVINGS.

BY M. L. WEEMS,
FORMERLY RECTOR OF MOUNT VERNON PARISH.

' The Author has treated this great subject with admirable
' success in a new way. He turns all the actions of Washing-
' ton to the encouragement of virtue, by a careful application of
' numerous exemplifications drawn from the conduct of the
' founder of our republic from his earliest life.'
H. Lee, Major-General, Army U. S.

PHILADELPHIA:
M. CAREY & SON.
1820.

Title page from *The Life of George Washington,* by Mason Locke Weems (Philadelphia, 1820)

3 John Trumbull to John Adams, December 26, 1818, Chicago Historical Society.

ment vaults for decades, displayed occasionally in the nineteenth century, and put on permanent display for the public only well into the twentieth century. As they are now preserved and displayed, the documents seem remote; they have been petrified and have lost the meaning they had in the passionate controversies and fierce debates they inspired when they first appeared.

Stories and poems written for children give us comparable idealized images of George Washington and of Paul Revere. George Washington comes down to us through a series of vignettes first told in 1805 in *The Life of George Washington; with curious anecdotes equally honorable to himself, and exemplary to his young countrymen,* by Mason Locke Weems, "formerly rector of Mount Vernon Parish." Here we see Washington as a boy confessing that he chopped down his father's cherry tree, as proof of his honesty; Washington throwing a dollar across the Rappahannock River, as proof of his physical prowess; Washington praying in the snow at Valley Forge, as proof of his piety.

Paul Revere also comes down to us in a story intended for children. His ride through the Massachusetts countryside to warn patriots that "the British are coming" was popularized in 1863 by Henry Wadsworth Longfellow's poem that begins:

*Listen, my children, and you shall hear
Of the midnight ride of Paul Revere*

According to Longfellow, Revere watched for lantern signals from the steeple of Old North Church in Boston to learn which way the troops would cross to the mainland ("One, if by land, and two, if by sea") and then galloped off to rouse patriots at Lexington and warn them of the impending attack.

What is wrong with such images? First, they are filled with what John Adams would call "Falsehoods": some little and inconsequential, some misleading in a larger sense. John Trumbull worked on his painting from 1786 to 1816. He painted each member of Congress from life or from another portrait. When he completed the painting in 1816, he wrote to Adams to solicit his support for a life-size version that now graces the wall of the rotunda of the Capitol in Washington, D.C.[3]

Trumbull got the date of the event wrong; Congress received the report of the drafting committee July 2. After debate Congress adopted the revised version July 4. This error is minor; more important, Trumbull's impression of unity is misleading. The delegates from several states refused to vote for independence; others were reluctant revolutionaries who had to be pushed to make the fateful decision. Moreover, Congress hacked out one of the passages most precious to

Jefferson, a sharp condemnation of Britain for refusing to allow a ban on the slave trade. The subject was too hot for the delegates from South Carolina and Georgia. Trumbull included four delegates who opposed independence, and he left out thirteen of the fifty-six signers. Thus he ignored the actual controversy, debate, and disunity. But as Trumbull wrote to Adams, his purpose was to show "those eminent patriots & statesmen who there laid the foundation of our Nation." And this he did in grand style.

Emanuel Leutze's painting in 1851 of Washington crossing the Delaware in 1776 is all imaginary. The flag that is shown was not yet used in the army. The boats too are entirely wrong. The Americans actually used boats specially constructed to navigate shallow rivers. Platforms ran the length of the boats, and sailors would pole, not row, the boats across the treacherous river. Had Washington stood as Leutze portrayed him he would have been the first one overboard. These errors, it could be argued, are minor. But by placing the action in daylight and not in the dark of the night, Leutze missed the whole point of the military operation: to surprise the Hessian soldiers at Trenton before dawn. Leutze's primary purpose was to inspire;

Paul Revere's Ride, April 19, 1775, drawn by Charles G. Bush, *Harper's Weekly*, 1867

he was not interested in realism. The original painting, a giant canvas twelve feet high and twenty-one feet wide, retains its capacity to inspire.

But how far does artistic or poetic license go? There is simply no credible evidence for any of the legends about Washington. They all were made up by Parson Weems, who claimed to be the rector of a nonexistent parish. An itinerant book peddlar, he knew what would sell, and his biography of Washington went through more than eighty editions in the nineteenth century. The cherry tree story was reprinted in the McGuffy readers, which sold in the millions. As Marcus Cunliffe, one of Washington's twentieth-century biographers, points out, the legends "were untrue in detail and unhistorical in a larger way." Washington, "as the man without faults," was "a copybook character" created by Weems for children to emulate.[4]

Longfellow's poem about Paul Revere is also wrong, in detail and in a larger way. Revere did not need the signals from Old North; he already knew the British plans. He was not the only rider; William Dawes also made the trip. Fortunately Dawes got through, for Revere was captured by the British, held for a few hours, and then let go. In a larger sense the legend "swallowed up the man" as Esther Forbes, Revere's modern biographer, expresses it. Revere's contributions to the patriot cause went beyond his rides as a courier. His engravings were especially important in stirring patriot emotions.[5]

The images and legends that perpetuate "Falsehoods" can be faulted further for portraying the history of the Revolution as the history of great men: the delegates in Congress led the people to independence; George Washington won the war; Paul Revere saved the Massachusetts countryside. Trumbull captured a moment when the leaders finally agreed to declare independence. His painting conveys none of the popular movement for independence that swept the colonies from January to June 1776, inspired in part by Thomas Paine's best-selling pamphlet, *Common Sense.* Leutze's painting celebrates the commander-in-chief. The sailors manning the oars, fishermen from the town of Marblehead, Massachusetts, are beyond the focal point. They received some recognition only in 1925 when J.O.J. Frost, an untrained Marblehead painter who did not know how to convey perspective in his painting but who knew his town's history, painted the same event. In bold lettering across the top he wrote, "Washington Crossing the Delaware / Boats Manned by Marblehead / Fishermen"; among the dozen boats filled with sailors and soldiers one has to look hard to find General Washington.[6]

In celebrating Paul Revere, an ordinary man and a skilled craftsman, the legend leaves out the rest of the group Revere was part of. He was a leader of the "mechanics," as the craftsmen of that day were called, and he began his own account of his since-famous ride with the words: "I was one of upwards of 30, chiefly mechanics," who kept track of the British soldiers in Boston.

[4] Marcus Cunliffe, *George Washington: Man and Monument* (New York, 1958), 19.

[5] Esther Forbes, *Paul Revere and the World He Lived In* (Boston, 1944), chaps. 5–7.

[6] Jean Lipman and Tom Armstrong, eds., *American Folk Painters of Three Centuries* (New York, 1980), 182–85.

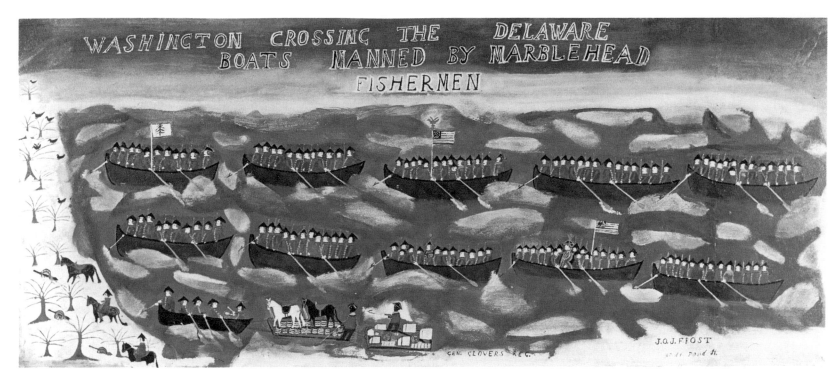

Within the image: WASHINGTON CROSSING THE DELAWARE BOATS MANNED BY MARBLEHEAD FISHERMEN · GEN. GLOVERS REG. · J.O.J. FROST

Washington Crossing the Delaware, Boats Manned by Marblehead Fishermen, oil painting by J.O.J. Frost, c. 1925. Collection of Bertram K. and Nina Fletcher Little

The dominant images, legends, and documents of the revolutionary era are so celebratory that they create a sacred aura around the founding fathers that permits no criticism. The parchment images of the Declaration, the Constitution, and the Bill of Rights convey them as sacred documents, like the Ten Commandments of Moses. The United States recently celebrated the two-hundredth anniversary of each document. In 1987 the major exhibition on the anniversary of the Constitution was entitled "Miracle at Philadelphia"; it asked viewers to cast a ballot either for or against ratifying the Constitution. But who can vote against a miracle?

If we view the Constitution of 1787 as sacred, we bestow on it the qualities of perfection and unchangeability. Thurgood Marshall, recently retired associate justice of the United States Supreme Court, does not believe that the meaning of the Constitution was forever "fixed" at the Philadelphia Convention. He acknowledges that the government devised by the framers was "defective from the start, requiring several amendments, a civil war, and momentous social transformation to attain the system of constitutional government, and its respect for individual freedoms and human rights, we hold as fundamental today."[7]

[7] *New York Times*, May 7, 1987.

The myths and the legends that dominate the popular vision of the Revolution are part of the all-perfect version of American history that dominates the high school and junior high school texts from which most Americans learn their history. Frances Fitzgerald, a skilled investigative journalist who published the results of her examination of the leading textbooks more than a decade ago, found the books to be devoid of controversy and unpleasantness, and devoid of anything that smacks of criticism of the founding fathers. Evils are always corrected in an unending tale of progress. Fitzgerald discovered that the goal of textbook publishers is to sell a product that will offend no one and that will meet with the approval of the state boards that certify textbooks. Consequently, the histories she examined are filled with silences. Large groups of people—women, African Americans, American Indians—are invisible or present only in token form. The result is a history that is not only misleading but bland and boring.[8] The dominant myths and legends thus contribute to a process by which the Revolution has "become trivialized," as Michael Kammen has put it, and in which Americans have unconsciously "derevolutionized the American Revolution."[9]

James Pike Carves the Tree of Liberty on His Powder Horn and Hannah the Weaver Asks Her Master for a Loom

Images and documents need not be clichés that deaden our sense of history. They need not focus exclusively on great men, encourage hero-worship, or convey "Falsehoods." Instead they can correct a distorted or unbalanced history. They can provoke us to think about the limitations as well as the achievements of the nation. Above all, new images and documents can help to rescue from oblivion the ordinary people who have so long been left out of conventional texts or treated as the extras on the stage of history.

Historians write history based on their research into primary sources—the records that people at the time left. When the text is complete, either they or their publishers select pictures from other sources to illustrate their findings. Because this book grew out of a museum exhibition, the images came first and remain central. We have used the objects as *evidence* rather than as illustrations. The result is a book of original sources interpreted to explore what the revolutionary era meant to ordinary people.

It is often assumed that ordinary people were inarticulate—that they expressed themselves rarely, and when they did they left little evidence that survives. The few educated men—the Washingtons, the Adamses, the Jeffersons, and the Madisons—left a full written record. And in the museum world, the material goods of the well-to-do—their furniture, silverware, and paintings—have survived far better than those of the poor and middling classes. Until very

[8] Frances Fitzgerald, *America Revised: History Schoolbooks in the Twentieth Century* (Boston, 1979).
[9] Kammen, *A Season of Youth*, 73, 211.

recently, museums have been more interested in collecting the objects demonstrating the lifestyles of the rich and famous than those of the poor and unknown.

But it is hardly true that ordinary people were voiceless. Especially in a time of revolution, they found their voices. But historians have not always listened to them, nor have they been very imaginative in interpreting the evidence that expresses the values, opinions, and activities of ordinary people. We offer this volume as an example of the materials that can be found in one historical society to produce a more inclusive, more balanced history.

In this book most of our sources are written records: letters, newspapers, documents, and books—the conventional sources of the historian. Other original sources are what museums traditionally collect: tools, clothing, the weapons of war, household furnishings, the objects crafted by artisans, and the objects woven, sewed, and embroidered by women in the domestic arts. This book is a sampler of both kinds of sources.

Original sources present special challenges to those who interpret the past. The letters by ordinary people become meaningful in the context of the events those people were part of. One person often exemplifies a larger trend. A minuteman named John Jones wrote to his wife on April 21, 1775, two days after his militia company rushed to the defense of Lexington and Concord. His letter is wonderfully prosaic—he is safe, please send some stockings—but it also reveals his deep religious faith.

Other letters by ordinary people provoke wonder. Hannah, a slave on one of Robert Carter's huge Virginia plantations, was a weaver by trade, about to be set free by her master in 1793 when she sent him a note that begins: "Dear master Hannah [begs] one favour that is to buy her loom." This document defies many preconceptions about slavery and voices the aspiration of African Americans to be free. We shall see that it also raises a host of questions.

A soldier's powder horn is a window into the world of the "G.I." of the revolutionary war. A militiaman who went into action with homemade uniform and equipment usually carved his name and a slogan or image onto the horn. James Pikc carved the Liberty Tree onto his horn with crude stick figures of "Regulars, the Aggressors" and "Provincials, Defending"; this is what the Revolution meant to him. The Liberty Tree symbol was widely used. It remains for us to figure out what it meant.

The images that portray the events of the Revolution present problems to Americans today. Living in the last quarter of the twentieth century, we are used to instant, realistic images through photography, either still shots reproduced in newspapers and magazines, or moving images in motion pictures and television. We assume they were taken on the spot and that they are accurate. In the last quarter of the eighteenth century the only way to copy an image was to draw or paint it, then reproduce it by engraving. But there were only a few artists in all of America.

Sometimes visual images are less valuable for the event they depict than for what they reveal of the points of view of the people who made them and, when they were popular, of the people who bought them or saw them. This is true of a host of drawings, oil paintings, line engravings, and nineteenth-century lithographs, many of which are in this book. To understand the creator's point of view, today's viewer has to ask who made the image, when and where was it made, for what purpose, and for what audience.

Paul Revere's engraving of the Boston Massacre is an example. Produced by an engraver who was one of the leaders of the Sons of Liberty in Boston, the engraving was rushed into print to win people to the patriot version of the event. In Revere's print British soldiers fire in unison at the command of their captain, with no apparent provocation from their victims. At the murder trials of the captain and soldiers, however, John Adams, lawyer for the defense, presented evidence for an entirely different version of the event and succeeded in winning acquittal for his clients.

Revere's print conveys the state of mind of the colonists as they justified revolution: the British were the aggressors; the colonists were defending their liberties. The same state of mind underlies Amos Doolittle's engraving of the Battle of Lexington and James Pike's engraving on his powder horn.

The original sources—letters, artifacts, visual images—in which common people expressed themselves or saw their ideas expressed often require the knowledge that has been accumulated by scholars to give them meaning, but viewers should not be intimidated by them. Sources challenge the viewer; they provoke the viewer; and they cut through the clichés that are a barrier to what John Adams called "the real revolution." These sources also make amply clear that there were revolutions other than what Adams was thinking of, just as they show us there are ordinary people to be heard along with the leaders Adams had in mind.

Americans Discover New Histories and the Past Looks Different

The major subjects covered in this book and the sequence of events will be familiar to people who have studied even a smattering of American history. But if the subjects are vaguely familiar, the approach may be unfamiliar. We have organized the history around the theme of ordinary people, asking two broad questions: What was the role of ordinary men and

*The Bloody Massacre
perpetrated in King Street,
Boston, on March 5, 1770,*
engraving by Paul
Revere, 1770 (Color
Plate 1)

*The Battle of Lexington,
April 19, 1775,* engraving
by Amos Doolittle,
December 1775 (Color
Plate 2)

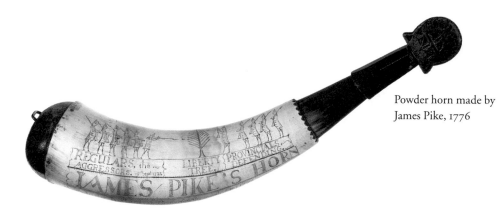

Powder horn made by
James Pike, 1776

women in shaping the events of the era? To what extent did they achieve the ideals of the Revolution asserted in the Declaration of Independence: that "all men are created equal" and that government is by "the consent of the governed"?

To study ordinary people means to deal with women as well as men, African Americans and American Indians as well as Anglo-Americans and recent immigrants from Europe. It means dealing with the common people, most of whom made their living with their hands as farmers or artisans, as well as with the merchants, plantation owners, and lawyers who comprised the political elite. It means dealing with the unfree as well as with the free.

"The study of American history today looks far different than it did a generation ago," Eric Foner writes in *The New American History*. History has been rewritten as a result of the "new histories," with their "emphasis on the experiences of ordinary Americans." Not only have black history and women's history "matured to the point where they are . . . recognized as legitimate subfields," but they "are seen as indispensable to any understanding of the broad American experience."[10]

Writing in this same volume, Linda Kerber states, "To a story once told in terms of political officeholders, lawyers, and pamphleteers we have added artisans, farmers, working women, middle-class women, Indians . . . the experiences of slaves and of free blacks." The new research has tended "to restore *rebellion* to histories of the American Revolution," stressing the ways that these various groups "shaped the revolution and were in turn affected by it." As a result the Revolution looks different.[11]

The changes in scholarship now appear in history that reaches a wider audience. The titles of recent college textbooks suggest the thematic changes: *The American People: Creating a Nation and a Society*, or *A People and a Nation*, or even more boldly *Who Built America? Working People and the Nation's Economy, Politics, Culture, and Society*. The exhibitions of leading historical museums are also contributing to this changing scholarship. The National Museum of American History at the Smithsonian offers a permanent exhibition entitled *After the Revolution: Everyday Life in America*. Major sections are devoted to the average farm household, African Americans, the artisans of Philadelphia, and the Seneca Indians. The Colonial Williamsburg Foundation, the largest restoration of American society in the era of the Revolution, which traditionally presented only the glowing aspects of colonial life, now grapples with portraying African Americans, who were the majority of the town's people.

Our intention is not to do a history of everyday life. We present a political history. The great men are here: Washington, Adams, Jefferson. The fundamental documents of the

[10] Eric Foner, ed., *The New American History* (Philadelphia, 1990), vii–viii.
[11] Linda K. Kerber, in *ibid.*, 26, 44.

founding era are here: the Declaration, the Constitution, the Bill of Rights, the Northwest Ordinance. But with the cast of characters in the drama enlarged, the "great men" and the great documents somehow look different. They have not lost their lustre; as the products of controversy, they have become even more vivid. By placing women, African Americans, American Indians, farmers, and artisans alongside the great men and the great documents, we can see the founders in perspective, their limitations as well as their achievements.

Readers may disagree with our conclusions. Indeed the original sources in this book are an invitation to readers to draw their own conclusions.

Between 1765 and 1820 the American people created a nation. From 1765 to 1775 they waged a political war against Great Britain that went from resistance to rebellion to revolution. From 1775 to 1783 they fought a successful military war. They created new political institutions, state and federal. In 1787–91, amid bitter controversy, they built the framework for a national government in the Constitution and the Bill of Rights. From 1789 to 1820 they put into practice a new republican government based on the will of the majority. They extended republican institutions to vast lands in the West. In the wake of the Revolution, they attempted to create a distinct national culture, including an American language, American symbols, American histories, and American heroes.

Americans of this era were a diverse people: slave and free; African American, Euro-American, and American Indian; men and women; rich, "middling," and poor. What part did these people play in creating a nation? We know the story best through the eyes of the extraordinary leaders of the day. But what roles did ordinary people, the vast majority, play in this half-century?

In 1776 the framers of the Declaration of Independence asserted as a fundamental principle that "all men are created equal" and are entitled to "Life, Liberty and the pursuit of Happiness." What did these ideals mean to the "unequals" and to what extent were the ideals achieved?

In 1787 the framers proclaimed a new government in the name of "We the People," the opening words of the Preamble to the Constitution. Who were the people in "We the People" and to what extent did they achieve government "by the consent of the governed," the principle of the Declaration of Independence?

Equality and self-government. Those were the ideals. To what extent were they realized?

PROLOGUE

Defending the Tree of Liberty

A Diverse and Aspiring People

I

John Mitchell's Map of the British and French Dominions in North America *is considered the most famous and influential of all eighteenth-century maps in American history. It was the map consulted by all officials in boundary disputes and was used by the British and American negotiators in setting the boundaries of the victorious United States in 1783.*

The British mapmaker John Mitchell, a physician and a botanist, lived in Virginia from the 1720s to 1746 and traveled in the colonies. He returned to Britain to spend five years working with official sources to render this detailed map. It was so large—four and one-half by seven feet—that it had to be engraved in eight sections. Published under the auspices of the Board of Trade, it was reprinted widely.

The map shows the stage upon which the dramatic history of the Revolution was played. Thirteen colonies lined the Atlantic seaboard and the river valleys that reached inward. A handful of major cities were established on the coast—Boston, New York, Philadelphia, and Charleston; the rest of the country was farmland, most of it uncultivated. Native American peoples possessed all the land beyond the Appalachian Mountains and much of the land east of them. Yet colonies held claims to boundaries that extended to the Mississippi River.

Few colonial Americans would have seen this or any other map of North America. But as more and more Americans traveled into the country's interior during the war with France (1754–63) or to settle on farms in the wilderness, they experienced what the map conveys: the vastness of the continent and the richness of its resources. Ultimately this knowledge contributed to the idea of an American empire independent of Great Britain.

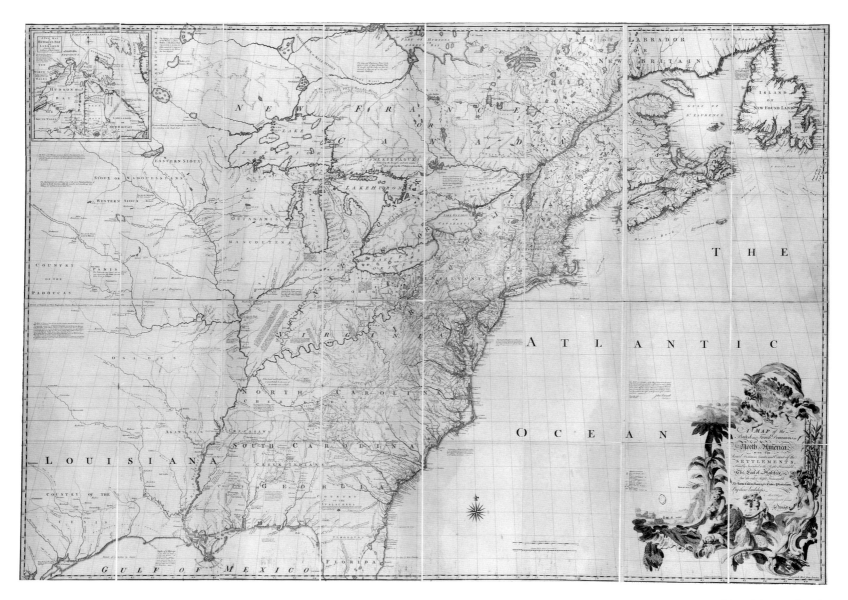

Map of the British and French Dominions in North America, by John Mitchell (London, 1755)

I n the era of the Revolution, ordinary Americans aspired to personal independence. The population of America grew from fewer than 250,000 people in 1700 to 2.5 million in 1765. By the first census in 1790 there would be 4 million people and by 1820 more than 9 million people.

Nine out of ten Americans made their living from the land. They were farmers or would-be farmers whose goal was to own land and pass it on to their children. One hundred thousand Americans lived in the major cities along the Atlantic seaboard. Half the population of these cities were artisans who aspired to become masters of their own trade.

Only a handful of colonists were wealthy: plantation owners in the South, landlord owners of tenanted estates in the Hudson Valley, or export-import merchants in the cities. Only a few thousand colonists were educated in one of the seven colonial colleges.

Personal independence was the aspiration of people wherever they lived: New England, the middle colonies, the South, or the growing backcountry. Recent immigrants from Scotland, Ireland, and Germany as well as descendants of the original English settlers also shared this goal.

Women, with few trades, little schooling, and no professions open to them, lived their lives as daughters, wives, and mothers. On the family farm women were indispensable co-workers.

A large proportion of working people were unfree: they were either slaves or indentured servants. In 1776 about half a million were slaves for life: either they had been brought to the colonies from Africa in shackles, or they had been born into slavery. Tens of thousands of white European immigrants were indentured servants who had sold their labor for periods of three to seven years to pay for their ship passage. In the cities there were large numbers of apprentices, boys under contract until age twenty-one to learn a trade. Americans who were unfree aspired to be free. Eighteenth-century newspapers were filled with advertisements for the return of runaway slaves, indentured servants, and apprentices.

The tools of ordinary Americans, free or unfree, tell the story of their lives of labor. These are tools that demanded heavy or constant labor: the plow, hoe, and sickle of farm men and women; the spinning wheel and butter churn of the housewife; the hammer and anvil of the blacksmith.

In the era of the Revolution, the individual aspirations of ordinary Americans for personal freedom and independence contributed in different ways to an aspiration for national independence.

Farmer's sickle, c. 1820

An eighteenth-century farmer knew what it meant to live "by the sweat of his brow." He tilled the fields by walking behind a wooden plow pulled by oxen, sowed seed by hand, and harvested with a hand-held sickle or scythe. Most farmers owned land; they were called freeholders or yeomen. Farmers' sons, tenants who worked the soil of their landlords, and squatters on frontier land all aspired to landownership.

Plow, c. 1760

Plows were used to break the sod and to cultivate between rows of corn and other grain crops. Four generations of the Armour family tilled the soil with this sturdy plow, first in Connecticut, then in New York, and finally in Illinois.

Artisans   en skilled in a craft were known as mechanics, tradesmen, or *leather aprons*, after the heavy leather aprons many wore to protect themselves from the hazards of work as a blacksmith, carpenter, or shipwright. A mechanic who owned his own shop was a master; a boy learning the trade was an apprentice. When an apprentice turned twenty-one he became a journeyman, with the right to earn wages working for a master. If he could accumulate enough capital, he might become a master, or "his own man."

Engraving from
The Book of Trades
(Philadelphia, 1807)

Artisan's half apron, c.
1800

Blacksmith's anvil,
c. 1810

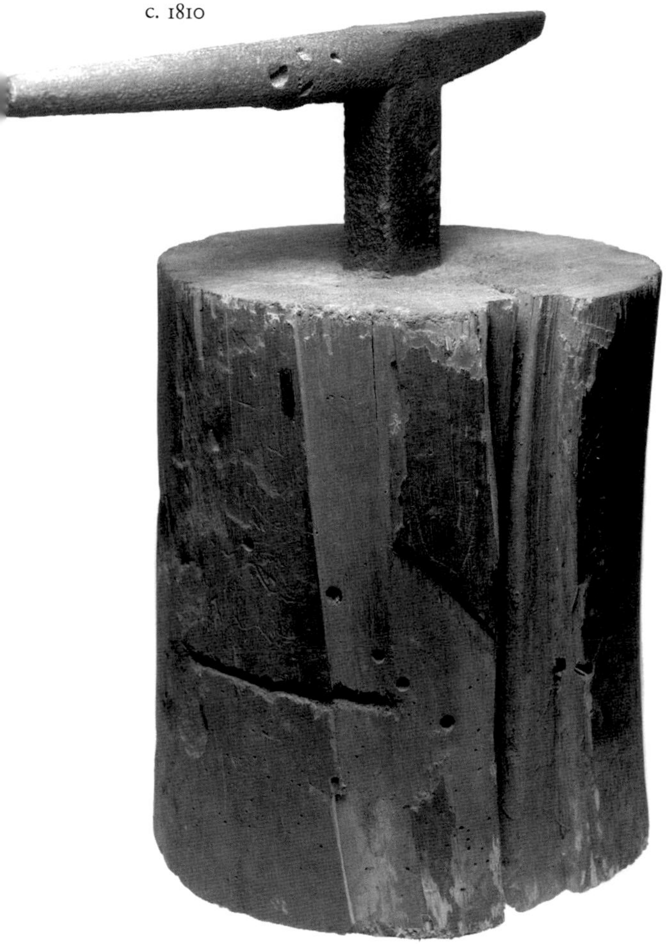

Indenture agreement,
August 1, 1768

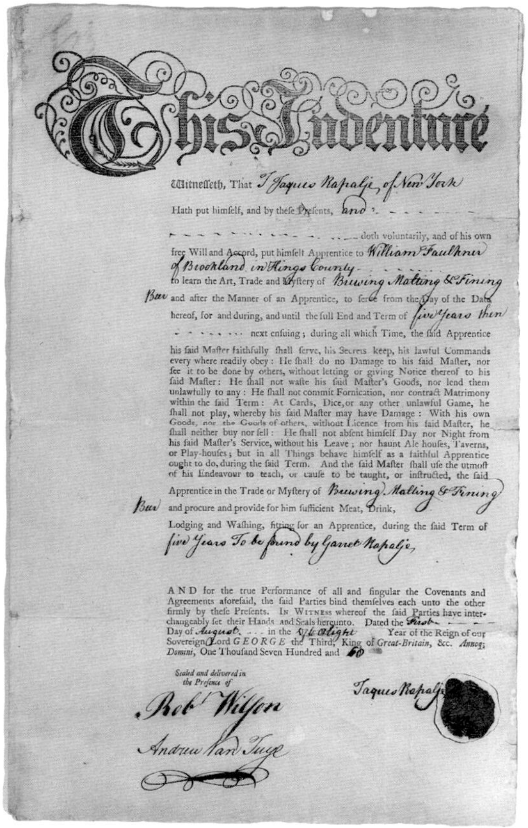

This Indenture

Witneſſeth, That I Jaques Rapalje, of New York Hath put himſelf, and by theſe Preſents, and .... doth voluntarily, and of his own free Will and Accord, put himſelf Apprentice to William Faulkner of Brookland in Kings County ...... to learn the Art, Trade and Myſtery of Brewing Malting & Fining Beer and after the Manner of an Apprentice, to ſerve from the Day of the Date hereof, for and during, and until the full End and Term of five Years then .... next enſuing; during all which Time, the ſaid Apprentice his ſaid Maſter faithfully ſhall ſerve, his Secrets keep, his lawful Commands every where readily obey: He ſhall do no Damage to his ſaid Maſter, nor ſee it to be done by others, without letting or giving Notice thereof to his ſaid Maſter: He ſhall not waſte his ſaid Maſter's Goods, nor lend them unlawfully to any: He ſhall not commit Fornication, nor contract Matrimony within the ſaid Term: At Cards, Dice, or any other unlawful Game, he ſhall not play, whereby his ſaid Maſter may have Damage: With his own Goods, nor the Goods of others, without Licence from his ſaid Maſter, he ſhall neither buy nor ſell: He ſhall not abſent himſelf Day nor Night from his ſaid Maſter's Service, without his Leave; nor haunt Ale houſes, Taverns, or Play-houſes; but in all Things behave himſelf as a faithful Apprentice ought to do, during the ſaid Term. And the ſaid Maſter ſhall uſe the utmoſt of his Endeavour to teach, or cauſe to be taught, or inſtructed, the ſaid Apprentice in the Trade or Myſtery of Brewing, Malting & Fining Beer and procure and provide for him ſufficient Meat, Drink, Lodging and Waſhing, fitting for an Apprentice, during the ſaid Term of five Years To be found by Garret Rapalje,

AND for the true Performance of all and ſingular the Covenants and Agreements aforeſaid, the ſaid Parties bind themſelves each unto the other firmly by theſe Preſents. In Witness whereof the ſaid Parties have interchangeably ſet their Hands and Seals hereunto. Dated the First Day of August ... in the Eight Year of the Reign of our Sovereign Lord GEORGE the Third, King of Great-Britain, &c. Annoq; Domini, One Thouſand Seven Hundred and 68

Sealed and delivered in the Preſence of

Robt Wilson

Andrew Van Tuyl

Jaques Rapalje

In this indenture, signed in New York in 1768, Jaques Rapalje apprenticed himself to William Faulkner for five years to learn the "Brewing, Malting & Fining" of beer. The practice of indenturing boys was so common that a tradesman could buy a printed legal form and fill in the blanks. The master promised to teach the apprentice "the trade or Mystery" and to provide him with food and lodging. The apprentice pledged not to get married, "commit Fornication," or "haunt Ale houses, Taverns, or Play-houses." The apprentice was at the mercy of his master.

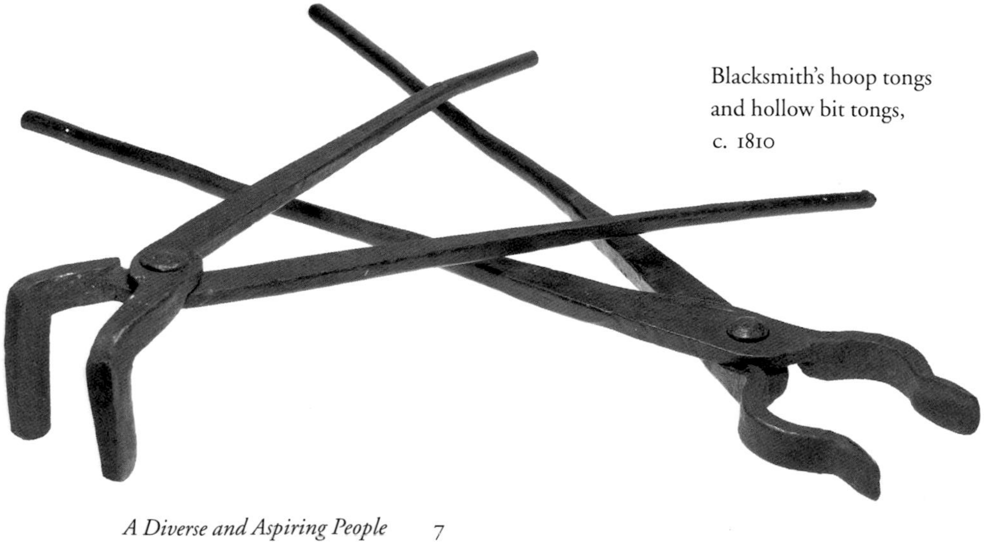

Blacksmith's hoop tongs
and hollow bit tongs,
c. 1810

George Washington's father willed ten thousand acres and forty-nine slaves to George's older brother, Lawrence. Upon Lawrence's death this document recorded "a Division of the Negroes" between Colonel George Lee and "the Brothers of the deceased Maj. Lawrence Washington," one of whom was George. George Washington acquired still more slaves when he married the widow Martha Custis. By the time of the Revolution he held about two hundred slaves at Mount Vernon. On his death in 1799 his will provided for their eventual emancipation after Martha's death.

Document dividing slaves between George Lee and the estate of Lawrence Washington, December 10, 1754

Irons like these were used to shackle slaves who were being transported or to punish slaves or confine prisoners in jail.

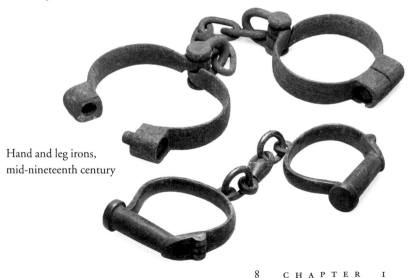

Hand and leg irons, mid-nineteenth century

A Division of the Negros made, and agreed to by between Colo. George Lee, and the Brothers of the deceasd Majr. Lawrence Washington the 10th day of Decemr. Anno Domini 1754—

Colo. Lee's part		The Estates Part	
Old Moll	125	Phebe	£125
Lawrence	60	Peter	60
Ben	40	Pharo	40
Will	40	Abram	40
Frank	40	Couta	40
Barbara	40	Nell	40
Moll	25	Sall	25
Milly	20	Bella	20
Hannah	15	Barbara	15
Jenny	10	Anteno	10
Will	10	Dicer	10
Nan	15	Aaron	15
Nan	35	Judah	35
James	40	Ned	40
Dula	40	Camero	40
Dublin	40	Sambo	40
Acco	40	Sando	40
Harry	35	Scipio	35
Roger	40	Tomboy	40
Grace	40	Lett	40
Phillis	40	Jenny	40
Kate	40	Judah	40
Cesar	25	Tom	15
Sarra	1 mth old £,5	Phill	£,5
Charles	A. 7½	Tom	A-1
Doll	3-A	Prince	3-7½
Sue	2-11½	Betty	3-1
George	3-7½	Lucy	A-1
Lydia	3-5½	Jin	2-9
Maria	5 mth old	Tom	A mths old
Glasgow		Tobey	1 Do

On the eve of the Revolution one out of five Americans was a slave. About 450,000 slaves lived in the South, and 50,000 in New England and the middle colonies. In Virginia about one in three were slaves and in South Carolina one in two. About half of the slaves were African-born; the other half African American. Plantation owners bought slaves, sold them, and passed them on in their wills as valuable property. Before the Revolution only a few thousand blacks were free, and very little sentiment existed among whites, northerners or southerners, to abolish slavery.

During the eighteenth century about half of the white immigrants to the colonies came as indentured servants from Germany or the British Isles, especially Ireland and Scotland. These were men, women, and children so poor that in return for their passage to the colonies, they signed a contract called an indenture, selling their labor for three- to seven-year terms on farms and in the cities. One group of indentured servants—as many as fifty thousand—were men and women convicted of crimes and sentenced by British judges to a certain number of years of hard labor in the colonies.

In this legal form Thomas Hodge, probably the captain of the ship Thornton, *assigned the convict Richard Golding to Samuel Love "for the Term of seven Years," beginning the day his ship arrived in Virginia. If he had a good master and good luck, Richard Golding survived the sentence.*

Sentence transporting Richard Golding "to his Majesty's Plantations in America," June 19, 1772

Women's Sphere

A woman in colonial society lived her life in the "domestic sphere," as a daughter, wife, or mother. Few careers were open to women. Women were midwives and teachers of little children in "dame schools." In the cities they were shopkeepers or tavernkeepers, or they worked in the needle trades as seamstresses.

A typical colonial woman who married in her early twenties spent nearly half of her child-bearing years either pregnant or nursing. Most women bore five to seven children; ten was not unusual. In a society where most men were farmers, women were indispensable to the household economy. They prepared food and tended to the chickens and the dairying. They were responsible for the never-ending production of clothing and linens, from spinning to weaving to sewing. They reared the children. As the saying went, "Man may work from sun to sun, but woman's work is never done."

Just imported in Capt. Partidge from LONDON and to be Sold by
Susanna Renken,
At her Shop in Fore-Street near the Draw-Bridge, BOSTON, Viz.
EARLY Charlton, Hotspur, Marrowfat, Golden Hotspur, and blue Marrowfat Peas; Large Windsor, early Hotspur, early yellow Kidney, early Spanish Beans:—Early Yorkshire, Dutch, Battersea, Red, and large Winter Cabbage: yellow and green Savoy; Purple and Colliflower Brocoli; white Goss-Cabbage, Marble, white Silesia, green Silesia, and scarlet Lettice, green and yellow Hyssop; Turkey Melons; and Winter Savory; with all sorts of other Garden Seeds, among which are a great Variety of Flower-Seeds;—Red and white Clover, Herd Grass and Trefoile.

Just Imported from LONDON, and to be Sold
By Sarah DeCoster,
At the Sign of the Walnut-Tree in Milk-Street, in Boston, a little below the Rev. Dr. Sewall's Meeting-House,
WINDSOR Beans; Early Peas of several Sorts; Early Cabbage-Seeds, and other Sorts of Garden-Seeds; too many to enumerate: All at reasonable Rates.

JUST IMPORTED from LONDON, In the last Ships, and to be Sold
By Ann Thomas,
At the Corner of Union-Street, opposite the Blue Ball,
ALL Sorts of Seed Peas & Beans and all Sorts of Garden Seeds, Canary and Hemp Seed; also split Peas by the Cask or smaller Quantity: Cheshire and Glocester Cheese, Raisins by the Cask, and all sorts of Grocery.
N. Stone-Ware by the Hogshead or Crate.

Women shopkeepers were common in the cities, especially in trades that required only a small investment. These three Boston women advertised imported garden seeds.

Boston Newsletter,
March 2, 1762

Mothers instructed daughters in the mechanics of spinning yarn from wool. In many rural households the younger women assumed much of the responsibility for textile production, beginning with carding and combing the wool to prepare it for spinning, then spinning the fiber, and weaving, bleaching, and dyeing the fabric. Many unmarried women were prodigious manufacturers of homemade cloth, and hence the name spinster.

Spinning wheel, c. 1800

Before dresses were made with sewn-in pockets, a woman tied a pocket, or a pair of pockets, on top of her first petticoat so that she could carry her personal necessities. This popular eighteenth-century nursery rhyme reminds us of this custom.

> Lucy Locket lost her pocket,
> Kitty Fisher found it.
> Not a penny was there in it,
> Only ribbon round it.

Woman's patchwork and calico pocket, c. 1775 (Color Plate 12)

The Pocket, Symbol of Women's Work

A historic object rarely speaks for itself. It takes on meaning in light of what we know about the society in which it was used. An old object can take on new meaning when historians interpret it in new ways.

Museums have long exhibited the spinning wheel as a symbol of women's work in the household economy of rural America during the era of the Revolution. Sturdily made spinning wheels have survived, and most Americans immediately associate them with women's work in a bygone era.

The historian Laurel Thatcher Ulrich, after investigating the daily lives of colonial women in northern New England, concluded, "Perhaps it is time to suggest a new icon for women's history." Spinning was only "one enterprise among many."

As an alternative symbol she suggests the pocket. Today the pockets of men and women are part of their clothing. In colonial days a woman's pocket was a separate garment that she tied around her waist. Whether ornately embroidered or patched together with scraps of fabric, pockets revealed the status and skills of their owners.

Pockets, along with most of the other plain, simple clothing worn by ordinary Americans, usually ended up in the rag bag. That this calico pocket was spared such a fate makes it even more powerful as a tangible symbol of eighteenth-century womanhood.

"Much better than a spinning wheel," Ulrich writes, "this homely object symbolizes the obscurity, the versatility and the personal nature of the housekeeping role. . . . A woman sat at a wheel but she carried her pocket with her from room to room, from house to yard, yard to street. . . . Whether it contained cellar keys or a paper of pins, a packet of seeds or a baby's bib, a hand of yarn or a Testament, it characterized the social complexity as well as the demanding diversity of women's work." The pocket may have been a mundane costume accessory, but, examining it, we can stretch our imaginations to visualize a day in the life of a colonial woman.

Children   The population of the nation-to-be was strikingly young. At the time of the Revolution almost one-half of all Americans, black and white, were under sixteen years of age, while today less than one-quarter of the population is so young. Large families were the rule in colonial America, but many children never survived childhood.

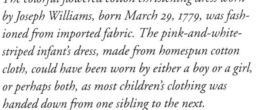

The colorful flowered cotton christening dress worn by Joseph Williams, born March 29, 1779, was fashioned from imported fabric. The pink-and-white-striped infant's dress, made from homespun cotton cloth, could have been worn by either a boy or a girl, or perhaps both, as most children's clothing was handed down from one sibling to the next.

This silver baby mug was made in England; the pewter porringers with the traditional crown handle were made in America. Inexpensive earthenware and wooden utensils were found in most American kitchens. Pewter, both elegant and practical, was often given as a gift by the "middling sort" to celebrate births and marriages, while silver was the province of "people of quality."

Christening dress of
Joseph Williams (Color
Plate II)

Infant's dress, early
nineteenth century

Baby mug, 1808

Presenting American nursery rhymes, as well as lessons in morality and proper behavior, this book was designed to fit the small hands of a child.

Although most American children played with less ornate homemade toys, this doll, with leather arms, a turned wooden head, and glass eyes, is of a type commonly manufactured in England in the late eighteenth century.

Doll, c. 1795

A Little Pretty Pocket-Book, Intended for the Instruction and Amusement of Little Master Tommy and Pretty Miss Polly, by Isaiah Thomas, 1787

Left: child's porringer, c. 1810; *right*: child's porringer, c. 1790

A Diverse and Aspiring People   13

People from Diverse Nations

In the decades prior to independence the colonies became less English. About 20 percent of Americans were African-born or of African ancestry. The first census in 1790 showed that about 10 percent of the white population was Scotch-Irish, 5 percent Scottish, 5 percent Irish, and 9 percent German. Germans made up about 40 percent of the population of Pennsylvania. Trunks and chests, Bibles, and other family heirlooms expressed the distinctions among the Old World arts and traditions of the immigrants.

This religious figure, made in France in the mid-eighteenth century, was used in French Canada, most of whose European inhabitants were Roman Catholic. In the thirteen colonies, in contrast, Catholics were a small minority who gained greater freedom of worship in the revolutionary era.

Ceramic figurine of
Madonna and child,
French, c. 1750

Ephrata Cloister
hymnal, c. 1750

Ephrata was a communal settlement near Lancaster, Pennsylvania, founded by German Seventh-Day Baptists, one of the many religious groups that flourished in Pennsylvania's climate of religious freedom. Entire families and two celibate orders, the Sisters and the Brethren, were part of the Ephrata community, which was known for its vocal music. The fine pen work for which the Sisters were famous is apparent in this hymnal.

German and Dutch immigrants often decorated their furniture with tulip and dove motifs, as on this chair, signed and dated by G. Keller. The tulip was revered as a variant of the Easter lily, while the dove stood for love and married bliss. This chair, one of a pair, was probably made as a wedding present.

The bird, tulips, and wedding scene painted on this hand-carved chest suggest that it was a dower chest brought from Holland or made in America by a Dutch craftsman for a bride-to-be.

Chair, painted wood and reed, 1784

Chest, hand-carved, Dutch, 1660

The People Who Were Here First

For thousands of years before the invasion of their lands by Europeans, the native peoples who became known as American Indians lived throughout the area of the present United States. Prior to the introduction of European disease and warfare, they numbered at least five million. By the 1760s the British and Americans had dispossessed the Indians of most of their land east of the Appalachian Mountains.

American Indian cultures were complex and varied. For example, North America had much greater linguistic diversity than Europe: American Indians spoke several thousand languages that can be grouped into about nine large classes. They lived in towns and seasonal settlements along rivers. Groups of allied or related communities were termed "tribes" or "nations" by Europeans.

Most white settlers looked on the native peoples as "savage," "warlike," and "pagan," as obstacles to settlement and civilization. As European settlement expanded, it met with armed Indian resistance. A pattern of Indian-white relations ensued with tragic consequences for the Indians—war, broken agreements, and social disruption.

Penn's Treaty with the Indians, 1682, painting by Benjamin West, c. 1771

Benjamin West's painting of William Penn, the proprietor of the land that became Pennsylvania, negotiating with the Lenape Indians for their land in 1682, is unusual in its compassionate portrayal of American Indian men, women, and children.

Penn, dressed in plain brown Quaker garb, is in the background, left of center. Indian chieftains are to the right, and the two young men kneeling in the foreground are merchants offering a bolt of cloth, a symbol of trade with the Indians.

The painting served a political purpose in the 1770s. West was an American-born painter mastering his craft in London. Thomas Penn, William's son and the current proprietor of Pennsylvania, commissioned the painting to bolster his control of the colony against the challenge of the Anti-Proprietary party. It celebrated his father's golden age. The original was six feet by ten feet; West made this reduced replica so that an engraver could copy it and the Penn family could disseminate its message in England.

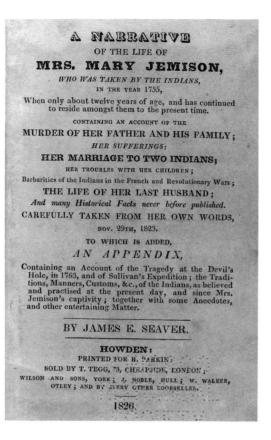

Title page from *A Narrative of the Life of Mrs. Mary Jemison*, by James E. Seaver, 1826

James Seaver's book tells the story of Mary Jemison, who was captured by American Indians in western Pennsylvania in the 1750s. White captives were sometimes adopted into an Indian family who had lost someone in battle. Mary Jemison, in keeping with this practice, replaced a brother of two Seneca women, who reared her as one of their own family. She grew to womanhood as an Indian, married twice, and reared eight children. After the Revolution an Indian brother offered her freedom, but she chose instead to remain with her tribe in upstate New York, adhering to Indian customs and manner of dress until her death in 1833.

James Seaver interviewed Mary Jemison when she was eighty years old and recorded her life's story. Her recollections give a sympathetic portrayal of Indians, whom she describes as "naturally kind, tender and peaceable towards their friends." Seaver's captivity narrative of Jemison's life was immensely popular with nineteenth-century readers. First published in 1824, it went through twenty-two editions.

Indian apron, Great Lakes region, c. 1760

This buckskin apron, probably worn for ceremonial occasions, is decorated with porcupine quills, feathers, and dyed deer-tail hairs.

The Road to Revolution, 1765–75

2

This British cartoon depicts an event that took place in Boston in January 1774, a few weeks after the Tea Party. The artist has taken the usual cartoonist's liberty. He refers to the earlier event (the dumping of the tea is shown in the background) and embellishes it with the pouring of tea down the victim's throat. He gives the reader an appropriate clue to the composition of the crowd—the man to the right is wearing an artisan's leather apron.

The victim is John Malcolm, an officer in His Majesty's customs service with the reputation of an informer who turned in ships as well as ordinary sailors who smuggled in a few bottles of gin to make some extra money. Giving a man a coat of tar and feathers was a centuries-old British custom that reappeared in the New England seaports in the late 1760s. It was a form of popular justice, usually carried out by crowds of workingmen on British officials whom they did not believe the courts would punish.

The steps in tarring and feathering were to strip a man, usually to the waist, cover him with a layer of tar (a tar bucket like the one in the foreground was readily available on the docks and on ships), and coat him with feathers from a featherbed or pillow. Then the victim was carted around town to public places such as the Liberty Tree, or he was made to sit on the gallows (the noose on the tree is an ominous reminder) until he repented his "crime." It was a harsh and cruel ritual of ostracism, but it invariably stopped short of death. Many patriot leaders opposed the custom because they disapproved of crowds taking the law into their own hands. Nevertheless, tarring and feathering became a popular method to intimidate Tories of all sorts or drive them out of town.

The Bostonians Paying the Excise-man, or Tarring & Feathering, engraving attributed to Philip Dawe, London, 1774

"What do we mean by the American Revolution?" John Adams asked many decades after the event. "Do we mean the American war? The Revolution was effected before the war commenced." The "real American Revolution," he wrote, was the "radical change in the principles, opinions, sentiments and affections of the people," and it occurred between 1760 and 1775, "before a drop of blood was drawn at Lexington."

The colonists did not begin with the goal of independence. They started out resisting what they considered "innovations" by the British Parliament and royal officials. In 1765 the Tree of Liberty in Boston was designated to symbolize the rights of Englishmen that colonists believed belonged to them.

Over the decade that followed resistance sank deep roots among the common people in the seaboard cities and spread to farmers in the countryside. Colonists began to question whether they could defend their rights and remain within the empire. Some predicted that independence was inevitable, but few advocated it.

By 1775 a movement that had begun ten years earlier to conserve existing rights had become a movement to expand rights. Patriots were ready to take up arms, and when the British cracked down with force, political resistance became armed rebellion, and in 1776 became a revolution. When the Continental Congress adopted the Declaration of Independence, the Tree of Liberty stood for the natural rights of all men to "Life, Liberty and the pursuit of Happiness."

"The Causes which Impel Them to the Separation"

The framers of the Declaration of Independence enumerated "the causes which impel them to the separation." A primary cause was the challenge to the colonists' self-government. The colonists had long exercised broad powers in their own representative houses, including the right to tax themselves, and they considered the right to self-government to be fundamental.

But in the decade gone by, from 1765 to 1775, royal governors had suspended or dissolved these bodies. Worst of all, Parliament had imposed taxes "without our Consent." Colonial legislative powers seemed an illusion. At risk was the political control of matters vital to the colonists' economic well-being: land, trade, currency, manufactures.

The rights of Englishmen were precious, even to those unrepresented in colonial government. British "Standing Armies" threatened civilian rule. The curtailment of the right to trial by jury threatened the rights of all to justice. The imposition of a tax on tea caused the colonists to wonder, will land be next?

In the Declaration of Independence colonial leaders listed "a long train of abuses and usurpations" to justify revolution. "Let Facts be submitted to a candid world," they wrote, summing up in phrase after phrase the "repeated injuries" of the years since 1765. Letters, proclamations, and pamphlets illustrate some of their most important grievances.

"A Tyrant . . . is unfit to be the ruler of a free people"

The Declaration, with its long list of grievances all beginning with "He," singled out George III as the villain. The colonists had come to this conclusion slowly. In 1761, when the twenty-two-year-old prince was crowned king, this British engraving would have circulated in the colonies. Colonists toasted the king each year on his birthday; they had no objection to monarchy in principle. But when the king, his ministers, and Parliament violated their rights as Englishmen, they came to see him as a tyrant.

George the III, King of Great Britain, mezzotint by James McCardle, 1761

"For imposing Taxes on us without our Consent"

Americans believed that they had the right to tax themselves through the representatives that voters of each colony elected to their assembly. In New England each town elected a delegate to the assembly and appointed a tax collector who went about collecting the taxes due. In Rowley, a town in north-eastern Massachusetts, the collector seems to have added up the current and back taxes for each person. His large X probably meant paid.

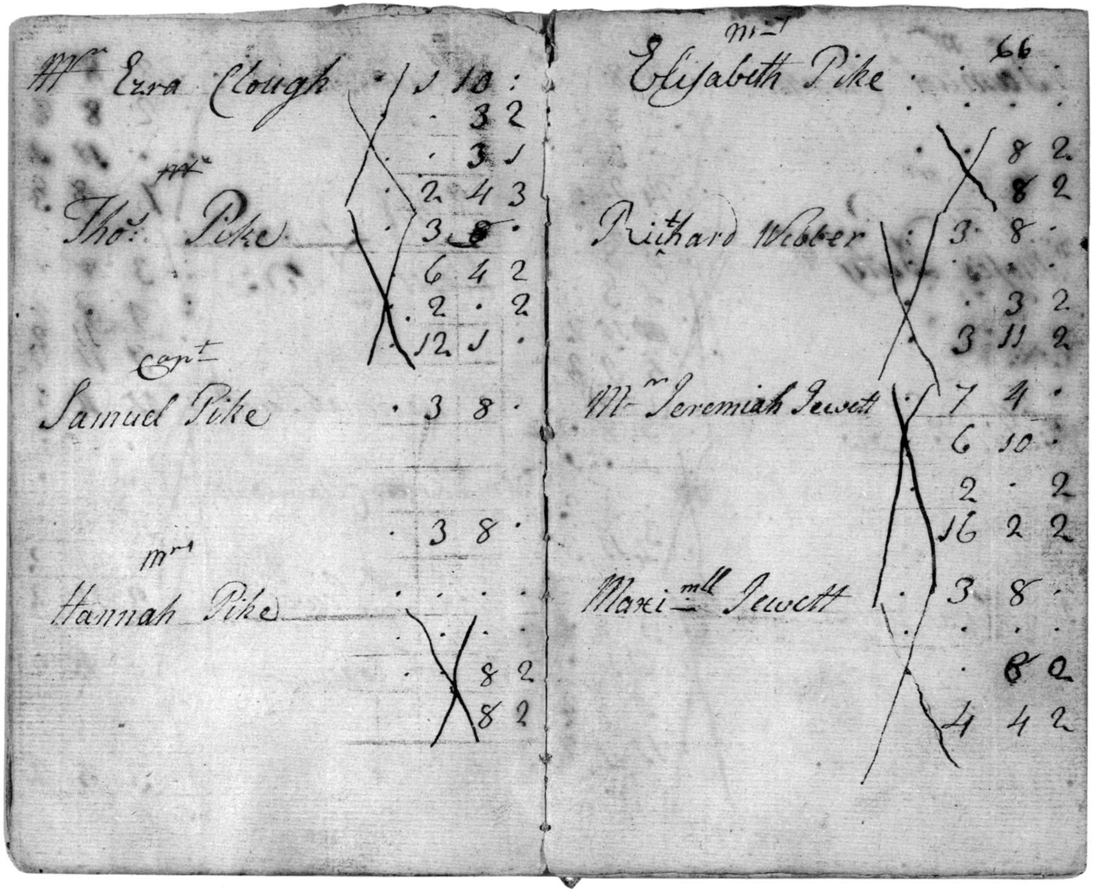

Tax Assessment Book,
Rowley, Massachusetts,
1772

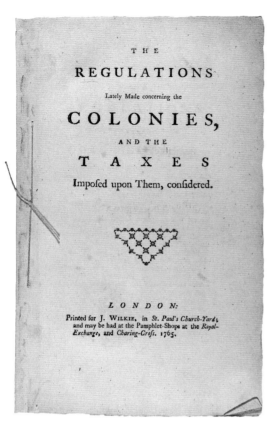

In 1764–65 Parliament imposed taxes on the colonies, a right it always believed it possessed but had never put into practice. The chief tax was the Stamp Tax on all printed matter—newspapers, pamphlets, legal documents, even playing cards. In this pamphlet George Grenville, the king's principal minister, justifies the right of Parliament to tax the colonists on the grounds that each member of Parliament legislates for everyone in the empire, not merely his own constituents. In America the Stamp Act Congress, composed of delegates from nine colonial assemblies, rejected the idea, asserting that "no taxes ever have been, or can be constitutionally imposed on them, but by their respective legislatures." Surrendering to the pressure, Parliament repealed the Stamp Act but retained the principle of its right to tax the colonists and adopted new taxes. The colonists continued to protest British measures but did not send delegates to another intercolonial congress until 1774.

Title page from *The Regulations Lately Made concerning the Colonies and the Taxes Imposed upon Them*, by George Grenville (London, 1765)

"He has dissolved Representative Houses repeatedly"

Colonial assemblies had the right to meet and to pass laws, but in the royal colonies (nine of the thirteen) the governor appointed by the king had the right to "prorogue" or dissolve the assembly. When the Stamp Act Congress met in New York City on October 7, 1765, in the chambers of the New York Assembly, the New York assemblymen passed a resolution in support of the Congress. The lieutenant governor thereupon dismissed the assembly. In the years that followed other royal governors would dissolve colonial legislatures that defied royal authority.

Proclamation dismissing the General Assembly, issued by Cadwallader Colden, the royal lieutenant governor of New York, October 9, 1765

"He has refused his Assent to Laws, the most wholesome and necessary for the public good"

Under the royal system, the elected colonial assemblies could pass laws, but all laws had to be approved first by the governor and the council appointed by the governor and then by the Board of Trade in England. The British either "allowed" or "disallowed" (vetoed) colonial laws.

The issuance of paper currency, such as these notes, by the colonists was a source of dispute. Faced with a shortage of gold or silver to pay their debts to British creditors, the colonists resorted to various types of paper money. Parliament restricted colonial assemblies from issuing such money through a series of currency acts, and British officials disallowed some but not all such currency in the colonies.

"Raising the conditions of new Appropriations of Lands"

Colonists and the British also clashed over the policy on land that was occupied by American Indians in the vast American interior. In 1763 a royal proclamation established a temporary western boundary for settlement and reserved for the crown the right to purchase land from the Indians. In this letter to the superintendent of Indian affairs, the British forbid "the Settlements lately projected near the Ohio" as "injurious to the Indians" and as an "audacious Defiance of . . . Royal Authority."

Paper currency issued by
colonial assemblies,
1765–75

ced, Practices. The Settlements lately projected near the Ohio by Persons from Maryland & Virginia, as appears by your last Letter, & ca. that of the 15 Jan.r to the Board of Trade, are so injurious to the Indians, so detrimental to the Interests of His Majesty's Provinces, & such an audacious Defiance of His Royal Authority repeatedly signified both in Proclamations, & Instructions to His Governors & Superintendant, that they can by no means be permitted; &

Letter from the Earl of Shelburne, British secretary of state for foreign affairs, to Sir William Johnson, superintendent of Indian affairs, June 20, 1767

"Altering fundamentally the Forms of our Governments"

This pamphlet caused a sensation throughout the colonies, where it was first printed in 1773. It contains private letters, secretly obtained by Benjamin Franklin, from leading royal officials of Massachusetts to their superiors in Britain. Governor Hutchinson wanted to free the executive and judicial branches of the colonial government from any economic dependence on the colonial legislature. He contended that ultimately either Parliament or the colonies had to be supreme. To Samuel and John Adams, as to other colonists, the letters were proof of an attempt to "subvert the constitution" of the colony of Massachusetts and of a long conspiracy to bring them under tyranny.

THE
LETTERS
OF
Governor HUTCHINSON,
Thomas
AND
Lieut. Governor OLIVER, &c.
Printed at BOSTON.
AND REMARKS THEREON.
With the ASSEMBLY'S ADDRESS,
And the PROCEEDINGS
Of the LORDS COMMITTEE of COUNCIL.
Together with
The SUBSTANCE of Mr. WEDDERBURN'S SPEECH
relating to those LETTERS.
And the REPORT of the LORDS COMMITTEE
to his MAJESTY in COUNCIL.
THE SECOND EDITION.

LONDON:
Printed for J. WILKIE, at Number 71, in
St. Paul's Church-yard. MDCCLXXIV.

Title page from *The Letters of Governor Hutchinson and Lieut. Governor Oliver* (London, 1774)

Patriots Take Action

Patriots took aggressive action against the British. "We have warned them," they wrote of their "British brethren" in the Declaration; "We have appealed." And so they had, in legislative resolutions, in petitions, in newspaper articles, and in pamphlets. To arouse their fellow citizens, patriots made speeches, preached sermons, and wrote songs and poems.

Patriots did much more than write and speak. In the cities they enforced boycotts against importers of British goods, conducted street demonstrations against British officeholders, fought with British troops, and dumped chests of tea into Boston harbor. They erected Liberty Poles as symbols of defiance.

At first the patriot leaders came from the ranks of educated gentlemen—the merchants, planters, lawyers, and ministers who had long dominated colonial political life. But crowds of artisans, shopkeepers, apprentices, and sailors in cities and towns often took action on their own or in response to their own leaders, as did farmers in the countryside. Joining the Sons of Liberty as Daughters of Liberty, women spun their own textiles and refused to buy British goods or drink imported tea.

Colonists were sharply divided. Patriots (or "Whigs") argued with Loyalists (called "Tories"), but large numbers played no part in the political conflict. Indeed, not all Americans considered the British a threat. African Americans knew slaveholders did not intend liberty for them. American Indians saw the British as their protectors against land-hungry settlers. Many poor backcountry farmers or tenant farmers refused to make common cause with aristocratic landholders.

Patriots further divided between what contemporaries called "cool" or "moderate" men and "hot-headed" or "violent" men. John Adams, a prominent Massachusetts lawyer, was representative of moderate leaders driven by events to become more radical. In 1770 when he defended the British soldiers on trial for the Boston Massacre, he was a foe of popular turbulence who saw the soldiers as victims of a mob. By 1773 he admired the illegal destruction of the tea at the Boston Tea Party as "necessary" and "magnificent." By 1776 he was a delegate to the Continental Congress and an advocate of independence.

As common people acquired a sense of their own strength, they refused to defer to their "betters," and they transformed what began as a movement to conserve existing rights into a revolution in which they would demand their natural rights, including a greater voice.

We the Subscribers in order to releive the Trade under those discouragements to promote Industry Frugality & Oeconomy & to discourage Luxury & every kind of Extravagence, do promise & Engage to and with each other as follows —

1st That we will not send for or Import from Great Britain either upon our own Account or upon Commissions this Fall any other goods than what are already ordered for the Fall Supply

2d That we will not send for or import any kind of Goods or Merchandize from Great Britain either on our own Account or on Commissions or any otherwise from the 1st Jany 1769 to the 1st Jany 1770 Except Salt, Coals, Fish hooks & Lines, Hemp & Duck, Bar Lead & Shott, Wool Cards & Card wire

Resolution by Boston merchants restricting the importation of British goods, August 1, 1768

In the Stamp Act crisis of 1765–66, colonists agreed not to import British manufactured goods. This effective tactic led British exporters to bring pressure on Parliament to repeal the act. In 1767 Parliament, insisting on the right to tax, adopted the Townshend duties on tea, lead, glass, paper, and painters' colors imported by the colonists. Once again, colonists adopted a nonimportation tactic. In this handwritten copy of the agreement that circulated for signatures in Boston, merchants agreed not to import British goods for one year, from January 1, 1769, to January 1, 1770. To enforce the boycott, patriot committees visited nonsigners and organized picket lines in front of their stores.

Mercy Otis Warren

As women took up patriotic activities, a few writers like Mercy Otis Warren (1728–1814) entered the male political world. Mercy Warren was a well-to-do woman from one of the leading families of Plymouth, Massachusetts, whose father, brother, and husband were patriot leaders. She wrote poems and verse plays that ran in the patriot press under a pseudonym. Her plays satirized Tory leaders in a sharp style considered inappropriate for women.

Before the revolutionary war, she used no female characters in what she called her "dramatic sketches." But in her poems, through the voices of women, she appealed to women to join the patriot cause. And she corresponded with other women, such as Abigail Adams, wife of John Adams, encouraging them to speak out for the patriot cause.

After the war, her verse plays featured as central characters women of earlier ages who had taken a role in the struggle for liberty. In one play a woman criticizes men who prefer in women "the fading, short lived, perishable trifle beauty" to "noble, exalted mental accomplishments."

In 1788 Mercy Warren wrote an influential pamphlet opposing the Constitution because it lacked a bill of rights. She used the pseudonym "A Columbian Patriot." In 1790 she published her collected poetry under her own name.

Her crowning achievement was a three-volume history published in 1805. The work celebrates the participation of ordinary people in the Revolution, but it has scarcely a word to say about women. Her accomplishments as a woman who dared to voice political opinions inspired the women of her own day.

Mercy Otis Warren, engraving from *The Women of the American Revolution,* vol. 1, by Elizabeth F. Ellet, 1848

Warren's book includes a poem written in 1774 that appeals to women to join in the boycott of imported British luxuries. She urges women to lay their *"female ornaments aside,"* foregoing *"feathers, furs, rich sattins and du capes / And head dresses in pyramidal shapes."*

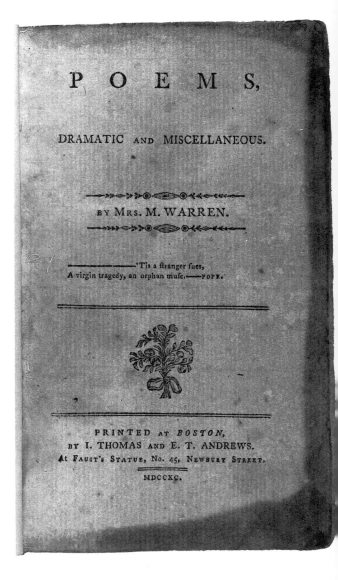

Title page from *Poems, Dramatic and Miscellaneous,* by Mercy Otis Warren (Boston, 1790)

Paul Revere, painting by
John Singleton Copley,
1768–70. Gift of Joseph
W., William B., and
Edward H. R. Revere.
Courtesy, Museum of
Fine Arts, Boston

Paul Revere

Paul Revere (1735–1818) is generally
remembered as the horseman who
carried the news that "the British are
coming" from Boston to Lexington.
But in his own day he was best
known as a leader of Boston's
mechanics, or skilled craftsmen. He
applied his skills as a silversmith and
engraver to the patriot cause. His work
appeared in newspapers, magazines, and
almanacs, on broadsides, and in public
displays. His engraving of the Boston Massacre was the most famous
of many illustrations he did to inspire patriots.

After the war Revere was a leader of the mechanics' campaign to
ratify the Constitution, and he became the first president of the
Massachusetts Mechanics Association. Later, he opened a copper and
brass factory, where he cast bells for New England churches and
fittings for the nation's early naval vessels.

In this portrait by John Singleton Copley, painted at a time
when he was using his skills in the patriot cause, Revere is depicted at
his workbench in his work clothes, a tool of his trade at hand. It was
unusual for an artisan to have his portrait painted. In colonial days, if
he were wealthy enough, he usually had himself painted in the clothes
of a gentleman, showing that he had arrived. Revere, by contrast, is
proud to be an artisan.

When he died in 1818 a friend wrote of him in a Boston paper:
"He was a Prosperous North End Mechanic, quietly but energetically
pushing his business interest. . . . He was a born leader of the people,
and his influence was pervading, especially among the mechanics and
workingmen of Boston, with whom his popularity was immense."

Detail from *Paul Revere's
Ride, April 19, 1775,*
drawn by Charles G.
Bush, *Harper's Weekly,*
1867

*The Bloody Massacre
perpetrated in King Street,
Boston, on March 5, 1770,
engraving by Paul
Revere, 1770 (Color
Plate 1)*

Engrav'd Printed & Sold by PAUL REVERE BOSTON

In 1767, the British established a Board of Customs in Boston and sent commissioners to enforce new stringent regulations of trade. Demonstrations and threats by crowds in effect nullified the laws, and so in 1768 the British sent troops to enforce them—four thousand soldiers (later reduced to about two thousand) in a city of fifteen thousand civilians. To patriot leaders, armies of professional soldiers— known as standing armies—were a threat to English liberties, since the soldiers could be used to overpower the legislature. To ordinary Bostonians, the soldiers were a constant source of tension in everyday life.

On March 5, 1770, tensions reached a climax in the event patriots called the "Boston Massacre." Contemporaries disagreed about causes, and historians still puzzle over the evidence. The event was precipitated by an incident in a rope factory a few nights before in which an off-duty soldier looking for work was insulted by a worker, and a brawl ensued in which the workingmen beat up a large group of soldiers. The soldiers wanted revenge; townsmen were ready to take them on.

Paul Revere's engraving, copied without permission from a painting by the Boston artist Henry Pelham, presents the patriot version of the shooting. The engraving by Alonzo Chappel, a mid-nineteenth-century artist who did dozens of paintings and engravings of the Revolution, presents a more realistic yet still dramatic version.

In Revere's version the soldiers are lined up, firing in unison at the command of Captain Thomas

Preston. Unarmed townspeople, most of them well dressed, are falling in the streets as a woman in widow's weeds mourns the death of the young men.

In Chappel's version the event is more chaotic. Aggressive townsmen—many in the clothes of laboring men, some with clubs—threaten the soldiers. The soldiers are firing in disarray, and Captain Preston has his hand raised as if to stop them. Horrified civilians watch as a soldier drives his bayonet into a wounded man. The man near the center with his club raised may be Crispus Attucks, a sailor who was half-black, half-Indian. Chappel also portrays the two men to Attucks's left as African Americans.

Chappel's version is a closer rendition of the evidence brought out at the trials of Preston and the soldiers. John Adams, lawyer for the defendants, told the jury the crowd was composed of "a motley rabble of saucy boys, negroes and molottoes, Irish teagues and outlandish jack tarrs" who threatened the soldiers. Revere's version is what Americans came to accept. It may not have been the way it happened, but it embodied a protest on an issue of principle.

The framers of the Declaration of Independence incorporated this grievance: in peace time, "Standing Armies without the Consent of our legislatures" rendered "the Military independent of and superior to the Civil power." Later, in framing the Constitution and Bill of Rights, Americans showed how much they cherished this principle by insisting on civilian supremacy over the military.

Spreading the Word

As John Adams worried about how to recover the "real revolution" in American opinion from 1765 to 1775, he thought it would be necessary to collect "all the records, pamphlets, newspapers and even handbills which in any way contributed" to this change.

Pamphlets, which usually ran from sixteen to sixty-four pages, appeared unbound with only a title page. Selling for a few cents, they were hawked around town by boys or in the country by peddlars. Some four hundred appeared in the decade before 1776.

Newspapers grew in number from twenty-three in 1764 to forty-four in 1775, and most were four-page tabloid-size weeklies. A circulation of five hundred copies was good, one thousand high. When Isaiah Thomas's *Massachusetts Spy* reached thirty-five hundred in 1775, he boasted that he had the largest circulation in New England.

A handbill or broadside was a single page that a printer could run off quickly to report the latest news just arrived from Europe or to rouse people to come to a meeting. These were often posted on trees or tavern doors.

In the list of sources that can reveal the "real revolution," John Adams forgot to include almanacs, the best sellers of their day, which were issued once a year. Amid useful information about the weather, the tides, or post office roads, almanac printers interspersed political jibes and crude pictures.

In a world without telephones, radio, or television, printers spread the word. They reported events and published opinions that reflected the popular temper and mobilized the people. The publications that poured from the printing presses were part of a revolution in communications.

Engraving (Paris, 1751–52) from Denis Diderot, *L'Encyclopédie, ou Dictionnaire raisonné des sciences, des arts, et des métiers*

Printer's composing stick, c. 1780

A printer's composing stick, which he held in one hand while he picked letters of type from the upper and lower cases, is a vivid reminder of the state of communications in the era of the Revolution. Letter by letter, line by line, the printer assembled words and sentences that would make up a column of a newspaper or the pages of a pamphlet. He would then place the type in a flatbed press, ink it, and press paper down on the type, one page at a time.

The Boston Post-Boy &
Advertiser, Boston, April
8, 1765

Top: facsimile of The
Massachusetts Spy Or,
American Oracle of
Liberty, Worcester, Mas-
sachusetts, May 3, 1775

Bottom: The Independent
Ledger and the American
Advertiser, Boston,
December 7, 1778

The Congregational ministers in New England, one Loyalist complained, preached from "pulpits of sedition." By contrast, the Anglican Episcopal Church, the Church of England, was generally Loyalist.

Congregational ministers were learned men who wrote out their sermons before reading them in the pulpit rather than delivering them extemporaneously. In this selection from the notebook of Rev. Isaiah Dunster of New Hampshire, the minister takes as his text a passage from Luke and ends with the clear message that Christians need not submit to the "great men [who] make it their chief Design to Oppress the Common People"—a message that in 1775 clearly could be taken to justify rebellion.

Sermon on Luke 4:18–19, by Isaiah Dunster, 1775

The Tea Act of 1773 led to the era's most sweeping and dramatic acts of resistance. American merchants violated the Townshend duty of 1767 imposed on tea, smuggling in tea from the Orient that was shipped by other countries, especially Holland. With the Tea Act, Parliament came to the aid of the powerful East India Company, which was stuck with eighteen million pounds of unsold tea. The act lowered the tax to make the tea more palatable to colonists—but allowed the company to sell through their own agents, thus undercutting American merchants. The action raised the ancient fear of monopoly among patriots: if Parliament could come to the aid of one special interest, why not others?

Resistance was strong in the seaports. If the tea was unloaded the tax would go into effect. The goal of patriot leaders in Boston was to force the East India Company ships carrying the tea to take it back to England. When three tea-laden ships docked in the harbor, patriots watched them closely. In November and December 1773 mass meetings of the "whole body of the people" debated a course of action with as many as five thousand men packed into Old South meetinghouse. When Loyalist officials refused to allow the ships to leave Boston harbor without unloading the tea, the meeting of December 16 sanctioned the only course of action they considered possible: destroying the tea to prevent paying the tax.

The British response to the Boston Tea Party set the stage for the final crisis that led to rebellion. Parliament passed the so-called punitive or coercive acts. Parliament closed the ports of Boston until Bostonians paid for the tea, and they altered the Massachusetts government, curtailing town meetings and giving the royal governor power to appoint the council. Parliament also gave the power to choose members of trial juries to the governor-appointed sheriff and expanded the military's power to quarter troops. Patriots called these measures the Intolerable Acts.

Patriots throughout the colonies came to the aid of the blockaded Bostonians by sending food and money. "The cause of Boston is the cause of America," wrote George Washington.

The Tea Party

Tea was the favorite nonalcoholic drink among all classes in the colonies, occupying the place that coffee holds today. The genteel classes imitated the British afternoon tea ceremonies. They stored their tea in well-crafted tea chests with compartments for Bohea, Hyson, and other types of tea.

English tea chest, c. 1775

In this mid-nineteenth-century lithograph Nathaniel Currier (later part of the team of Currier and Ives) got almost everything wrong about the event of December 1773. In reality, the action took place at night, and only a few of the participants were disguised as Indians (most had time only to smear some soot on their faces as a disguise). The work was hard, and only apprentices and artisans could raise the heavy chests from the holds; they did not throw the chests overboard but broke them open with axes, spilling the tea into the harbor; the crowd assembled on the docks did not cheer but stood in awed silence. No matter, the Boston Tea Party was a bold, defiant act that caught the imagination of Americans at the time and ever since has symbolized civil disobedience to unjust laws.

The Destruction of Tea at Boston Harbor, lithograph by Nathaniel Currier, 1846

THE DESTRUCTION OF TEA AT BOSTON HARBOR.

To help the blockaded Bostonians, leaders in New York City collected money ward by ward, recording the receipts and disbursements on this ledger page. The page on the right lists the donations for each ward. The page on the left lists the money paid from these donations to various suppliers of provisions, mostly for "barrels of flour" and "firkins of butter" but also for iron and nails.

Accounting of cash received from New York contributors for Boston's poor, 1774–75

Many people in Great Britain sympathized with the colonists, especially reformers who sought to change the corrupt, unrepresentative British political system. Political opinions were often expressed on broadsides hawked through the streets of London and displayed in taverns. These caricatures were the popular political cartoons of their day. This drawing mocks the government's policy of starving Boston into submission. Bostonians are locked in a cage like common criminals or slaves and are being fed fish by the American sailors. Troops and cannon face them below. The cage hangs on the Liberty Tree, symbol of the patriot cause.

The Bostonians in Distress, engraving by Philip Dawe, 1774

In this American-made engraving the colonies are represented by an Indian maiden—long a symbol of the American continent—and the British by a well-dressed gentleman pouring tea down her throat, the Boston Port Bill stuffed in his back pocket. The maiden has been stripped half-naked. She is being restrained by one Briton while another lecherously peers up her dress. Britannia, the symbol of Great Britain, hides her head in shame at this rape of America. The original cartoon appeared in London, where it appealed to the British who sympathized with the American cause. Paul Revere copied it in Boston, and a printer in New London, Connecticut, copied it again for the cover of his Almanack, *an example of a cheap form of literature that circulated widely in the countryside.*

Title page from
*Freebetter's New-England
Almanack* (New London,
1776); *right*: detail

After the enactment of the Intolerable Acts in the spring of 1774, events moved swiftly toward war. In Massachusetts the British appointed a general as royal governor and moved in enough troops to make Boston an armed camp. In the fall, a Continental Congress met in Philadelphia and sponsored associations in every community to boycott British imports.

In Massachusetts, patriots formed a provincial congress, an illegal revolutionary government, that met at Concord. The local militia drilled, pledged to be ready at a minute's notice (hence the name "minutemen"), and stored up arms.

On the night of April 18, 1775, seven hundred British troops marched out of Boston to seize military stores at Concord. Boston's patriots sent Paul Revere and William Dawes to alert the country towns.

When the British arrived at Lexington Green at dawn on April 19, they encountered only about forty minutemen. The commander of the American militia ordered his men to disperse. Someone fired a shot. The British charged, wounding ten Americans and killing eight.

The British then marched into nearby Concord, setting buildings on fire. The four hundred minutemen assembled at Concord Bridge saw their burning homes and marched toward town. A skirmish ensued.

As the British retreated, several thousand enraged farmers swarmed toward the retreating army to repel the invasion. All the way back to Boston they sniped at the British, guerrilla style, from behind stone walls and trees. The war had begun.

Amos Doolittle's engraving presents the patriot version of what happened at Lexington on the morning of April 19, 1775: British troops are attacking, firing a volley of shots on the orders of their commander; they are mowing down the Lexington minutemen, who are dispersing, not returning fire.

Doolittle's version supports the sworn deposition of John Parker, captain of the Lexington militia, who on hearing the news that the British regulars were on the march from Boston ordered the militia to muster in order "to consult what to do." As the British appeared Parker "immediately ordered our militia to disperse and not to fire. Immediately said British troops made their appearance and rushed furiously, fired upon and killed eight of our party without receiving any provocation therefore from us."

Establishing who fired the first shot has been important to Americans in every war because it seems to determine who is the aggressor and who is the defender. Historians who have studied many eyewitness testimonies see a more complex event at Lexington. The militia was indeed dispersing, but it is likely that militiamen behind stone walls or in the town tavern fired the first shots. It also seems that the British troops, in a wild frenzy and out of control of their officers, charged into the retreating militia, some of whom fired back.

Who fired the first shot matters less than the fundamental issues at stake. But blaming the British added strength to the cause of patriots who took up arms.

Amos Doolittle's four engravings of the battles of Lexington and Concord (Color Plates 2–5) are the first pictorial war reporting in America. Doolittle, a twenty-one-year-old apprentice silversmith who had taught himself how to engrave on copper, was in the New Haven militia that marched to the aid of Massachusetts. He visited Lexington and Concord soon after the battles, and by the end of the year, he had engraved four views, which he advertised as being "from original paintings taken on the spot," possibly by Ralph Earl. Crude and distorted in perspective though they may be, the engravings present the sense of outrage that inspired patriots to take up arms.

The Battle of Lexington, April 19, 1775, engraving by Amos Doolittle, December 1775 (Color Plate 2)

The Battle of Lexington, April 19th 1775. Plate I.

A. Doolittle Sculpt.

1. Major Pitcarn, at the head of the Regular Granadiers.
2. The Party, who first fired on the Provincials at Lexington.
3. Part of the Provincial Company of Lexington.
4. Regular Companies on the road to Concord.
5. The Metinghouse at Lexington.
6. The Public Inn.

John Jones was in a militia unit from Princeton, Massachusetts, that marched to the aid of their countrymen as soon as they heard of the encounter at Concord, but his unit did not see action. Three days after the encounter he wrote to his wife to report that he was safe and that his regiment was "stationed in one of ye Colleges" at Cambridge (Harvard), to send his love to her and his family, and to pray that "our God . . . may save us from Ruin."

Militiamen were outfitted in clothing made by their wives and family. "If you have an Opportunity," Jones asked his wife, "you may find Brother Hapgoods a Shirt and pair of Stockings." And, mindful that his wife was now in charge of the farm and that it was planting time, he added a postscript telling her where she could get some seed to grow the flax she needed to make linen.

Cambridge Apr 22 1775
Loving Wife—

There was a hot Battle fought Between the Regulars that march'd to Concord and our People, on Wednesday the 19 of this Instant in which many on both sides were slain / but most of the Enemies / as we heard before we march'd. As we marched to Concord we were often Inform'd that the Enemy had marched from Boston a second time had got as far as Lincoln—we hurried on as fast as Possible Expecting to meet them in Concord but when we arrived there we were Inform'd that they had Return from their first Engagement to Charleston—from which they are gone to Boston—we are now stationed in one of ye Colleges as are many more of ye Army—all in good health Through ye Divine goodness and hope for ye Blessing of Heaven.

In ye first Combat among those that were slain were Lieut John Bacon of Newham two mills, Nat Chamb^n and 2 others from Needham—Elias Haven from Springfield—

If you have an Opportunity you may find Brother Hapgoods a Shirt and pair of Stockings—Tis uncertain when we shall Return may we all be Enabled to Repent & turn to our God that he may save us from Ruin.

I am with the Greatest Respect your Affectionate & Loving Husband till Death.
John Jones
N.B. my Best Love to Brother Jones & Children—Let us all be Patient & Remember that it is ye hand of God

Capt Moore has sold his flaxseed but if you apply in season you may get some of M^r. Woods—

Cambridge Apr.: 22. 1775 ———

Loving Wife — There was a hot Battle fought
between the Regulars that march'd to Concord
and our People on wednesday the 19 of this Instant
in which many on both sides were Slain, but
most of the Enemies / as we heard before we march'd
as we marched to Concord we were often Inform'd
that the Enemy had marched form Boston a second
time had got as far as Lincoln — we hurried on
as fast as Possible Expecting to meet theon in
Concord but when we arrived there we were
Inform'd that they had Return from their first
Engagement to Charleston — from which they are
gone to Boston — we are now Stationed in one
of ye Colleges are are many more of ye Army —
all in good health Through ye Divine goodness
and in hope for ye Blessing of Heaven ———

In ye first Combat among those that were Slain
were Lieut: John Bacon of Needham two millers
Nat. Chamb.n and 2 others from Needham ———
Elias Haven from Springfield —

If you have an Opportunity you may send
Brother Hapgoods a Shirt and pair of Stocki-
-gs — Tis uncertain when we shall Return
may we all be Enabled to Repent & turn to
our God that he may Save us from Ruin —

I am with the Greatest Respect your
Affectionate & Loving Husband till Death

John Jones

N.B. my Best Love to
Brother Jones & Children — Let us all
be Patient & Remember that it is ye hand of
God ———

Capt. Moore has Sold his flax seed
but if you apply in Season you may get
Some of Mr. Wood —

Declaring Independence

Opposite: Pulling Down the Statue of George III, engraving by John McRae, c. 1860

In celebrating independence from Great Britain in 1776, Americans rejected not only King George III but the principle of monarchy. After the Declaration of Independence was read aloud in the seaboard cities, crowds destroyed every symbol of royal authority and kingship they could lay their hands on.

New York City witnessed the most dramatic action: citizens pulled down an equestrian statue of King George III, an event that was depicted in an oil painting in the mid-nineteenth century and later reproduced in this engraving. The statue, erected in 1770, was made of lead, but it was "very elegant and richly gilded" so that it looked like gold. It stood in Bowling Green near the tip of Manhattan Island, and before its completion it was so often a target of the Sons of Liberty that the royal government passed a law to "prevent the defacing of statues."

On July 9, 1776, after the public reading of the Declaration, troops and civilians went to work on the statue. The artist used his imagination to recreate the scene, for which he probably had no eyewitness accounts. Soldiers at the right pull down the statue with ropes and a worker with a sledge hammer approaches on the left. A gentleman and a lady stand to the right, somewhat aghast at this mob action, while at the left a workingman joyfully waves his hat in the air.

Elsewhere other symbols of monarchy were attacked. In Savannah, after hearing the reading of the Declaration at the Liberty Pole, Georgians paraded an effigy of the king to the courthouse, where they buried it. In Boston Abigail Adams reported to her husband, John, "The Kings Arms were taken down from the State House, together with all shop signs and inn signs with royal symbols, and burnt in King Street."

Even after the colonists began fighting they did not adopt independence as their goal. The war that began at Lexington April 19, 1775, went on for more than a year before Americans declared their independence. Patriots were divided politically; many moderate leaders held out for reconciliation, doubtful about winning a war and fearful of what the internal upheavals of revolution might bring.

What now seems inevitable was the result of bitter debate between advocates of independence and of reconciliation. Thomas Paine's decisive pamphlet *Common Sense*, published in January 1776 and reprinted through the spring, won many patriots to his ideals of independence under a republican government. Popular opinion welled up, and the Continental Congress at Philadelphia moved toward independence. In June the delegates at the congress appointed a committee to draft a statement, and in July they adopted a declaration of independence that expressed their fundamental principles.

Common Sense: *Independence and No King*

The harsh military actions of the British and their rejection of American appeals paved the way in 1776 for Thomas Paine's *Common Sense*, the most influential pamphlet of the era. In common language Paine ridiculed every argument for reconciliation with the parent country, condemning not only King George III as the "royal brute" but also the very idea that mankind should be ruled by kings.

While *Common Sense* effectively ended the debate over independence, it stimulated another debate over how America should be ruled. Paine supported giving power to ordinary people in large, elected representative assemblies based on a broad male suffrage.

John Adams, although a strong advocate of independence, rushed the pamphlet *Thoughts on Government* into print, arguing for constitutions that would check and balance popular majorities and preserve "respect for persons of authority."

Controversy over how democratic or how aristocratic the new America would be continued through the revolutionary era and beyond.

Thomas Paine, artist unknown, copied from the 1792 portrait by George Romney

"I know not whether any man in the world has had more influence on its inhabitants or affairs for the last thirty years than Thomas Paine," wrote John Adams in 1805. Paine wrote three of the most popular pamphlets of the eighteenth century: Common Sense *(1776),* The Rights of Man *(1791), and* The Age of Reason *(1795). Paine lived the first thirty-seven years of his life in England, where he worked as an artisan (a corsetmaker by trade), a tobacconist, and a tax collector. A self-educated man, he emigrated from England to Philadelphia in 1774 in search of opportunity. He became a magazine editor and associated with artisans who were at the forefront of the movement for independence and democracy.*

After the success of Common Sense, *he wrote a series of pamphlets during the war to rally patriots, the first of which began, "These are the times that try men's souls." In 1786 he returned to England to garner support for his invention of an iron bridge. In 1791 he wrote* The Rights of Man, *a defense of the French Revolution and a scathing attack on the English system of monarchy and the corrupt aristocratic government.*

In 1792, about the time George Romney painted the original of this portrait, in which Paine is holding a manuscript marked "The Rights of Man," the British government charged Paine with sedition, and he fled to France. There he was made an honorary member of the revolutionary convention. When he was imprisoned during the Reign of Terror, he wrote his third great pamphlet, The Age of Reason, *attacking organized religion for being in league with aristocracy and monarchy.*

In the nineteenth century many paid homage to Paine; this painting was copied either from the original or from an engraving based on it. It was a flattering tribute to a man who could say of himself, "A share in two revolutions is living to some purpose."

Common Sense *first appeared in January 1776, only fourteen months after Paine arrived from England. It went through two dozen printings, selling as many as 150,000 copies by July. At the time, a circulation of five thousand was considered large for a pamphlet.*

To win his readers to the cause of independence, Paine tried to break the ties that bound them. "Britain is the parent country say some. Then the more shame upon her conduct. Even brutes do not devour their young nor savages make war upon their families."

To attack monarchy he tried to open people's eyes to the historical record: since the Norman conquest England "hath known some few good monarchs but groaned beneath a much larger number of bad ones." He challenged the origins of monarchy: "William the Conqueror a French Bastard landing with an armed banditti and establishing himself king of England is in plain terms a very paltry original. It certainly hath no divinity in it." Above all he appealed to the principle of equality: "Of more worth is one honest man to society and in the sight of God than all the crowned ruffians that ever lived."

He ended with a stirring appeal to idealism: "We have it in our power to begin the world over again. A situation similar to the present, hath not happened since the days of Noah until now. The birthday of a new world is at hand."

This copy of the pamphlet was reprinted in England in 1791 by the same reform movement that circulated The Rights of Man. *By then reformers in Great Britain and France regarded the American Revolution as a successful example to follow.*

Title page from *Common Sense*, by Thomas Paine, London edition, 1791

COMMON SENSE;

ADDRESSED TO THE

INHABITANTS

OF

AMERICA,

On the following interesting

SUBJECTS:

I. Of the Origin and Design of Government in general, with concise Remarks on the English Constitution.
II. Of Monarchy and Hereditary Succession.
III. Thoughts on the Present State of American Affairs.
IV. Of the present Ability of America, with some miscellaneous Reflections.

A NEW EDITION, with several Additions in the Body of the Work. To which is added, an APPENDIX; together with an Address to the People called QUAKERS.

N. B. The New Edition here given, increases the Work upwards of One-Third.

By THOMAS PAINE,

Secretary for Foreign Affairs to Congress during the American War, and Author of *The Rights of Man*, and a *Letter to the Abbe Raynal.*

LONDON:
PRINTED FOR J. S. JORDAN, NO. 166, FLEET-STREET.
M,DCC,XCI.

"A view to independency is growing in the Colonies,"
Cogswell *wrote from Stamford, Connecticut, to
Major Joseph Ward early in March 1776.* Common
Sense *"has made many proselytes, and I believe will
open the eyes of the common people."*

Ward, a Boston schoolteacher serving as aide-
de-camp to General Artemas Ward in Washington's
new army outside of Boston, agreed. A week later he
wrote to his friend John Adams, *"I hope* Common
Sense *will convince every doubting mind, with
regard to the propriety and necessity of forming a*
Government in *America."*

Another correspondent informed Adams that in
the South they speak of nothing *"but* Common
Sense *and independency."* And still another reported
that ordinary people were asking why *"their superiors"* in the Continental Congress were so slow to
follow *"the dictates of common sense."* By June Congress acted. Never had a single pamphlet moved so
many Americans.

The Philosophy of the Declaration

In announcing the separation from Britain, the framers of the Declaration of Independence felt compelled to justify the extreme act of revolution with a statement of their political philosophy. The Declaration was written by Thomas Jefferson, who was assisted by a committee that included John Adams and Benjamin Franklin. Jefferson was chosen, wrote Adams, "for the elegance of his pen."

Their reasoning was concise and eloquent. They assumed a state of nature, before governments existed, in which "all men are created equal" and have "certain unalienable Rights, that among these are Life, Liberty and the pursuit of Happiness." To protect these rights, men come together to form governments that require the "consent of the governed."

If any form of government repeatedly took away the peoples' rights, aiming to put them under "absolute despotism," then it was "the Right of the People to alter or abolish it." Indeed it was "their duty." A long "train of abuses and usurpations" was offered as evidence that Americans were now entitled to exercise this natural right.

What did the framers mean by "all men are created equal"? Did they mean blacks as well as whites, women as well as men? Who gave the "consent of the governed"? The Congress that adopted the Declaration included slaveholders from the plantation South who had no intention of abolishing slavery; indeed Congress forced Jefferson to eliminate a statement condemning the king for refusing to allow states to ban the slave trade. Instead Congress chastised the king for "exciting domestic insurrections," a specific reference to the efforts of the British commander in Virginia to recruit slaves by promising freedom.

The ringing phrases meant one thing to the leaders, most of whom took for granted a political world composed of white male property holders, who had a right to hold slaves as property, but they meant something more to the unequals in American society. The Declaration, as it inspired many colonists to the cause of independence, inspired others to seek equality and a voice in their government.

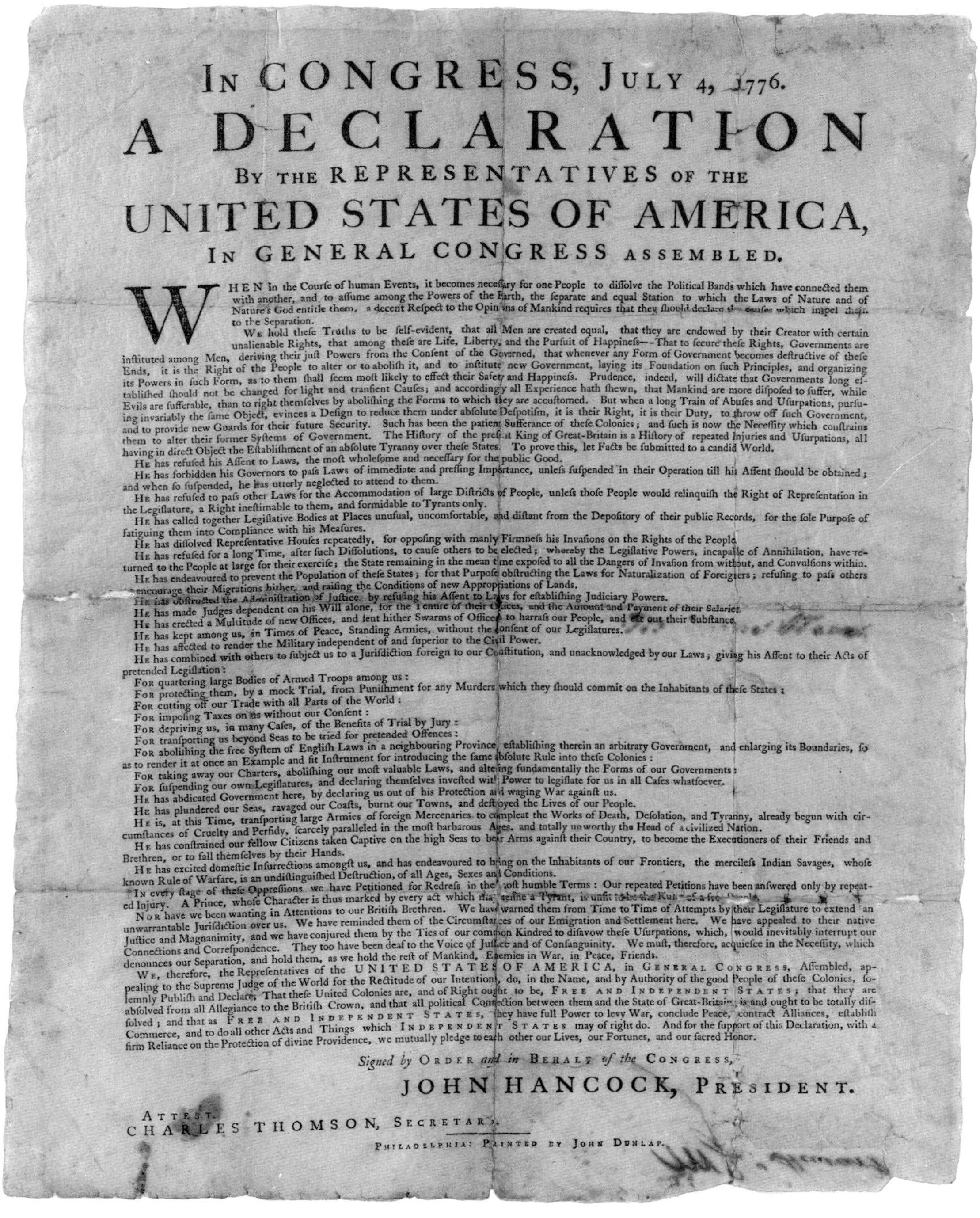
IN CONGRESS, JULY 4, 1776.

A DECLARATION

BY THE REPRESENTATIVES OF THE

UNITED STATES OF AMERICA,

IN GENERAL CONGRESS ASSEMBLED.

WHEN in the Course of human Events, it becomes necessary for one People to dissolve the Political Bands which have connected them with another, and to assume among the Powers of the Earth, the separate and equal Station to which the Laws of Nature and of Nature's God entitle them, a decent Respect to the Opinions of Mankind requires that they should declare the causes which impel them to the Separation.

WE hold these Truths to be self-evident, that all Men are created equal, that they are endowed by their Creator with certain unalienable Rights, that among these are Life, Liberty, and the Pursuit of Happiness—That to secure these Rights, Governments are instituted among Men, deriving their just Powers from the Consent of the Governed, that whenever any Form of Government becomes destructive of these Ends, it is the Right of the People to alter or to abolish it, and to institute new Government, laying its Foundation on such Principles, and organizing its Powers in such Form, as to them shall seem most likely to effect their Safety and Happiness. Prudence, indeed, will dictate that Governments long established should not be changed for light and transient Causes; and accordingly all Experience hath shewn, that Mankind are more disposed to suffer, while Evils are sufferable, than to right themselves by abolishing the Forms to which they are accustomed. But when a long Train of Abuses and Usurpations, pursuing invariably the same Object, evinces a Design to reduce them under absolute Despotism, it is their Right, it is their Duty, to throw off such Government, and to provide new Guards for their future Security. Such has been the patient Sufferance of these Colonies; and such is now the Necessity which constrains them to alter their former Systems of Government. The History of the present King of Great-Britain is a History of repeated Injuries and Usurpations, all having in direct Object the Establishment of an absolute Tyranny over these States. To prove this, let Facts be submitted to a candid World.

HE has refused his Assent to Laws, the most wholesome and necessary for the public Good.

HE has forbidden his Governors to pass Laws of immediate and pressing Importance, unless suspended in their Operation till his Assent should be obtained; and when so suspended, he has utterly neglected to attend to them.

HE has refused to pass other Laws for the Accommodation of large Districts of People, unless those People would relinquish the Right of Representation in the Legislature, a Right inestimable to them, and formidable to Tyrants only.

HE has called together Legislative Bodies at Places unusual, uncomfortable, and distant from the Depository of their public Records, for the sole Purpose of fatiguing them into Compliance with his Measures.

HE has dissolved Representative Houses repeatedly, for opposing with manly Firmness his Invasions on the Rights of the People.

HE has refused for a long Time, after such Dissolutions, to cause others to be elected; whereby the Legislative Powers, incapable of Annihilation, have returned to the People at large for their exercise; the State remaining in the mean time exposed to all the Dangers of Invasion from without, and Convulsions within.

HE has endeavoured to prevent the Population of these States; for that Purpose obstructing the Laws for Naturalization of Foreigners; refusing to pass others to encourage their Migrations hither, and raising the Conditions of new Appropriations of Lands.

HE has obstructed the Administration of Justice, by refusing his Assent to Laws for establishing Judiciary Powers.

HE has made Judges dependent on his Will alone, for the Tenure of their Offices, and the Amount and Payment of their Salaries.

HE has erected a Multitude of new Offices, and sent hither Swarms of Officers to harrass our People, and eat out their Substance.

HE has kept among us, in Times of Peace, Standing Armies, without the consent of our Legislatures.

HE has affected to render the Military independent of and superior to the Civil Power.

HE has combined with others to subject us to a Jurisdiction foreign to our Constitution, and unacknowledged by our Laws; giving his Assent to their Acts of pretended Legislation:

FOR quartering large Bodies of Armed Troops among us:

FOR protecting them, by a mock Trial, from Punishment for any Murders which they should commit on the Inhabitants of these States:

FOR cutting off our Trade with all Parts of the World:

FOR imposing Taxes on us without our Consent:

FOR depriving us, in many Cases, of the Benefits of Trial by Jury:

FOR transporting us beyond Seas to be tried for pretended Offences:

FOR abolishing the free System of English Laws in a neighbouring Province, establishing therein an arbitrary Government, and enlarging its Boundaries, so as to render it at once an Example and fit Instrument for introducing the same absolute Rule into these Colonies:

FOR taking away our Charters, abolishing our most valuable Laws, and altering fundamentally the Forms of our Governments:

FOR suspending our own Legislatures, and declaring themselves invested with Power to legislate for us in all Cases whatsoever.

HE has abdicated Government here, by declaring us out of his Protection and waging War against us.

HE has plundered our Seas, ravaged our Coasts, burnt our Towns, and destroyed the Lives of our People.

HE is, at this Time, transporting large Armies of foreign Mercenaries to compleat the Works of Death, Desolation, and Tyranny, already begun with circumstances of Cruelty and Perfidy, scarcely paralleled in the most barbarous Ages, and totally unworthy the Head of a civilized Nation.

HE has constrained our fellow Citizens taken Captive on the high Seas to bear Arms against their Country, to become the Executioners of their Friends and Brethren, or to fall themselves by their Hands.

HE has excited domestic Insurrections amongst us, and has endeavoured to bring on the Inhabitants of our Frontiers, the merciless Indian Savages, whose known Rule of Warfare, is an undistinguished Destruction, of all Ages, Sexes and Conditions.

IN every stage of these Oppressions we have Petitioned for Redress in the most humble Terms: Our repeated Petitions have been answered only by repeated Injury. A Prince, whose Character is thus marked by every act which may define a Tyrant, is unfit to be the Ruler of a free People.

NOR have we been wanting in Attentions to our British Brethren. We have warned them from Time to Time of Attempts by their Legislature to extend an unwarrantable Jurisdiction over us. We have reminded them of the Circumstances of our Emigration and Settlement here. We have appealed to their native Justice and Magnanimity, and we have conjured them by the Ties of our common Kindred to disavow these Usurpations, which, would inevitably interrupt our Connections and Correspondence. They too have been deaf to the Voice of Justice and of Consanguinity. We must, therefore, acquiesce in the Necessity, which denounces our Separation, and hold them, as we hold the rest of Mankind, Enemies in War, in Peace, Friends.

WE, therefore, the Representatives of the UNITED STATES OF AMERICA, in GENERAL CONGRESS, Assembled, appealing to the Supreme Judge of the World for the Rectitude of our Intentions, do, in the Name, and by Authority of the good People of these Colonies, solemnly Publish and Declare, That these United Colonies are, and of Right ought to be, FREE AND INDEPENDENT STATES; that they are absolved from all Allegiance to the British Crown, and that all political Connection between them and the State of Great-Britain, is and ought to be totally dissolved; and that as FREE AND INDEPENDENT STATES, they have full Power to levy War, conclude Peace, contract Alliances, establish Commerce, and to do all other Acts and Things which INDEPENDENT STATES may of right do. And for the support of this Declaration, with a firm Reliance on the Protection of divine Providence, we mutually pledge to each other our Lives, our Fortunes, and our sacred Honor.

Signed by ORDER *and in* BEHALF *of the* CONGRESS,

JOHN HANCOCK, PRESIDENT.

ATTEST.
CHARLES THOMSON, SECRETARY.

PHILADELPHIA: PRINTED BY JOHN DUNLAP.

The Declaration of Independence, Philadelphia, July 4, 1776, broadside (Color Plate 7)

The Declaration as History and as Icon

There are two historic versions of the Declaration of Independence: the one adopted by the Continental Congress on July 4, 1776, and the handwritten "engrossed" copy on parchment signed by the delegates a month later. The printed version was distributed and read aloud to tens of thousands all over the colonies. The parchment version was stored away in government offices and not put on permanent public display for almost 150 years. The parchment version has become a sacred icon. The printed broadside is all but forgotten.

The broadside reproduced here (p. 53) is one of the rare first printings of the Declaration. Congress adopted a resolution for independence on July 2, and after two days of debate adopted a Declaration of Independence on July 4, 1776. That night John Dunlap, official printer to Congress, set the type and printed it on a single sheet, a broadside, running off from eighty to one hundred copies. This is one of only twenty-three copies known to have survived.

On July 5 delegates rushed copies to their home states and to the army. Couriers on horseback would have put copies in their saddlebags, which may account for the folds down the middle and across this copy that ended up in Goshen, a small town in the Hudson Valley of New York. On the reverse side, John Steward, a local political leader, signed his name.

On July 19 Congress resolved that the Declaration "be fairly engrossed on parchment," which meant handwritten in a large, clear hand, and that it "be signed by every member of Congress." It was not until August 2 that Timothy Matlack, a Philadelphia patriot leader, had the parchment ready, and delegates walked to the front of the hall to sign it. Days later there were fifty-six signatures, although a few prominent members withheld their names. For a while the names of the signers were kept secret—"to alter or to abolish" the government was an act of treason.

It was some time before Americans made an icon out of the engrossed version. Nobody saw it, because the parchment was stored away for decades. Fifty years later a facsimile was made and widely distributed, but the original was not displayed until the 1876 centennial. It did not go on permanent public display in Washington until 1921, and not until 1952 was it installed at the National Archives.

The parchment version is what most Americans think of as the Declaration, but the plain printed broadside proclaimed the principles of the Revolution directly to the people at the time.

HISTORIAN'S VOICE

Congress ordered that the Declaration be sent to "the several Assemblies, Conventions & Committees or Councils of Safety and to the several commanding officers of the Continental troops that it be proclaimed in each of the United States & at the head of the army."

This engraving is a British artist's depiction of the Declaration being read in Philadelphia by a man on horseback. In most places the throngs that heard the Declaration were large and enthusiastic. In Boston, Abigail Adams wrote her husband, John, that she was among "the multitude" on King Street in front of the State House, the site of the Boston Massacre. The troops and "all the inhabitants" assembled. After the Declaration was read "the church Bells rang . . . cannon were discharged and every face appeared joyfull."

The Manner in which the American Colonies Declared themselves Independent; engraving by G. Noble, from *New, Comprehensive and Complete History of England*, by Edward Barnard (London, 1783)

In a notice from before July 4, 1776, the Malden town clerk notified the town constable "In His Majesty's name." After independence was declared, the same official addressed the constable "In the name of the Government and People of the Massachusetts State."

Legal notices announcing town meetings in Malden, Massachusetts, February 19, 1773, and April 14, 1777

Winning the War, 1775–83

Battles appear one way to artists years later but quite another way to participants at the time. Even when participants record the event, they can report only what they experienced.

The battle at the Brandywine, September 11, 1777, was a disaster for the Americans, but this is hardly apparent in the account by George Weedon, a brigadier general of the Virginia line.

Weedon sketched the line of American troops on the morning of the battle, and that evening recorded the events of the day. His map reveals one of the reasons Gen. George Washington lost the battle. Gen. William Howe, who had just landed in the Chesapeake Bay with 12,500 British troops, was on the march to capture Philadelphia, the capital city. Washington decided to stop the troops at the Brandywine River, several miles southwest of Philadelphia.

In the foreground Weedon drew the "High ground on which our army formed in the Morning," some eleven thousand troops. In the background are "the High grounds" from which the Americans expected Howe's army to cross the Brandywine at one of several fords, low water points in the river. But Washington lacked good maps of the topography, and his intelligence of British troop movements was faulty. The British crossed the Brandywine at several points, including fords not shown on Weedon's crude map. They outflanked the Americans, capturing the high ground behind them, and sent them into full retreat.

Weedon reported "not more than 600 [Americans] killed and missing"; in reality there were twelve hundred American casualties. He also expected the battle to continue, but it was over in one day, and the British marched on to take Philadelphia.

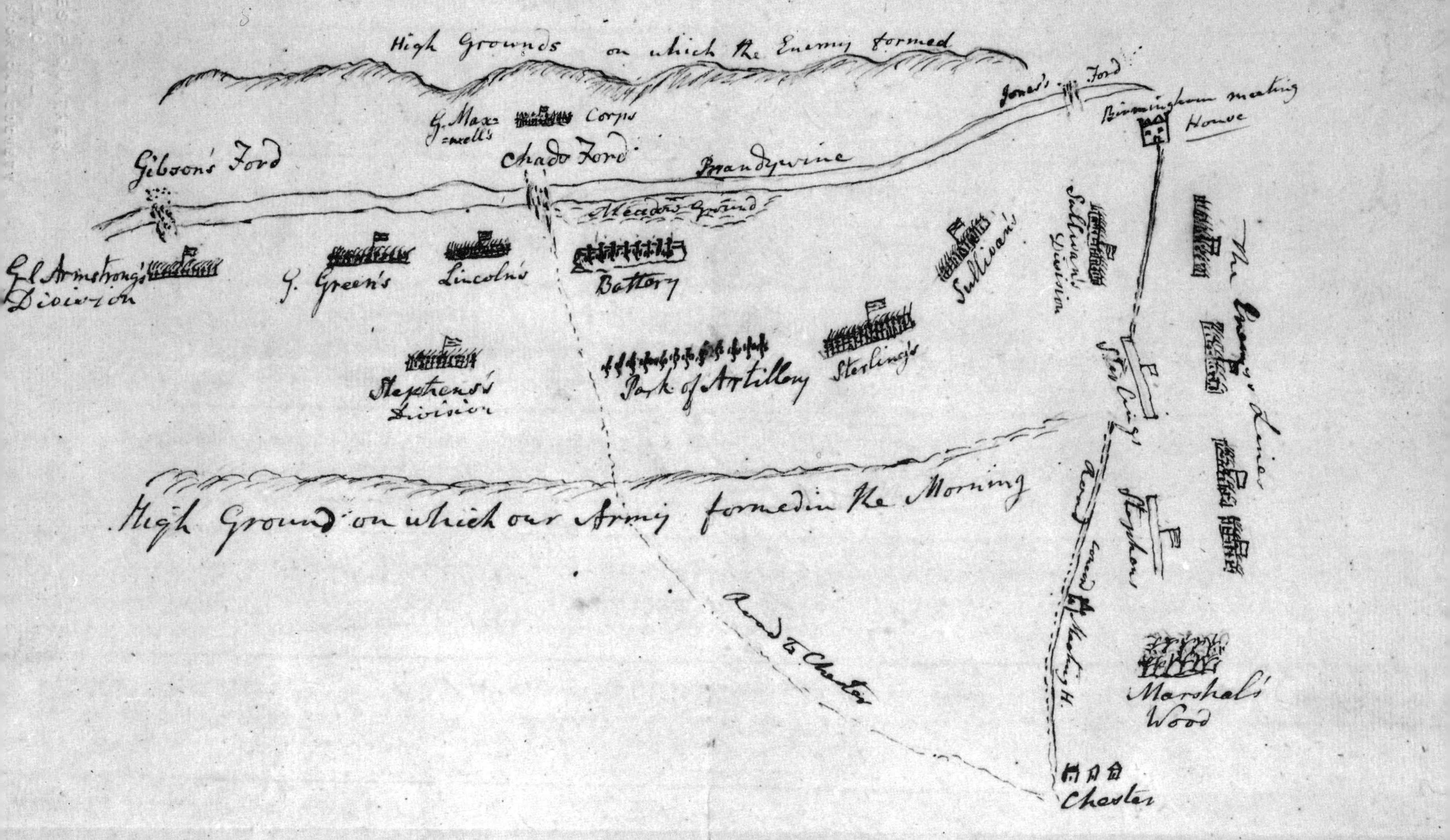

High Grounds on which the Enemy formed

Jones's Ford

Birmingham meeting House

G. Maxwell's Corps

Chadd's Ford

Brandywine

Gibson's Ford

Meadow Ground

Gl. Armstrong's Division

G. Green's

Lincoln's

Battery

Sullivan's Division

Sullivan's

The Enemy's Line

Stephen's Division

Park of Artillery

Sterling's

High Ground on which our Army formed in the Morning

Road to Chester

Stephen

Dilworth H.

Marshal's Wood

Chester

r.d. 4. 11th. 1777. The American Army drawn up as above opposite to Chadds Ford; & General Maxwell posted on the Enemy Side in a wood with 800 light Infantry — At ½ past 8, the Enemy appeared & formed on the high Grounds in Front, the soon engaged Maxwell & he with great Firmness repulsed them twice with much Loss; they were reinforced & he retreated in good Order about 10, crossed & formed on the Banks of the River — The rest of the Army were Spectators of Gallantry of this little Corps, who frequently crossed & skirmished with the Enemy in the Course of the Day — Our Battery was on Eminence which commanded the Ford, & in the Cannonading made the Enemy retire several times, it was better served than theirs — About 11 O'Clock, the General received Intelligence that a considerable Part of the Enemy's Army had filed off to right towards, that the meant to cross at Jones's Ford. Sterling's & Stephen's Divisions were to march to Birming

From 1775 to 1783 Americans fought a long, bitter war for independence. It was the first successful revolution of modern times, won through popular support. As in David's biblical challenge of Goliath, the odds were against the colonists to defeat Britain, the major power in Europe. The odds changed in 1777 when France, Europe's number two power, entered the war against her old enemy.

Americans were far from united. Many men and women remained loyal to Great Britain. Some rich Loyalists feared falling under the rule of "the rabble"; some poor Loyalists considered upper-class patriots their oppressors. Several tens of thousands of Americans took up arms with the British, turning the Revolution into a bloody civil war in parts of the middle states and the southern backcountry. Still others who felt no stake in either side chose to be neutral or made up their minds according to who gained control in their area, the patriots or the British.

To many at the bottom of American society, the patriots were not their champions. For African Americans the war was primarily an opportunity to win freedom. Most American Indians sided with the British because they considered the land-hungry frontiersmen their enemies.

Patriots won the war because several hundred thousand men and women contributed to the effort. David Ramsay, the first American historian of the Revolution, wrote that the war set people "to thinking, speaking and acting in a line far beyond that to which they are accustomed." It "not only required but created talents."

Soldiers

Why did men fight in the Revolution? Some volunteered for love of country. Some were induced by promises of land or money. Some were drafted—they had no choice.

In 1775–76, tens of thousands of men went off to war with their local militias, enraged at the British "butchery" at Lexington and aroused by the threat to their liberties. Representing a cross section of their hometowns, these citizen-soldiers served for stints of three months, then returned to their farms and workshops, and often enlisted again.

The Continental army, or *regulars*, required men to enlist for three years or the duration. As the war dragged on, the poor and landless filled the military ranks: mechanics, indentured servants, runaway apprentices, and unmarried sons of farmers. Congress and the states offered recruits bounties of money and promised land, typically one hundred acres. They also resorted to a form of the draft that allowed a well-to-do individual to hire a substitute. The ranks of the regulars were filled with ordinary men who combined a love of country with the hope of a better future for themselves.

Three months after Lexington and Concord twenty-seven men from upstate New York voluntarily enlisted in the militia, pledging to "take up arms" in defense of their "Rights and Privileges" against "the heavy and tyrannical Hand of Power." Most of the twenty-seven volunteers from a frontier farm community, where few people had a formal education, signed with an X because they could not write their names.

A roster of enlisted men from Tryon County, New York, July 16, 1775

At a General Assembly of the Governor and Company of the State of Connecticut, holden at Hartford, (by special Order of his Excellency the Governor) on the 21st Day of February, A. D. 1781.

An ACT, in addition to an Act; for filling up and compleating this State's Quota of the Continental Army.

WHEREAS Doubts have arisen on the Construction of said Act: Which Doubts to remove,

BE it Enacted, by the Governor, Council and Representatives, in General Court assembled, and by the Authority of the same, That each Class, divided as in said Act, meeting for the Purposes mentioned in the same, or the major Part of such as shall meet for said Purpose, shall have full Power to Tax themselves and the Class, in Proportion to their several Lists, in such Sum or Sums as they shall deem necessary, to procure a Recruit, or to pay such Recruit, as may have been by them procured; which Tax, when laid and agreed to, shall be collectable, as though laid by any other Authority.

Provided always, That whenever any Individual or Individuals, of any Class, shall neglect or refuse to pay or furnish his Proportion, towards obtaining a Recruit, it shall be the Duty of the Select-Men of the Town, where such Delinquent dwells, on Application to them made (and Citation by them given to said Persons to appear, if they see Cause, with their Reasons) to assess and doom said Delinquents, in such Sum, as said Select-Men shall think proper, the Circumstances and Nature of the Refusal being duly considered; which Assessment shall be laid agreeable to Circumstances, on the List mentioned in said Act, and shall be collected by Warrant, as in other Cases, in said Act, is provided.

A true Copy of Record,

Examined, by

GEORGE WYLLYS, Secretary.

~~~~~~~~~~~~~~~~~~~

HARTFORD:

PRINTED BY HUDSON AND GOODWIN.

Late in the war, Congress and the states resorted to a form of conscription in which a draftee, chosen by lottery, could pay for a substitute. In Connecticut this broadside announcing penalties for failure to obtain recruits would have been posted in local taverns.

Broadside, act of the Connecticut General Assembly to fill the state's quota of soldiers for the Continental army, February 21, 1781

In this certificate, issued by Patrick Henry as governor of Virginia, Thomas Meriwether certified that John Barnes was entitled to "a proportion of land allowed a Private in the Continental line enlisted for the war." Individual states set aside land for soldiers that was confiscated from Tories or the crown, but they were so slow in distributing it that many veterans often sold their certificates to land dealers.

Certificate for land due John Barnes, March 1, 1785

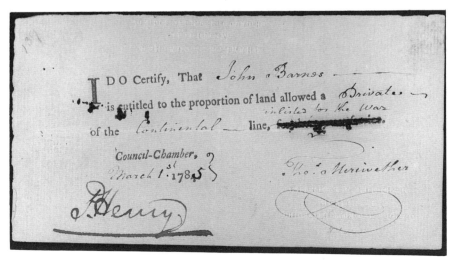

The British artist who drew these pictures of American soldiers during the war insisted on their accuracy, calling one "A real representation of the Dress of An American Rifle-man." He inscribed the word "Liberty" on the hats of both the general and the rifleman. Perhaps he had been in the colonies and seen the war firsthand, but he would have seen few riflemen in the Continental army clothed like this in a clean, new uniform. Many militia riflemen supplied and wore their own loose-fitting hunting shirts.

Engravings from *New, Comprehensive and Complete History of England*, by Edward Barnard (London, 1783)

Portrait & Uniform of An
AMERICAN GENERAL.

A real reprefentation of the Drefs of An
AMERICAN RIFLE-MAN.

Roberts Sculp

The Tools of War

Along with his gun, a rifleman carried a cartridge pouch and a cow or ox horn containing the precious stock of coarse gunpowder needed to charge the muzzle. The powder horns that soldiers carried were no different from the ones they used for hunting in civilian life. Carving decorative motifs on powder horns had been a common practice for centuries when these revolutionary soldiers personalized their horns.

The army and militia suffered from a chronic shortage of weapons and equipment. The states and the army contracted with independent artisans and iron foundries to produce the goods of war. But many soldiers made do with what they had, often bringing their own hunting rifles and handcrafted swords into battle.

The soldier named Ira West who carved "Roxbury Camp, 1775" on his powder horn was undoubtedly the Connecticut man who is on record as having filed for a pension in 1832. West had served as corporal in the town militia of Toland. He reported that his company had marched to Roxbury, a camp outside of Boston, in May 1775 and had been fired upon by the British during the Battle of Bunker Hill. For seven months and nine days of service, he was awarded an annual pension of $23.33.

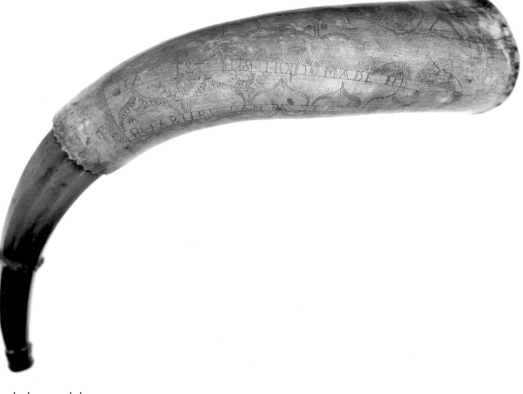

Powder horn made by
Ira West, 1775

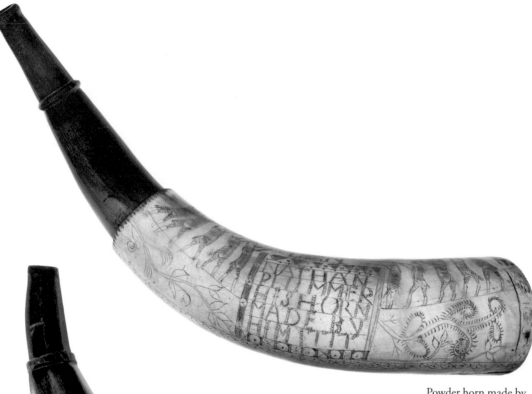

Powder horn made by
Nathan Plummer, 1777

Nathan Plummer carved British soldiers attacking
and Americans defending a pine tree marked
"Liberty," but he recorded no place name on his
horn. It is likely that he is Nathan Plummer of
Londonderry, New Hampshire, who filed for a
pension under an 1818 act of Congress that required
proof of poverty. Plummer, a "laborer in agriculture," listed assets of $47.20 and a mortgage for
thirty-three acres of land. For serving three years in
the regular army he was awarded an annual pension
of $48.

Jonathan Dibble carved into his horn these words:
"Jonathan Dibble, his Horn in the Year A.D. 1775. If
I lose it and you find it return it to me for it is mine."
Because he did not record either the town of his
origin or his army camp, it is difficult to trace him in
the military rosters of the thirteen states. Apparently
he did not live long enough to file for a pension, and
no record exists of his descendants applying for
membership in the Daughters of the American
Revolution.

Powder horn made by
Jonathan Dibble, 1775

James Pike

The scene James Pike carved into his powder horn illustrated the convictions of tens of thousands of New Englanders who sprang to arms in 1775–76. The Tree of Liberty symbolized the rights of self-government and individual liberty that the colonists considered the rights of all Englishmen and the natural rights of man.

Who was James Pike who lettered on his horn, "Made by Him at Somersworth, March 10, 1776"? Somersworth was a small town in southeastern New Hampshire. Soldiers often carved on their horn the name of their hometown or military camp.

Most likely the horn belonged to the James Pike who was born in New Hampshire, served in the Massachusetts militia, and lived out his life in New Hampshire, his residence when he applied for a pension in 1832. This James Pike was born in Plaistow, in southern New Hampshire not far from Somersworth, and as a boy moved with his farming family across the border to Haverhill, Massachusetts. In the latter part of May 1775, he testified in his pension application, "I joined the army at Cambridge. . . . I was one of the militia or Provincials [the word used on the powder horn] as we were then called." On June 17, 1775, at age twenty-three, he was in the thick of the Battle at Bunker Hill. "I worked all night digging with a shovel preparing the entrenchments," he wrote in 1832. Facing waves of British attackers, he saw his older brother Simeon killed, and he himself was wounded in the right shoulder by a musket ball. He wrote proudly, "I was among the last of the Americans that retreated."

Granted a few days furlough "in consequence of my wound," he returned to active duty and was discharged late in January 1776 after nine months of service. He married, and then in August 1776 he enlisted again as a private in the Haverhill militia for three more months. On March 10, 1776, the date carved on the horn, he would have been between tours of duty.

After seeing service, in the midst of the war he went back to southern New Hampshire, where he was a farmer at Gofftown until 1795 and then at Andover for the rest of his life. Alice George Pike bore twelve children, the first son named for Simeon. James Pike received a pension of $37.50 a year in 1833. He died in 1837. Not much more is known about him, but if James Pike left no more than his powder horn, he left a rich legacy.

Who Is the Real James Pike?

How does one trace a soldier of the Revolution? James Pike's powder horn was donated to the Chicago Historical Society in 1932 by Charles Pike, president of the Society, but no relation to James Pike. The powder horn itself provided the only clues to its possible owner: the date and place where it was carved.

The horn could have belonged to Rev. James Pike, minister of the Congregational Church of Somersworth beginning in 1730. But Reverend Pike, born in 1702, would have been seventy-four in 1776, and although men of his age rallied to "the spirit of '76," there is no record of him going off to war. He was hearty—he lived to be eighty-nine—but none of the accounts of his life mentions military service.

The military records for the Revolution are incomplete and uneven. The historian on the trail of James Pike—a fairly common name—has three major sources to work with. First are the long, published lists of men who served, compiled for each state in the nineteenth century. Second are the federal pension applications filed by veterans in 1818 (when the government required proof of the poverty of the applicant) and in 1832 (when it required a detailed account of service). In all some eighty thousand filed applications, copies of which are preserved on microfilm or are available at the National Archives in Washington. Third are the applications filed by descendants of veterans for membership in the Daughters of the American Revolution (D.A.R.), which detail the military service of their ancestors.

The military rosters for New Hampshire produced no James Pike, but those for Massachusetts produced a dozen. The federal pension applications produced the only James Pike from New Hampshire. The D.A.R. descendants all traced themselves to this James Pike. The only mystery is what he was doing at Somersworth, March 10, 1776, the date he carved on the horn. He does not seem to have been a relative of Rev. James Pike. Other historical detectives may solve this puzzle.

Six British soldiers, identified as "Regulars, the Aggressors," are firing at five "Provincials, Defending." In the center is the Liberty Tree, symbol of the natural rights a young militia man believed were at stake in the war.

Powder horn made by James Pike, 1776; *below*: detail

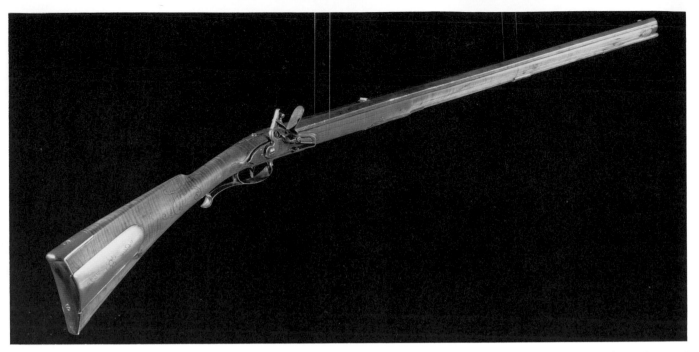

American long rifle,
c. 1780

Also known as the Pennsylvania or Kentucky flint-lock rifle, this gun (above) was used during the Revolution and on the postwar frontier.

British-American
musket, c. 1775

This regulation "Brown Bess" musket (below) began its life in the service of the British army. During the Revolution, an American soldier took it as his own and decorated it with distinctive tiger stripes.

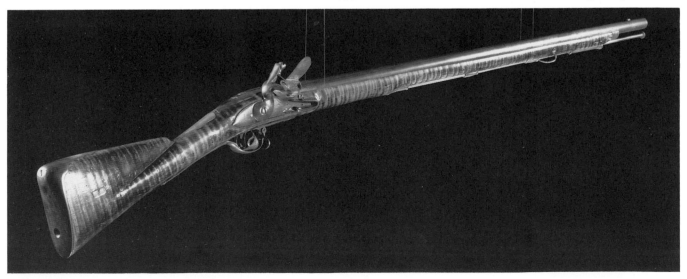

Cartridge box, c. 1775

This leather pouch with a wooden block bored for twenty-four cartridge rounds is fitted with loops for attachment to a waist belt. Although prescribed cartridge boxes for men armed with muskets were fitted to hold twenty-nine cartridges, necessity required the soldier to use whatever was available.

Tinderbox with flint, c. 1775

This small wooden water barrel was the kind farmers took out to the fields when they mowed hay. Judging by the carving on the side, "Ticonderoga 1775," this barrel saw service with Vermont troops at the Battle of Ticonderoga as a canteen for water or a soldier's ration of rum.

Since regulation equipment and supplies were scarce, soldiers often brought household items into battle with them, such as this tinderbox for striking a fire.

Canteen, 1775

Fifes and drums provided rousing music as well as signals on the fields of battle for both sides. These instruments were probably used during the Revolution.

Fifes, dates unknown

Drum, date unknown

The task of feeding and equipping an army was overwhelming. To feed fifteen thousand soldiers for one year, Gen. George Washington estimated the military needed one hundred thousand barrels of flour and twenty million pounds of meat, but he never came close to meeting those needs. Congress set quotas for the states to fill. When desperate, the army requisitioned supplies by force.

With men away at battle, farm women often plowed the fields and harvested the crops. To clothe their husbands and sons they continued to spin and weave, to sew and knit. Artisans produced cannons in local iron foundries, gunsmiths and blacksmiths hammered out small arms, and shipwrights constructed ships. But even after badly needed supplies arrived from France there was never enough of anything to go around.

Inflation was rampant. Prices skyrocketed, and the value of paper currency, issued by Congress and the states to pay for the war, depreciated drastically. The states passed laws to control prices but with little success. Men and women took part in angry riots against sellers who refused to abide by the laws. For many the war brought profit and a new affluence; for others it was a bitter, impoverishing experience.

The Home Front

At Valley Forge, Pennsylvania, digging tools were essential to construct the army's quarters, which were often huts dug into the hillside. This receipt records Mark Bird's amazing achievement: supplying the army with five hundred picks, one thousand spades, and one thousand shovels for the encampment. Bird was the owner of Hopewell Furnace in northeastern Pennsylvania, where artisans may have cast the picks, spades, and shovels. It is also possible that he purchased some of the tools from the numerous iron furnaces in Pennsylvania and New Jersey or that he produced pig iron that local blacksmiths then hammered into tools. Hopewell Furnace also provided cannons and shot for the Continental army.

Receipt for tools sent by Mark Bird to Col. Jonathan Mifflin at Valley Forge, December 22, 1777

Patriots made cartridges at home by melting lead and ladling it into molds, a task often performed by women. The lead statue of King George III that patriots in New York City pulled down and broke up on July 9, 1776, was sent to Litchfield, Connecticut. There half a dozen women melted the lead and turned it into 42,228 cartridges for use by patriot forces.

Bullet molds, c. 1780

Kettle and ladle, c. 1780

Inflation

Inflation racked the country during the war. The hardship posed by this rapid decline in the value of money, even for those relatively well-off, is illustrated by the shopping practices of Sarah Franklin Bache. During the war she sent her servants to market with two baskets, one empty to carry the items they bought, a second filled with continental money to pay for the purchases. "If I was to mention the prices of the common necessaries of life it would astonish you," she wrote to her father in 1778.

Hard money was in such short supply that coins were commonly shaved, and their filings recycled. In daily transactions merchants and others weighed their coins on fold-up pocket scales to guarantee their value.

Pocket scale, English, c. 1760

This chart reveals the extraordinary extent of currency depreciation. In January 1777 it took $105 in continental currency to equal $100 in gold and silver. Less than two years later it took $634; by April of 1780, $4,000 in continental currency was needed to purchase $100 of gold and silver.

Scale of Depreciation, Agreeable to an Act of the (now) Commonwealth of Massachusetts, passed September 29, 1780

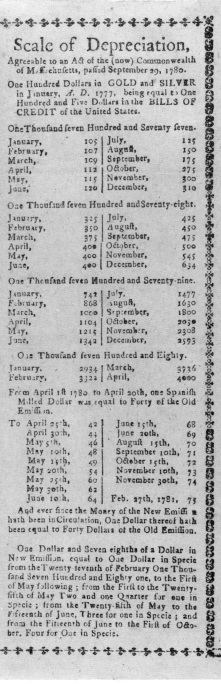

Scale of Depreciation,
Agreeable to an Act of the (now) Commonwealth of Massachusetts, passed September 29, 1780.

One Hundred Dollars in GOLD and SILVER in January, A. D. 1777, being equal to One Hundred and Five Dollars in the BILLS OF CREDIT of the United States.

One Thousand seven Hundred and Seventy seven.

Month		Month	
January,	105	July,	125
February,	107	August,	150
March,	109	September,	175
April,	112	October,	275
May,	115	November,	300
June,	120	December,	310

One Thousand seven Hundred and Seventy-eight.

Month		Month	
January,	325	July,	425
February,	350	August,	450
March,	375	September,	475
April,	400	October,	500
May,	400	November,	545
June,	400	December,	634

One Thousand seven Hundred and Seventy-nine.

Month		Month	
January,	742	July,	1477
February,	868	August,	1630
March,	1000	September,	1800
April,	1104	October,	2030
May,	1215	November,	2308
June,	1342	December,	2593

One Thousand seven Hundred and Eighty.

Month		Month	
January,	2934	March,	3736
February,	3322	April,	4000

From April 1st 1780, to April 20th, one Spanish Milled Dollar was equal to Forty of the Old Emission.

To April 25th,	42	June 15th,	68
April 30th,	44	June 20th,	69
May 5th,	46	August 15th,	70
May 10th,	48	September 10th,	71
May 15th,	49	October 15th,	72
May 20th,	54	November 10th,	73
May 25th,	60	November 30th,	74
May 30th,	62		
June 10th,	64	Feb. 27th, 1781,	75

And ever since the Money of the New Emission hath been in Circulation, One Dollar thereof hath been equal to Forty Dollars of the Old Emission.

One Dollar and Seven eighths of a Dollar in New Emission, equal to One Dollar in Specie from the Twenty seventh of February One Thousand Seven Hundred and Eighty one, to the First of May following; from the First to the Twenty-fifth of May Two and one Quarter for one in Specie; from the Twenty-fifth of May to the Fifteenth of June, Three for one in Specie; and from the Fifteenth of June to the First of October, Four for One in Specie.

Continental currency, 1775–83

Women of the Revolution

When Elizabeth Ellet compiled her three-volume history *The Women of the American Revolution* (1848–50), she wrote: "It is almost impossible now to appreciate the vast influence of woman's patriotism upon the destinies of the infant republic." Her aim was "to render a measure of justice" to the women who had been left out of conventional histories. She took a biographical approach, reading unpublished letters and interviewing the descendants of both famous and lesser known women. The result was two hundred anecdotal sketches that reveal women's wide-ranging activities during the war.

Engravings from *The Women of the American Revolution*, 3 vols., by Elizabeth Ellet, 1848–50

Esther De Berdt Reed (1746–80)

In 1779 Esther De Berdt Reed, wife of a prominent patriot leader, helped organize women in Philadelphia to collect donations for soldiers in Washington's army. Women went from door to door in every ward, soliciting money from other women. They collected $300,000 in continental currency, worth $7,500 in gold or silver, from fifteen hundred donors. She corresponded with General Washington and insisted to no avail that the money be donated directly to the soldiers. In the fall of 1780, she died before the project could be completed.

Sarah (Sally) Franklin Bache (1744–1808)

After the death of Esther Reed, Sarah Franklin Bache, the daughter of Benjamin Franklin, took on the leadership of the wartime work initiated by the women of Philadelphia. The money that the women collected was used to purchase linen for 2,200 shirts that they donated to the city's soldiers. Much of the cutting and sewing was done at Sarah Bache's house and, according to Elizabeth Ellet's account, "on each shirt was the name of the married or unmarried lady who made it."

Rebecca Brewton Motte (1738–1825)

A well-to-do southern widow, Rebecca Motte sacrificed her South Carolina mansion to the patriot cause. Her large house, also known as Fort Motte, served as a depot for American troops waging war with the British between Camden and Charleston. In the course of battle, Mrs. Motte's house was destroyed by fire. Upon being told of the destruction of her property, she declared to the American officer in charge that she was "gratified with the opportunity of contributing to the good of her country."

Many women held political opinions of their own during the Revolution, sometimes differing sharply with their husbands. In this petition, Elizabeth Graeme Ferguson of Philadelphia identified herself as "warmly attached to the American cause," although her British-born husband, Commissary of Prisoners in the British Army, had been declared a traitor and his property confiscated by the state of Pennsylvania.

In common law, the property that a married woman owned before marriage became the property of her husband. When Pennsylvania confiscated Henry Ferguson's property, it took the country estate that his wife had inherited from her father. The Supreme Council of Pennsylvania denied Mrs. Ferguson's request to restore her inheritance. After the war ended she and her husband separated. Elizabeth Ferguson renewed the struggle and eventually recovered her own "little estate."

Petition of Elizabeth Ferguson to the Supreme Executive Council of Pennsylvania, June 26, 1778

Washington and His Officers

After a series of military routs in 1776, American leaders decided that if they were to fight a long, drawn-out war against a powerful British army they would have to create their own professional army; they could not rely on the militia alone.

George Washington's strategy as commander-in-chief was to organize and discipline a regular army, using the militia as auxiliaries. He would retreat when necessary and keep the cause alive by harassing the enemy. Ultimately, he hoped to defeat the British with French military support in large-scale army engagements.

At the outset few American officers had military skills. Many, like Washington, were gentlemen: plantation owners, landlords, or merchants who were in positions of authority in their local communities. Some had been farmers, artisans, or shopkeepers; Gen. Henry Knox, the artillery commander, had been a bookseller.

American officers displayed many traditional aristocratic military traits, including a love of rank, glory, and honor. But to succeed they had to learn to command enlisted men who had democratic notions. Baron Friedrich von Steuben urged each officer to "gain the love of his men."

Before Washington was appointed commander-in-chief at the age of forty-three, his only military experience had been on the frontier as a colonel in the Virginia militia during the French and Indian War. Little in his background foreshadowed the historic role he would play.

Plate 1
The Bloody Massacre perpetrated in King Street, Boston, on March 5, 1770, engraving by Paul Revere, 1770

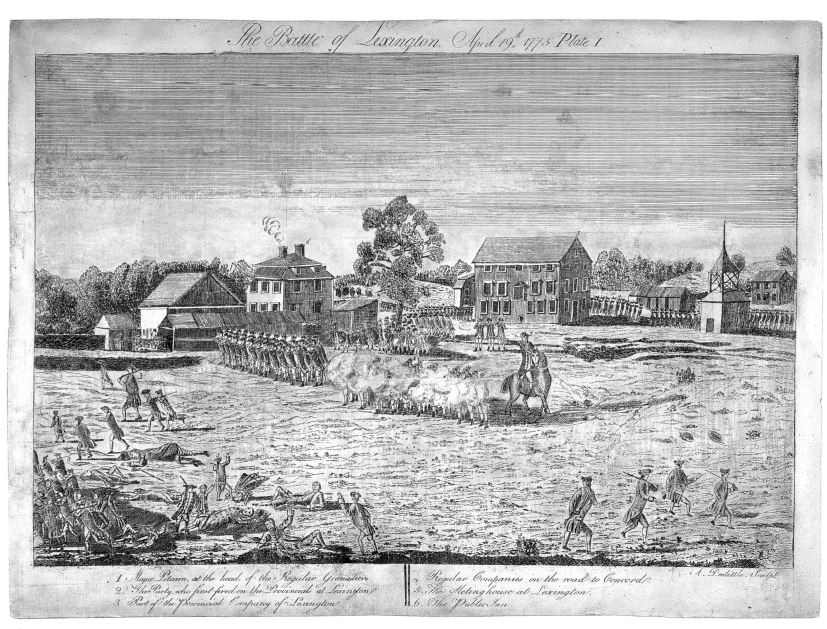

The Battle of Lexington, April 19th 1775. Plate I.

1. Major Pitcarn, at the head of the Regular Granadiers.
2. The Party, who first fired on the Provincials at Lexington.
3. Part of the Provincial Company of Lexington.
4. Regular Companies on the road to Concord.
5. The Metinghouse at Lexington.
6. The Public Inn.

A. Doolittle Sculpt.

Plate 2
The Battle of Lexington,
April 19, 1775, engraving
by Amos Doolittle,
December 1775 (Plate I)

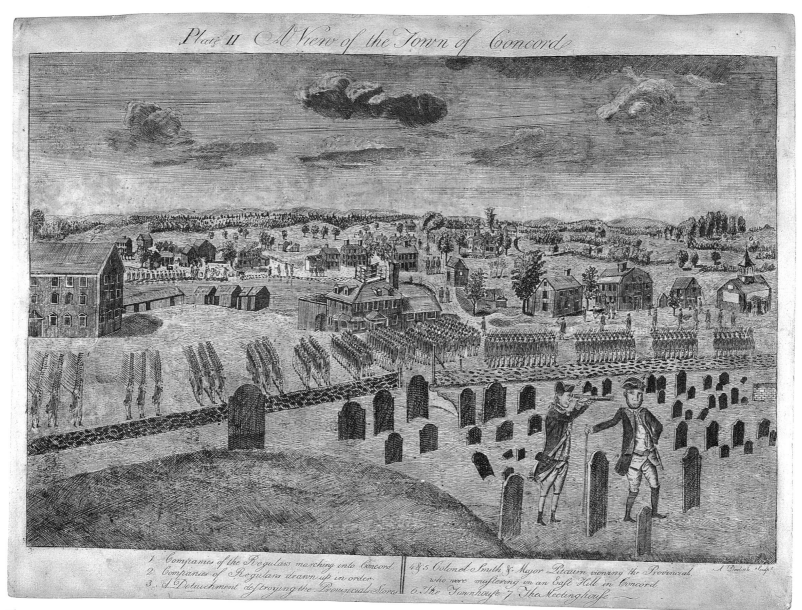

Plate 3
A View of the Town of Concord, April 19, 1775, engraving by Amos Doolittle, December 1775 (Plate II)

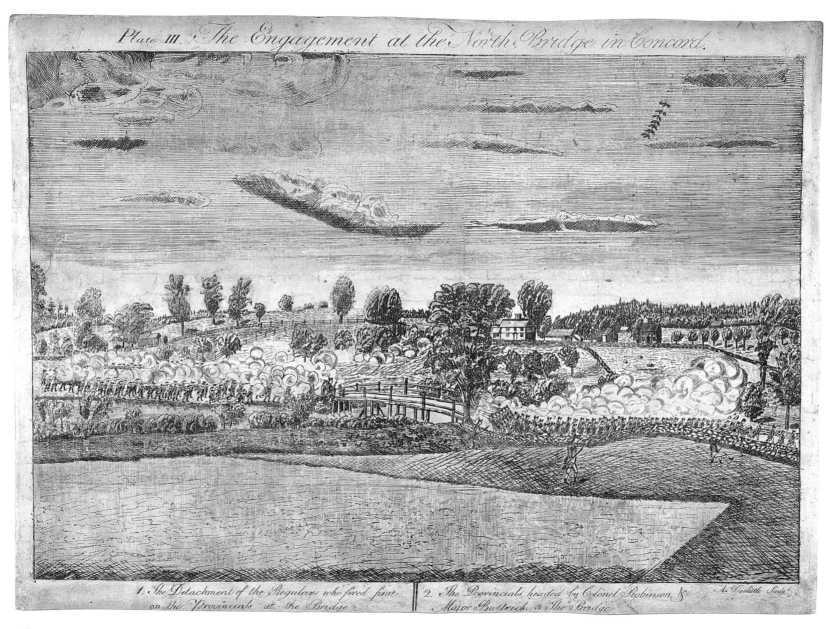

Plate III. The Engagement at the North Bridge in Concord.

1. The Detachment of the Regulars who fired first on the Provincials at the Bridge
2. The Provincials headed by Colonel Robinson & Major Buttrick 3. The Bridge

A. Doolittle Sculpt

Plate 4

The Engagement at the North Bridge in Concord, April 19, 1775, engraving

by Amos Doolittle, December 1775 (Plate III)

Plate IV   A View of the South Part of Lexington

1. Colonel Smith's Brigade retreating before the Provincials.
2. Earl Percy's Brigade meeting them.
3. & 4. Earl Piercy & Col Smith. 5 Provincials.
6. & 7. The Flank-guards of Percys Brigade.
8. A Field-piece pointed at the Lexington Metinghouse.
9. The Burning of the House in Lexington.

A. Doolittle Sculpt

Plate 5

A View of the South Part   Doolittle, December
of Lexington, April 19,   1775 (Plate IV)
1775, engraving by Amos

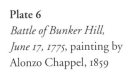

Plate 6
Battle of Bunker Hill,
June 17, 1775, painting by
Alonzo Chappel, 1859

In CONGRESS, July 4, 1776.

A DECLARATION

BY THE REPRESENTATIVES OF THE

UNITED STATES OF AMERICA,

IN GENERAL CONGRESS ASSEMBLED.

WHEN in the Courſe of human Events, it becomes neceſſary for one People to diſſolve the Political Bands which have connected them with another, and to aſſume among the Powers of the Earth, the ſeparate and equal Station to which the Laws of Nature and of Nature's God entitle them, a decent Reſpect to the Opinions of Mankind requires that they ſhould declare the cauſes which impel them to the Separation.

We hold theſe Truths to be ſelf-evident, that all Men are created equal, that they are endowed by their Creator with certain unalienable Rights, that among theſe are Life, Liberty, and the Purſuit of Happineſs—That to ſecure theſe Rights, Governments are inſtituted among Men, deriving their juſt Powers from the Conſent of the Governed, that whenever any Form of Government becomes deſtructive of theſe Ends, it is the Right of the People to alter or to aboliſh it, and to inſtitute new Government, laying its Foundation on ſuch Principles, and organizing its Powers in ſuch Form, as to them ſhall ſeem moſt likely to effect their Safety and Happineſs. Prudence, indeed, will dictate that Governments long eſtabliſhed ſhould not be changed for light and tranſient Cauſes; and accordingly all Experience hath ſhewn, that Mankind are more diſpoſed to ſuffer, while Evils are ſufferable, than to right themſelves by aboliſhing the Forms to which they are accuſtomed. But when a long Train of Abuſes and Uſurpations, purſuing invariably the ſame Object, evinces a Deſign to reduce them under abſolute Deſpotiſm, it is their Right, it is their Duty, to throw off ſuch Government, and to provide new Guards for their future Security. Such has been the patient Sufferance of theſe Colonies; and ſuch is now the Neceſſity which conſtrains them to alter their former Syſtems of Government. The Hiſtory of the preſent King of Great-Britain is a Hiſtory of repeated Injuries and Uſurpations, all having in direct Object the Eſtabliſhment of an abſolute Tyranny over theſe States. To prove this, let Facts be ſubmitted to a candid World.

He has refuſed his Aſſent to Laws, the moſt wholeſome and neceſſary for the public Good.

He has forbidden his Governors to paſs Laws of immediate and preſſing Importance, unleſs ſuſpended in their Operation till his Aſſent ſhould be obtained; and when ſo ſuſpended, he has utterly neglected to attend to them.

He has refuſed to paſs other Laws for the Accommodation of large Diſtricts of People, unleſs thoſe People would relinquiſh the Right of Repreſentation in the Legiſlature, a Right ineſtimable to them, and formidable to Tyrants only.

He has called together Legiſlative Bodies at Places unuſual, uncomfortable, and diſtant from the Depoſitory of their public Records, for the ſole Purpoſe of fatiguing them into Compliance with his Meaſures.

He has diſſolved Repreſentative Houſes repeatedly, for oppoſing with manly Firmneſs his Invaſions on the Rights of the People.

He has refuſed for a long Time, after ſuch Diſſolutions, to cauſe others to be elected; whereby the Legiſlative Powers, incapable of Annihilation, have returned to the People at large for their exerciſe; the State remaining in the mean time expoſed to all the Dangers of Invaſion from without, and Convulſions within.

He has endeavoured to prevent the Population of theſe States; for that Purpoſe obſtructing the Laws for Naturalization of Foreigners; refuſing to paſs others to encourage their Migrations hither, and raiſing the Conditions of new Appropriations of Lands.

He has obſtructed the Adminiſtration of Juſtice, by refuſing his Aſſent to Laws for eſtabliſhing Judiciary Powers.

He has made Judges dependent on his Will alone, for the Tenure of their Offices, and the Amount and Payment of their Salaries.

He has erected a Multitude of new Offices, and ſent hither Swarms of Officers to harraſs our People, and eat out their Subſtance.

He has kept among us, in Times of Peace, Standing Armies, without the Conſent of our Legiſlatures.

He has affected to render the Military independent of and ſuperior to the Civil Power.

He has combined with others to ſubject us to a Juriſdiction foreign to our Conſtitution, and unacknowledged by our Laws; giving his Aſſent to their Acts of pretended Legiſlation:

For quartering large Bodies of Armed Troops among us:

For protecting them, by a mock Trial, from Puniſhment for any Murders which they ſhould commit on the Inhabitants of theſe States:

For cutting off our Trade with all Parts of the World:

For impoſing Taxes on us without our Conſent:

For depriving us, in many Caſes, of the Benefits of Trial by Jury:

For tranſporting us beyond Seas to be tried for pretended Offences:

For aboliſhing the free Syſtem of Engliſh Laws in a neighbouring Province, eſtabliſhing therein an arbitrary Government, and enlarging its Boundaries, ſo as to render it at once an Example and fit Inſtrument for introducing the ſame abſolute Rule into theſe Colonies:

For taking away our Charters, aboliſhing our moſt valuable Laws, and altering fundamentally the Forms of our Governments:

For ſuſpending our own Legiſlatures, and declaring us out of his Protection and waging War againſt us.

He has abdicated Government here, by declaring us out of his Protection and waging War againſt us.

He has plundered our Seas, ravaged our Coaſts, burnt our Towns, and deſtroyed the Lives of our People.

He is, at this Time, tranſporting large Armies of foreign Mercenaries to compleat the Works of Death, Deſolation, and Tyranny, already begun with circumſtances of Cruelty and Perfidy, ſcarcely paralleled in the moſt barbarous Ages, and totally unworthy the Head of a civilized Nation.

He has conſtrained our fellow Citizens taken Captive on the high Seas to bear Arms againſt their Country, to become the Executioners of their Friends and Brethren, or to fall themſelves by their Hands.

He has excited domeſtic Inſurrections amongſt us, and has endeavoured to bring on the Inhabitants of our Frontiers, the mercileſs Indian Savages, whoſe known Rule of Warfare, is an undiſtinguiſhed Deſtruction, of all Ages, Sexes and Conditions.

In every ſtage of theſe Oppreſſions we have Petitioned for Redreſs in the moſt humble Terms: Our repeated Petitions have been anſwered only by repeated Injury. A Prince, whoſe Character is thus marked by every act which may define a Tyrant, is unfit to be the Ruler of a free People.

Nor have we been wanting in Attentions to our Britiſh Brethren. We have warned them from Time to Time of Attempts by their Legiſlature to extend an unwarrantable Juriſdiction over us. We have reminded them of the Circumſtances of our Emigration and Settlement here. We have appealed to their native Juſtice and Magnanimity, and we have conjured them by the Ties of our common Kindred to diſavow theſe Uſurpations, which, would inevitably interrupt our Connections and Correſpondence. They too have been deaf to the Voice of Juſtice and of Conſanguinity. We muſt, therefore, acquieſce in the Neceſſity, which denounces our Separation, and hold them, as we hold the reſt of Mankind, Enemies in War, in Peace, Friends.

We, therefore, the Repreſentatives of the UNITED STATES OF AMERICA, in GENERAL CONGRESS, Aſſembled, appealing to the Supreme Judge of the World for the Rectitude of our Intentions, do, in the Name, and by Authority of the good People of theſe Colonies, ſolemnly Publiſh and Declare, That theſe United Colonies are, and of Right ought to be, FREE AND INDEPENDENT STATES; that they are abſolved from all Allegiance to the Britiſh Crown, and that all political Connection between them and the State of Great-Britain, is and ought to be totally diſſolved; and that as FREE AND INDEPENDENT STATES, they have full Power to levy War, conclude Peace, contract Alliances, eſtabliſh Commerce, and to do all other Acts and Things which INDEPENDENT STATES may of right do. And for the ſupport of this Declaration, with a firm Reliance on the Protection of divine Providence, we mutually pledge to each other our Lives, our Fortunes, and our ſacred Honor.

Signed by ORDER *and in* BEHALF *of the* CONGRESS,

JOHN HANCOCK, PRESIDENT.

ATTEST.
CHARLES THOMSON, SECRETARY.

PHILADELPHIA: PRINTED BY JOHN DUNLAP.

Plate 7
The Declaration of
Independence,
Philadelphia, July 4,
1776, broadside

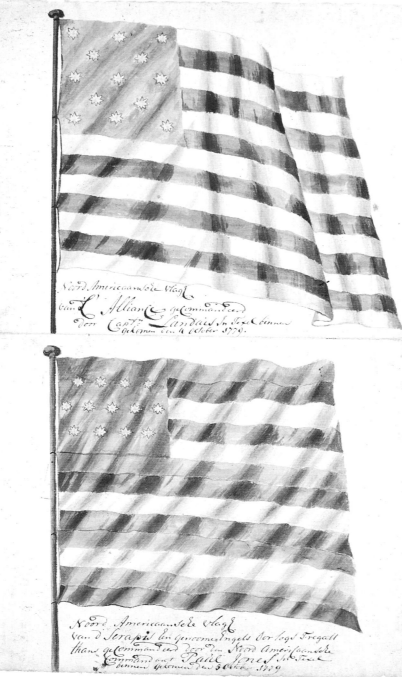

Plate 8
Watercolor sketch of
flags, artist unknown,
1779

General Washington is depicted at Princeton, New Jersey, in 1777, after the Battle of Princeton, one of the first American victories following a long series of retreats. In the background are Princeton University's Nassau Hall and sticklike figures of soldiers in military tents.

Charles Peale Polk painted this portrait of Washington in 1795, copying the original his uncle Charles Wilson Peale had painted from life in 1778. This version of Washington was widely reproduced in engravings during and after the war for a public eager to see or to own an image of the commander-in-chief.

This was the way General Washington was first known to Americans. In the uniform of an officer of the Continental army, his hand on his sword, he conveyed the strength and determination indispensable to keeping the patriot cause alive.

George Washington, painting by Charles Peale Polk, c. 1795

Telescope made by J. A. Chapman, English, c. 1775

Baldric, c. 1770

Compass, c. 1775

This compass, telescope, leather baldric, and sword knot are thought to have belonged to George Washington and have been authenticated as having been made and used during his lifetime. A baldric was worn over one shoulder to support a sword. This sword knot, a decorative tassel that dates from the French and Indian War, was tied to the hilt of a sword. It was accompanied by a note testifying that it was once owned by a niece of Washington's, Harriet Parks, but there is no way to be certain that these relics belonged to George Washington.

Sword knot, c. 1755

History by Association

Museum collections teem with real things that allegedly belonged to famous people. Among the artifacts in the Chicago Historical Society's collections attributed to famous people are George Washington's telescope and compass, Benjamin Franklin's typesetting stick, Martha Washington's sewing box, Samuel Adams's shoe buckles, the spurs Andrew Jackson wore at the Battle of New Orleans, and the gloves of someone who shook the hand of Lafayette on his tour of the United States in 1824.

History by association is appealing but problematic. Something is uniquely moving about seeing the telescope George Washington held to his eye, or the suit John Adams wore when he was received by the king of England after the American victory in the Revolution. But for every object with a proven or likely association there is another with a dubious connection. Hard evidence is often lacking. The tendency of people to claim fame for an object they possess by associating it with a famous person is notorious. Over the course of two centuries many of these attributed pieces have changed hands a number of times, sometimes through antique dealers for whom an association with the famous was money in the bank.

Some objects can be verified by checking acquisition records and experts. For example, John Adams's suit stayed in the family and is indeed his. Some objects clearly did not check out. Inside the sewing box that supposedly belonged to Martha Washington was a piece of sample stitchery signed "Ann Holt" and dated 1762. It is possible that the box once belonged to the First Lady but we present it simply as a woman's workbox of the period, alongside other objects women used in the "domestic arts."

The typesetting stick that Benjamin Franklin is supposed to have used, an expert informed us, clearly was from Franklin's time, but there is no way of knowing whether Franklin actually used it. Thus we present it as a period composing stick to illustrate the important role printers played in the Revolution, something Franklin himself would surely approve.

The sewing box and the typesetting stick are nonetheless significant without the claims that they once belonged to famous people. As tangible pieces of the past such objects can remind us that people whose names we do not know also made history.

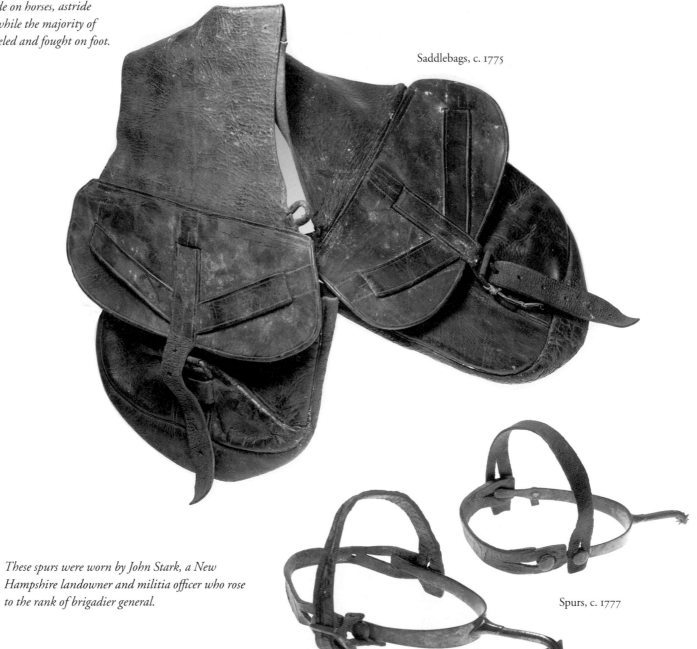

Officers and cavalry units rode on horses, astride well-crafted leather saddles, while the majority of soldiers—infantrymen—traveled and fought on foot.

Saddlebags, c. 1775

These spurs were worn by John Stark, a New Hampshire landowner and militia officer who rose to the rank of brigadier general.

Spurs, c. 1777

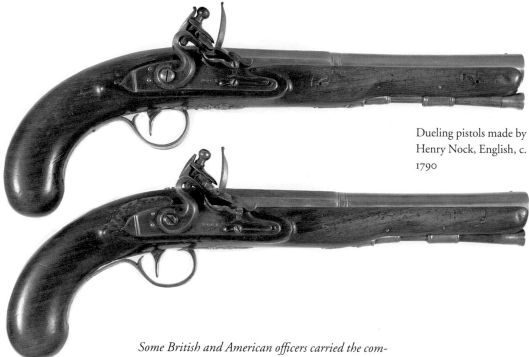

Dueling pistols made by Henry Nock, English, c. 1790

As officers of the new army became more conscious of themselves as professionals, they took on the European custom of dueling in defense of their honor as gentlemen, using handsome pistols like these.

Some British and American officers carried the comforts of home with them into the military camp. An officer attached to the Twenty-sixth British Regiment dined on this china plate, kept warm when its base was filled with hot water.

Canteen, c. 1785

The initials TRC on this canteen could refer to either a regiment or the canteen's owner.

Hot-water plate made by Josiah Spode, English, c. 1776

Europeans in the American Cause

The American Revolution was an international event. France was Britain's traditional enemy, defeated in a war fought in North America and Europe that ended in 1763. But would the French monarchy come to the aid of a revolutionary republic? After the American victory at Saratoga in 1777, France recognized American independence and entered into an alliance with the United States to advance her own imperial interests. French aid was indispensable for the ultimate American victory.

The Revolution inspired individual volunteers from Europe, glory-seeking soldiers of fortune as well as political sympathizers. They lent a variety of much-needed skills to create a professional army. Thaddeus Kosciuszko, a Pole, was an accomplished military engineer; his countryman Casimir Pulaski, a skilled cavalry officer. The Prussian Baron Friedrich von Steuben became drillmaster to the American army. Others came from Denmark, Sweden, and Hungary.

The impact of America on Europe was revolutionary. Many of the volunteer officers who returned were imbued with a "zeal for liberty." Kosciuszko led an unsuccessful Polish rebellion against Russian rule. French soldiers returned from the Battle of Yorktown to take part in the rural uprisings of their own revolution in 1789. The Marquis de Lafayette, a young French nobleman who fought under George Washington, became a leader of the French Revolution. He sent the key to the Bastille, symbol of the hated old regime, to George Washington, symbol of the new.

Appointed inspector general of the army, von Steuben wrote the guide that summarized for each rank of officer their responsibilities in drilling and disciplining the Continental army. The Regulations *impressed upon officers that they must win "obedience through Love and Affection rather than through Fear and Dread." Popularly known as the* Blue Book, *it went through seventy editions. While von Steuben did not eliminate punishment, he warned against harsh treatment, arguing that officers should gain the respect of enlisted men by demonstrating concern for them and appreciation of their competence.*

Regulations for the Order and Discipline of the Troops of the United States, by Baron Friedrich von Steuben, 1782

Thaddeus Kosciuszko,
engraving by Gabriel
Fiesinger, 1798

Kosciuszko, as a military engineer, supervised the
fortifications at the key Battle of Saratoga and in
defense of West Point, a strategic site on the Hudson
River. After the war Kosciuszko returned to his
native Poland, where he led an unsuccessful uprising
against the king. Thomas Jefferson called him "as
pure a son of liberty as I have ever known."

Congress appointed Pulaski, a nobleman with military experience in his native Poland, as chief of
cavalry. This accounting was made the day after he
was fatally wounded in a charge to retake Savannah
from the British. The purpose of this printed military
form was to keep the commander informed of the
strength of the regiment. It lists, from left to right,
twenty-one commissioned and noncommissioned
officers, fifty-four "rank and file" soldiers, and forty-
nine horses.

An accounting of the
men and horses in
Count Casimir Pulaski's
regiment of light horse,
October 10, 1779

*Major General Baron
Steuben,* engraving by
B. B. Ellis, 1783

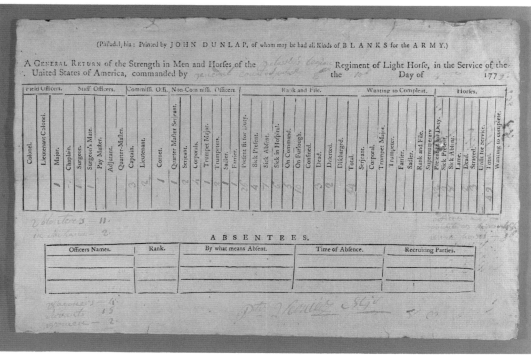

Lafayette, a young French nobleman, served in the Revolution as Washington's aide-de-camp and as military commander. In 1789, inspired by the success of the American experience, he helped draft the French Declaration of the Rights of Man and was one of the most popular leaders in the early years of the French Revolution.

Following the overthrow of the French monarchy in 1792 Lafayette, a constitutional monarchist, avoided charges of treason by defecting to the Austrians, who held him prisoner until 1797. This broadside, issued in Paris about 1798, laments his cruel fate and celebrates his service as commander of the National Guard of Paris (1789–91) and in the American war for independence. The American Congress voted to give Lafayette money in 1794 and land in 1803 because he had refused all payment for his services during the Revolution. In 1824 he returned to America for a triumphal tour of the country.

Gilbert du Motiér Lafayette, engraving by Levacher, 1798

Sent by his government to reinforce the Continental army, Rochambeau commanded a force of more than five thousand French soldiers. This support was instrumental to the American victory in the war's final battle at Yorktown.

As ambassador to France, Franklin, depicted here in his American beaver hat, negotiated crucial war loans and military aid, as well as the Treaty of Alliance. He became a popular symbol of America in France. The French put his image on a variety of souvenirs, and Franklin made the most of his fame.

Miniature of the Comte de Rochambeau, by Alexandre Alaux, c. 1875

Medallion of Benjamin Franklin, by Giovanni Battista Nini, French, 1777

In April 1777 the privateer brig Fanny *captured the British merchant ship* Caesar *in the waters off Barbados. As prize master of the* Fanny, *William Warner was responsible for sailing the* Caesar *to the port of Dartmouth, Massachusetts. As soon as he landed, he sent this letter to his parents to reassure them that he had safely returned from his journey.*

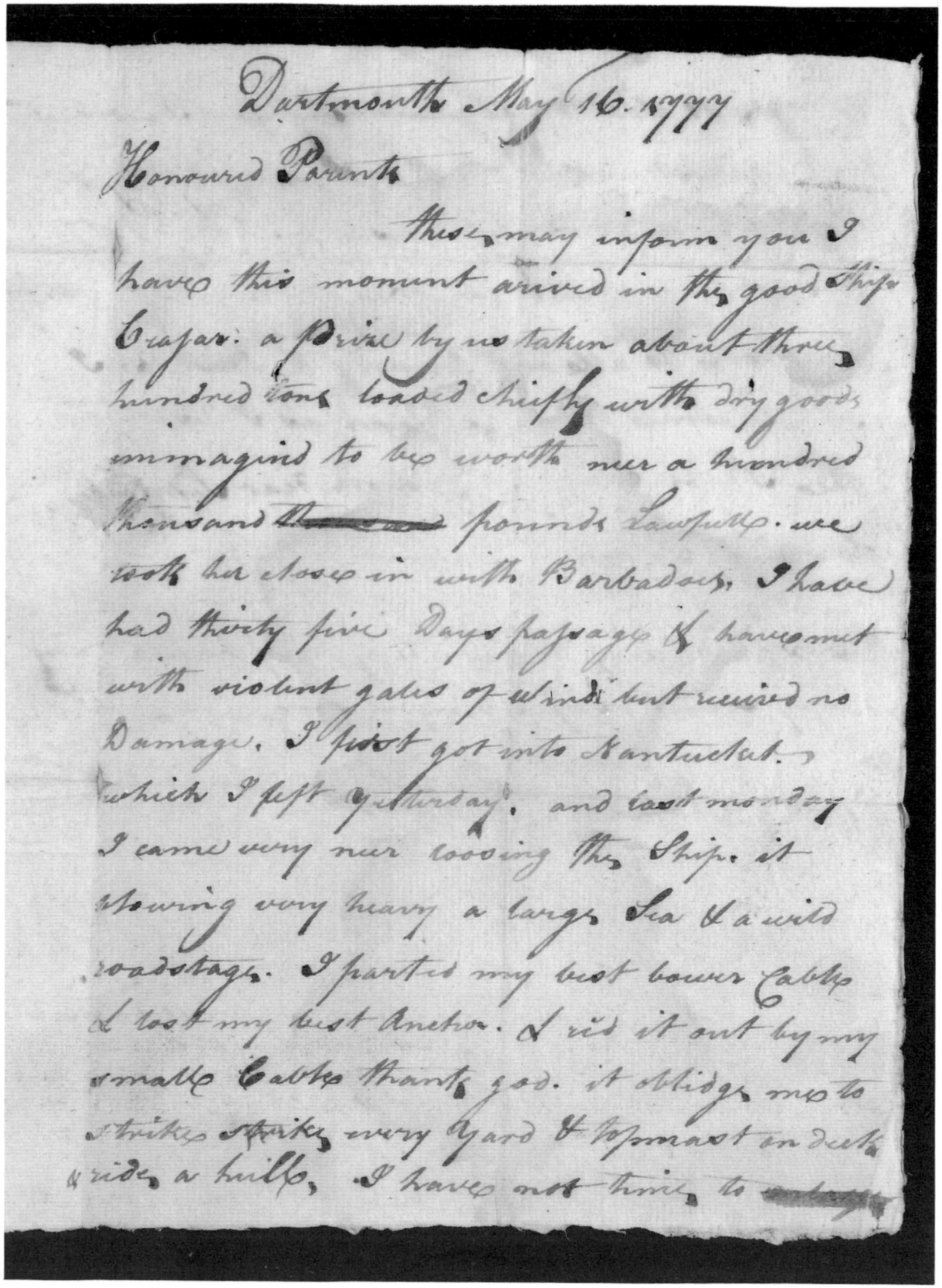

Dartmouth May 16, 1777

Honoured Parents

This may inform you I have this moment arrived in the good ship Caesar, a prize by us taken about three hundred tons loaded chiefly with dry goods immagind to be worth over a hundred thousand pounds Lawfull. we took her close in with Barbadoes. I have had thirty five Days passage & have met with violent gales of wind but received no Damage. I first got into Nantucket, which I left yesterday, and last monday I came very near loosing the ship, it blowing very heavy a large Sea & a wild roadstage. I parted my best bower Cable & lost my best anchor. I rid it out by my small Cables thank god. it oblige me to strike every yard & topmast on deck & ride a hull. I have not time to enlarge, so conclude acquainting you I am well but almost wore out. these come by Capt Phillips, who is likewise Just arived & has lost his mast in one of the gales I was in. my love to all our family & friends. I shall come home as soon as I discharge the Ships Cargo. I am dear Sir your loving Son Wm Warner Please excuse my bad writing my hands being very stif & fingers sore

Dartmouth May 16. 1777
Honoured Parents
these may inform you I have this moment arived in the good Ship Caesar: a Prize by us taken about three hundred tons loaded chiefly with dry goods immagind to be worth neer a hundred thousand pounds Lawfull. we took her close in with Barbadoes. I have had thirty five Days passage & have met with violent gales of Wind but received no Damage. I first got into Nantucket. which I left yesterday. and last monday I came very neer loosing the Ship. it blowing very heavy a large Sea & a wild roadstage. I parted my best bower Cable & lost my best Anchor. I rid it out by my small Cables thank god. it oblidge me to strike strike every Yard & topmast on deck & ride a hull. I have not time to

Letter from William Warner to his "Honoured Parents," May 16, 1777

Hopelessly outmatched by the British navy, Americans at sea concentrated on defending American shores, harassing the enemy, and plundering British commerce. Congress built a small navy of fifty to sixty ships commanded by local sea captains who recruited crews from their home ports. American ships saw action not only off American shores but also in the Caribbean and off the coast of Britain. The navy successfully captured enemy merchant vessels but seldom engaged in battle with British warships.

The government also commissioned some two thousand merchant vessels as privateers, legal pirates with the right to seize enemy merchant vessels. A share of the prize money was supposed to be divided among officers and crew. If the navy recruited no more than three thousand seamen, it was because seventy thousand men and boys flocked to privateering in response to the recruiting sergeant's plea to make their fortunes and "serve the glorious cause of their country."

Yet few ordinary seamen made their fortunes. Several thousand spent years as prisoners of war in wretched British prisons. Given an opportunity to defect, however, very few did. After the war, Benjamin Franklin singled out these proven patriot seamen for their "virtue and public spirit."

Sailors charted their course by using the quadrant to plot the changing altitudes of the sun, moon, and stars.

Quadrant of reflection made by Clark Elliott, 1784

A bosun, the officer in charge of riggings and sails, piped his orders. With high-pitched whistles that carried over the noise of a battle or a thunderstorm, he summoned sailors to man the cannons or to hoist, heave, and lower the sails.

Bosun's whistles, dates unknown

On board ship sailors used fids made of bone to stretch the eyes of sails and to part strands of rope for splicing.

Fids and fid case, dates unknown

John Paul Jones was the most celebrated naval hero of the war. Born in Scotland, the son of a gardener, he went to sea at age thirteen and rose to be master of a vessel. Congress gave him several commands, and he successfully captured British prize ships and raided British ports.

The encounter of his squadron, Bonhomme Richard *and* Alliance, *with the British frigate* Serapis *in September 1779 was the greatest naval battle of the war. The crew that Jones recruited in France was international. The 180 ordinary seamen were from nine different countries. The 20 officers included 17 Americans and 3 Irishmen; most of the 43 petty officers were British. The crew also included 137 Royal French marines.*

Bonhomme Richard *and* Serapis *exchanged fire for hours; the seamen then grappled on board ship in hand-to-hand combat. Jones and his crew triumphed, although their ship eventually sank. Jones then transferred the flag of the* Bonhomme Richard *to the captured* Serapis *and sailed it and the* Alliance *into the Dutch island port of Texel.*

This hand-colored line engraving is based on a painting by Richard Patin, who dedicated his work to the British commander of the Serapis, Captain Richard Pearson. The engraving was published by John Boydell in London in 1780.

The Memorable Engagement of Captn. Pearson of the Serapis, with John Paul Jones of the Bonhomme Richard *& His Squadron, Sep. 23, 1779,* engraving by Lerpiniere & Fittler, 1780

While the Alliance *and* Serapis *lay anchored at Texel, Holland, in October 1779, the British ambassador claimed that the United States were provinces in rebellion, not a recognized nation. Therefore, he charged, these ships were not entitled to the rights accorded belligerents in a neutral nation, and Jones was a pirate sailing under an unrecognized flag.*

The Dutch government sent an artist out in a small boat to draw the flags on the American-held ships. These sketches illustrate the stars-and-stripes flag that Congress had authorized in 1777 for American naval vessels. The labels on the drawings, written in Dutch, identify the top flag as that of the Alliance *and the bottom flag as that of the* Serapis. *These watercolors, very likely the first portrayals of the American flag in color, were evidence that the ships were not pirate ships. Thus the Dutch recognized the United States as an independent nation.*

Watercolor sketch of flags, artist unknown, 1779 (Color Plate 8)

Vessels commissioned as privateers customarily divided a portion of the prize money from their captures among the crew. United States naval vessels seem to have done the same, probably because the navy could offer no other incentive to recruit crews. This list of the crew members—one of the few such lists to have survived—aboard John Paul Jones's two ships records the division of prize money. Payment corresponded to rank. Ordinary seamen, boys, and cooks, listed here on the left-hand page, received six or twelve livres in French money, while commissioned officers, some of whom are listed on the right-hand page, received five, ten, and twenty times as much.

Account of the prize money paid by American merchants in France to the crews of the *Bonhomme Richard* and the *Alliance*, February 23, 1780

African Americans

Letter from David Lyman to Col. Henry Jackson, June 5, 1779

For African Americans, the war was an opportunity to free themselves from slavery. A few thousand, mostly in New England, fought in the patriot militia or army, especially when the Americans were desperate for soldiers. Peter Salem was one of a score or so of African Americans who fought at the Battle of Bunker Hill.

In the South and in the middle states, large numbers of African Americans joined the British. Thomas Peters was one of several hundred slaves who responded to an offer from the British commander in Virginia: freedom in return for military service. He joined a black regiment, some of whose members wore the words "Liberty to Slaves" on their uniforms. British promises of freedom were not always kept. Many African Americans simply fled from slavery. The largest number—tens of thousands—took advantage of the chaos of war in the South to run away.

The small number of free African Americans followed varying paths during the Revolution. Some joined the patriots in the army or on privateering vessels at sea. In the West, Jean Baptiste Point du Sable, a fur trader who operated at the mouth of the Chicago River, a site that later became Chicago, was imprisoned by the British for a year and then set free to pursue his fur trade.

Whatever their chosen course of action—patriot, Loyalist, runaway, or neutral—the common goal of African Americans was to win their freedom.

Although the Americans were vastly outnumbered in their unsuccessful attempt to defend Bunker Hill, sharpshooters like Peter Salem picked off a number of British officers. Salem, together with Barzillai Lew, Salem Prince, and other black patriots, fought valiantly against the redcoats in this legendary battle of the Revolution.

Alonzo Chappel was a prolific mid-nineteenth-century painter and engraver whose scenes of the Revolution, such as of the Boston Massacre, fill many history books. He patterned this painting of Bunker Hill after a more famous romantic canvas by Jonathan Trumbull. But where Trumbull portrayed Peter Salem as a servant carrying his master's gun, Chappel portrayed him (lower right corner) as a soldier on his own priming his rifle.

Battle of Bunker Hill,
June 17, 1775, painting by
Alonzo Chappel, 1859
(Color Plate 6)

THE

COLORED PATRIOTS

OF THE

AMERICAN REVOLUTION,

WITH SKETCHES OF SEVERAL

DISTINGUISHED COLORED PERSONS:

TO WHICH IS ADDED A BRIEF SURVEY OF THE

Condition and Prospects of Colored Americans.

By WM. C. NELL.

WITH AN INTRODUCTION BY
HARRIET BEECHER STOWE.

BOSTON:
PUBLISHED BY ROBERT F. WALLCUT.
1855.

Title page from *The Colored Patriots of the American Revolution,* by William C. Nell (Boston, 1855)

William C. Nell, an African American and a leading abolitionist, wrote this first history of African Americans in the Revolution. He wanted to establish their patriotism as part of their ongoing struggle for equal citizenship. The frontispiece in his book portrays Crispus Attucks, a sailor who was part American Indian and part African American, as a central figure leading an attack on the British troops in the Boston Massacre. Paul Revere left Attucks out of his version, and Alonzo Chappel was ambiguous in his rendition.

Nell, who had been educated in a segregated grammar school in Boston, was active in a long crusade to desegregate the city's schools, a victory won the year this book was published. He launched a campaign in 1858 to erect a memorial to Attucks. Wendell Phillips, a leading white abolitionist, placed Attucks "in the foremost rank of men that dare." As an associate of William Lloyd Garrison and for a time of Frederick Douglass, Nell fought for the rights of African Americans to participate equally in the Civil War. In 1888 Boston unveiled a monument, known as the Crispus Attucks monument, in memory of the victims of the massacre.

*Poems on Various Subjects
Religious and Moral, by
Phillis Wheatley, 1793*

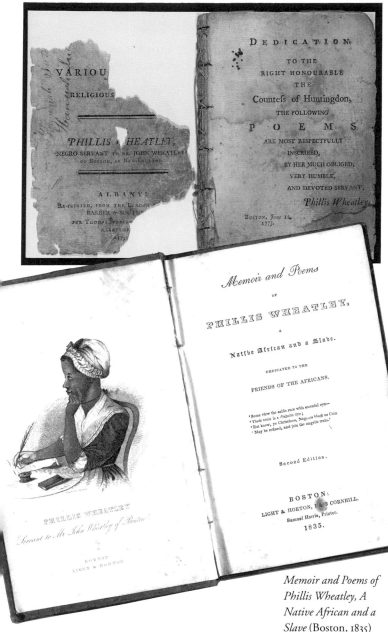

*Memoir and Poems of
Phillis Wheatley, A
Native African and a
Slave* (Boston, 1835)

Phillis Wheatley

Phillis Wheatley (1754–84) so impressed George Washington with her poem celebrating his appointment as "Generalissimo of the armies of North America" that in 1775 he invited her to his headquarters. The poem, when published, was introduced by Thomas Paine as written by "the famous Phillis Wheatley, the African poetess."

Enslaved in Africa as a child, Phillis was sold as a house servant to Thomas Wheatley, a Boston tailor. She was educated by the religious Wheatley family and wrote her first poem when she was fourteen. In 1773 she traveled to England, where her collection of thirty-nine poems was published.

Her master freed her in 1774, and she married Richard Peters, a free African American; they had three children. She died when she was only thirty years old, leaving a second volume of poems prepared but unpublished. Her 1773 book of verse was frequently reprinted by foes of slavery as proof of the abilities of African Americans.

Most of her poems were on evangelical Christian themes. Many were funeral elegies comforting Bostonians. But she also wrote verses on political events, siding with the patriots. And in subtle ways she expressed her identity as an African and a slave.

In one poem Phillis recalls being captured in Africa:

*I, young in life, by seeming cruel fate
Was snatch'd from Afric's fancy'd happy seat:
What pangs excruciating must molest,
What sorrows labour in my parent's breast?
Steel'd was that should and by no misery mov'ed
That from a father seiz'd his babe belov'd:
Such, such my case. And can I then but pray
Others may never feel tyrannic sway?*

In another poem she denounces racism:

*Some view our sable race with scornful eye,
"Their colour is a diabolic die."
Remember, Christians, Negros, black as Cain,
May be refin'd, and join th' angelic train.*

"In every human Breast," she wrote in a letter widely printed in 1774, "God has implanted a Principle which we call Love of Freedom; it is impatient of Oppression, and pants for Deliverance. . . . I will assert that the same Principle lives in us."

American Indians

During the war, almost all American Indians allied themselves with the British, whom they viewed as their protectors against American expansion. Many Indians shared the bitter feelings of the Mingo leader Logan (Tah-gah-jute), whose relatives were killed in a senseless slaughter by white frontiersmen in Virginia. In the war Logan sought vengeance against Americans.

Unlike most other Indian peoples, the Oneidas of western New York, whose warriors were strongly influenced by a Presbyterian missionary, supported the Americans at the outset of the war. In the dreadful winter of 1777–78 at Valley Forge, they sent two hundred pairs of snow-shoes to the American troops.

Colonial Americans generally looked on Indians as savages who scalped and tortured enemies in time of war. But American troops, who burned Iroquois villages in New York and Shawnee villages in Ohio during the Revolution, also committed atrocities. Corn-planter, a Seneca leader, said to George Washington: "When your army entered the country of the six nations, we called you town destroyer."

No matter which side American Indians supported, during and after the war they faced relentless American pressure for their land.

The story of the death of twenty-four-year-old Jane McCrae in upstate New York in the summer of 1777 became a legendary tale, in many different versions, of Indian atrocity. The story spread like prairie fire and became the subject of numerous paintings.

Some of Jane McCrae's family were patriots, some Loyalists. On the way to meet her fiancé, David Jones, a Tory enlisted in the British army, she was escorted by a group of Loyalist Indians. During an encounter with the war party of another Indian group, a quarrel broke out over sharing the reward that Jones had paid for the escort service. During the dispute McCrae, mistaken for a prisoner, was shot to death and then scalped. She was not scalped alive as the painting suggests.

The American general Horatio Gates exploited the story to stir outrage against the British for allying themselves with Indians. This sensationalized painting, a copy of the original by John Vanderlyn in 1804, is a product of an artist's imagination.

Murder of Jane McCrae by the Indians, artist and date unknown

Although British-American warfare ceased in 1781, frontier fighters like George Rogers Clark continued aggressive campaigns against the British-backed American Indians. Writing about a recent punitive attack he led on a Shawnee village in Ohio, Clark boasts that his troops "got a few Scalps" and left five Indian villages, as well as a British trading post, "in ashes." Americans eagerly exchanged stories of Indian atrocities, but they too engaged in the practice of scalping and perpetrated atrocities like Clark's remorseless annihilation of five Indian villages, home to women and children as well as warriors.

Letter from George
Rogers Clark, November
13, 1782

A silver armlet was typical of the ornaments given by the British to seal their alliance with Indian allies. This one was crafted by a well-known Philadelphia silversmith, Joseph Richardson.

Half-armlet made by
Joseph Richardson, Sr.,
c. 1765

Tayadaneega, or Joseph Brant as he was commonly known, was the major leader of the Mohawks during the revolutionary era. He played a key role in convincing most of the Six Nations of the Iroquois confederation to ally themselves with the British. Brant's older sister Molly had married Sir William Johnson, the British superintendent for Indian affairs, and Brant was educated at a school for whites in Connecticut.

In 1775 Brant traveled to Great Britain, where he was wined and dined by royal officials. His portrait, from which this engraving was made, was painted by George Romney. He appears in the regalia of a Mohawk chieftain, including the silver armlet and gorget (neck piece) the British bestowed on their Indian allies.

He took a leading part in the war in British-Indian raids on American frontier settlements in New York and Ohio, but when an American army invaded the Iroquois country, scorching the countryside, Brant fled with thousands of Mohawks to the protection of the British at Fort Niagara. After the American victory, he secured land from the British in Canada for the Mohawks.

Joseph Tayadaneega called the Brant, engraving by J. R. Smith, 1779

This standard printed form for a military commission records the name of an individual who, unlike the majority of the Indians, sided with the United States in the Revolution.

Military commission designating Tewaghtahkothe as "captain of the Indians," issued by the United States Congress, June 5, 1779

Brother: We wish you to listen—at the commencement of the late war you came to us and desired us to set still while the Father and son wrestled together. you told us that if we would set still and the son should out wrestle the Father, we should be partakers in all the privileges which the son might enjoy. we did not set still. we took an active part in favor of the son. we fought by his side, spilt our Blood and lost many of our brave men in his defence.

Brother: Now let us consider those who fought for the Father lack for nothing, they come among us covered with silver, they have presents made them every year. we are poor. look on us and see our poverty. we think it hard that although the son beat the Father the promises made to us are disregarded and we do not enjoy privileges equal to those who were your enemies. we think there is partiality shown, and those who fought against you receive the most favors even from the U States.

Transcription of speeches of the Oneida chiefs to Israel Chapin, September 29, 1792

Victory and Peace

The dramatic moment of the British surrender after their defeat at the Battle of Yorktown in October 1781 stayed in people's memories for years. Sarah Osborn, who had followed her husband in the army as cook and washerwoman, described it vividly in her 1837 pension application: "The British . . . marched out beating and playing a melancholy tune, their drums covered with black handkerchiefs and their fifes with black ribbons tied around them. [They] grounded their arms and then returned into town again to await their destiny."

The decisive victory at Yorktown, a combined French and American operation, forced the British to the peace table. During the negotiations in Paris, the shrewd American diplomats John Adams and John Jay broke with France, which did not want to see a strong United States emerge. In the Treaty of Paris (1783) they won from the British the vast Indian-held territory that stretched from the Appalachian Mountains west to the Mississippi River.

The British fear of an independent America came true. Independence opened up new worlds for farmer and planter, merchant and artisan, seaman and fisherman, to fulfill their aspirations for personal independence and prosperity.

This cartoon, published in London, satirizes a failed British attempt in 1778 to persuade the American colonies to stay within the empire. The peace commissioners bow before an Indian princess, long the symbol of America, who is perched on bales of tobacco, indigo, and rice bound for Europe. Her eyes are fixed on the Liberty Pole. Some in Great Britain rightly feared they would lose American trade unless they ended the war.

The Commissioners, etching by M. Darly, 1778

This is a French artist's version of the surrender of the British army under Lord Cornwallis at Yorktown in 1781. He clearly made French forces stand out in what was a combined French and American operation. Admiral de Grasse's fleet blocking the Chesapeake Bay dominates to the right, and a French army under General Rochambeau, the officers parading on horseback, dominates to the left. The artist had no knowledge of the rural American landscape, and so he fancifully depicted Yorktown, Virginia, in the background as a medieval walled town.

The artist was right, however, about the magnitude of the French contribution to the American victory. Beginning in mid-September, the combined French and American armies and the French fleet, which had arrived from the West Indies, laid siege to Yorktown. Cornwallis, isolated in a hopeless military position, surrendered his eight-thousand-man army on October 19. The arrival of Admiral Clinton on October 24 with seven thousand British reinforcements was too late; Yorktown proved to be the decisive military engagement of the war.

Surrender of the British Army commanded by Lord Count Cornwallis to the Combined Armies of the United States of America and France . . . at Yorktown, Virginia, the 19th of October, 1781, engraving by Mondhare, c. 1782

Reddition de l'Armée Angloises Commandée par Mylord. Comte de Cornwallis aux Armées Combinées des Etats unis de l'Amerique et de France aux ordres des Generaux Washington et de Rochambeau à Yorck town et Gloucester dans la Virginie, le 19 Octobre 1781. Il s'est trouvés dans ses deux postes 6000 hommes de troupes reglées Angloises ou Hessoises et 22 Drapeaux 1500 Matelots 160 Canons de tout Calibre dont 75 de Fonte & Mortiers 40 Batimens dont un Vaisseau de 50 Canons qui a été Brulé 20 Coules Bas. Ce jour à jamais memorable pour les Etats unis en ce qui assura definitivement leurs independances

A. Yorck Town   C. Armée Angloise sortant de la place   E. Armée Francaise   G. Armée naval de France aux Ordres du Comte de Grace   I. Riviere d'Yorck
B. Gloucester   D. Les Armées des ennemis posée en Faisceaux   F. Armée Americaine   H. Baye de Chesapeack

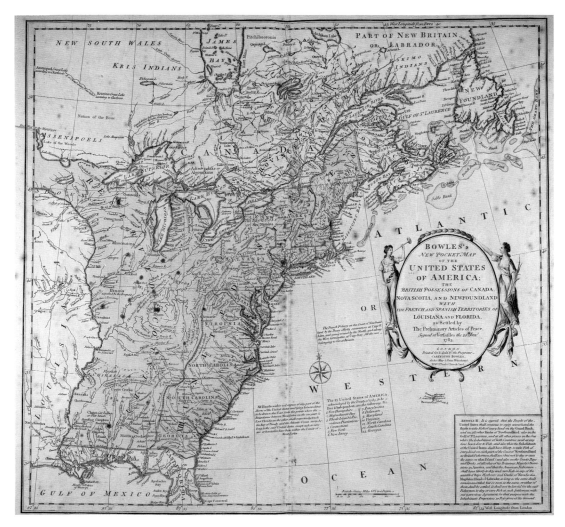

Bowles's New Pocket Map
of the United States of
America (London, 1784)

This map, published by Carrington Bowles, was one of the first British maps to show how much the Americans had won in the war. The boundaries of the United States extended west to the Mississippi River and north as far as the present boundary with Canada.

In the lower right-hand corner, the map reprints Article III of the treaty, which guaranteed American fishing rights off Newfoundland and Nova Scotia. As one of the negotiators, John Adams wrote, "There was a constant Scuffle Morning noon and night about Cod and Haddock on the Grand Bank, Deer skins on the Ohio and Pine Trees at Penobscat." He was proud of his role in winning the fishing rights this map acknowledges.

Technically this map is based on the preliminary accords between Britain, France, and Spain signed January 20, 1783. The definitive peace treaty was signed in Paris on September 3, 1783.

The Constitution and Bill of Rights, 1787–91

The Constitution of the United States, drafted in Philadelphia from May to September 1787, was presented to the people through a newspaper. This first printing of the document was the work of John Dunlap and David Claypoole. It appeared in their daily newspaper, The Pennsylvania Packet and Daily Advertiser. *Dunlap and Claypoole scooped other papers because they were the official printers to the Constitutional Convention and had already set the document in type as it went through successive revisions by the delegates. The convention approved the final version on September 18. That night the printers reset the preamble in larger type and printed the entire document, filling all four pages of their paper. Fewer than twenty copies of this issue have survived.*

Eleven years earlier, on the night of July 4, 1776, Dunlap, with Claypoole as his apprentice, had printed the first broadside of the Declaration of Independence. Since then David Claypoole had come of age and had become a partner.

Within twenty-four hours after Dunlap and Claypoole printed the Constitution, five other Philadelphia printers brought it out, and within two months some seventy-five newspapers from Maine to Georgia had reprinted the document. People arguing the pros and cons of the new form of government in a nationwide debate used these newsprint versions. The handwritten copy on parchment ordered by the convention to be signed by the delegates was, like the Declaration, stored out of sight until it went on display in Washington in the twentieth century.

Opposite: The Pennsylvania Packet and Daily Advertiser, September 19, 1787

The Pennsylvania Packet, *and Daily Advertiser.*

[Price Four-Pence.]   WEDNESDAY, September 19, 1787.   [No. 2690.]

WE, the People of the United States, in order to form a more perfect Union, establish Justice, insure domestic Tranquility, provide for the common Defence, promote the General Welfare, and secure the Blessings of Liberty to Ourselves and our Posterity, do ordain and establish this Constitution for the United States of America.

ARTICLE I.

Sect. 1. ALL legislative powers herein granted shall be vested in a Congress of the United States, which shall consist of a Senate and House of Representatives.

Sect. 2. The House of Representatives shall be composed of members chosen every second year by the people of the several states, and the electors in each state shall have the qualifications requisite for electors of the most numerous branch of the state legislature.

No person shall be a representative who shall not have attained to the age of twenty-five years, and been seven years a citizen of the United States, and who shall not, when elected, be an inhabitant of that state in which he shall be chosen.

Representatives and direct taxes shall be apportioned among the several states which may be included within this Union, according to their respective numbers, which shall be determined by adding to the whole number of free persons, including those bound to service for a term of years, and excluding Indians not taxed, three-fifths of all other persons. The actual enumeration shall be made within three years after the first meeting of the Congress of the United States, and within every subsequent term of ten years, in such manner as they shall by law direct. The number of representatives shall not exceed one for every thirty thousand, but each state shall have at least one representative; and until such enumeration shall be made, the state of New-Hampshire shall be entitled to chuse three, Massachusetts eight, Rhode-Island and Providence Plantations one, Connecticut five, New-York six, New-Jersey four, Pennsylvania eight, Delaware one, Maryland six, Virginia ten, North-Carolina five, South-Carolina five, and Georgia three.

When vacancies happen in the representation from any state, the Executive authority thereof shall issue writs of election to fill such vacancies.

The House of Representatives shall chuse their Speaker and other officers; and shall have the sole power of impeachment.

Sect. 3. The Senate of the United States shall be composed of two senators from each state, chosen by the legislature thereof, for six years; and each senator shall have one vote.

Immediately after they shall be assembled in consequence of the first election, they shall be divided as equally as may be into three classes. The seats of the senators of the first class shall be vacated at the expiration of the second year, of the second class at the expiration of the fourth year, and

The Constitution adopted in 1787–88 and the Bill of Rights added in 1789–91 fulfilled different principles of the Revolution. The Constitution met the aspirations of those people who sought a strong national republican government. The Bill of Rights spoke to those who sought to protect their individual liberties from an overly powerful central government.

Under the Articles of Confederation, the first constitution passed in 1781, each state retained its "sovereignty, freedom, and independence." This first central government achieved much. But most Americans agreed that the Confederation Congress lacked adequate power to deal with foreign nations and to bring prosperity to American commerce and manufactures. Some leaders were alarmed at the "excesses of democracy" in the states, especially at laws that state legislatures passed favoring debt-ridden farmers at the expense of the wealthy.

The Constitution of 1787 struck a balance. Renewing the debate opened in 1776 between followers of Thomas Paine's democratic principles and those, like John Adams, who favored checks and balances upon unpopular majorities, the Constitution was more a victory for Adams. Yet Paine, while critical of the Constitution, supported it, convinced of the need for a strong central government.

The Constitution provoked opposition from those whose ideal was local government close to the people. It curbed the powers of the states, creating a strong central government. It protected slavery, but it lacked adequate protection for individual liberties. Opponents of the Constitution forced the adoption of a Bill of Rights. These first ten amendments protected freedom of speech and the press, freedom of religious expression, the rights of states to maintain a militia, and the rights of individuals to due process of law.

To "last for the ages," wrote James Madison, a constitution must conform to the spirit of the people. Ultimately, with the addition of the Bill of Rights, the new Constitution did conform to the spirit of the American people: it met their aspirations for a national government, and it protected their liberties.

When the Constitution was submitted to the states for ratification, it led to a debate on a wide range of issues, the likes of which the country had never seen. Among people of all classes, the proposed new government aroused deep fears and new hopes. The American Revolution was being defined.

Did new government allow for rule by the people? In the Massachusetts ratifying convention Amos Singletary, a farmer, was convinced that "men of learning and moneyed men . . . will swallow us little folks just as the whale swallowed up Jonah." Jonathan Smith, a fellow farmer, had no such fears, nor did the artisans of the cities who were convinced that the Constitution fulfilled their aspirations for a strong government that would develop commerce and manufacturing.

Democracy was an issue to many. In New York Melancton Smith doubted that the House of Representatives was large enough to allow the election of the "middling class." Alexander Hamilton thought a larger house was not necessary. Others feared that the powers vested in the president made him a king; not so, replied Hamilton, pointing to the many limitations on the office.

The powers of the central government were a related issue. In Virginia, Patrick Henry called it a "consolidated" government that "annihilated" the states. James Madison called it a "mixed" government, explaining that the powers of the central government were enumerated and limited.

Henry, like other spokesmen for southern slaveholders, feared that the new government might use its "implied powers" to abolish slavery. Madison denied any such intention. There were other sides to the debate. In the North foes of slavery were critical of the many ways the Constitution protected slavery. In the South, many slaveholders agreed with Charles C. V. Pinckney of South Carolina, who said, "We have made the best terms possible for slavery."

Why was there no Bill of Rights in the Constitution? This was a crucial question. "The rights of individuals ought to be the primary object of all government," wrote Mercy Otis Warren. Many sympathizers to the new plan, including Thomas Jefferson, concurred. James Wilson, Madison, and Hamilton argued that in a government whose powers were strictly enumerated, a Bill of Rights was not necessary. But before long they relented to the political pressure and supported amendments.

Never before had so many Americans debated so many fundamental questions. The Constitution was ratified, but the debate continued. After two hundred years both Federalists and anti-Federalists continue to speak to issues that concern contemporary Americans.

Who Will Rule: The "Moneyed Men" or the "Little Folks"?

Amos Singletary, farmer, Anti-Federalist

These lawyers, and men of learning, and moneyed men, that talk so finely, and gloss over matters so smoothly, to make us poor illiterate people swallow down the pill, expect to get into Congress themselves; they expect to be the managers of this Constitution, and get all the power and all the money into their own hands, and then they will swallow up all us little folks, like the great *Leviathan*, Mr. President; yes, just as the whale swallowed up *Jonah*. This is what I am afraid of.

Massachusetts Ratifying Convention,
January 25, 1788

Jonathan Smith, farmer, Federalist

I am a plain man, and get my living by the plough. I am not used to speak in public, but I beg your leave to say a few words to my brother ploughjoggers in this house. . . . I did not go to any lawyer, to ask his opinion; we have no lawyer in our town, and we do well enough without. I formed my own pinion, and was pleased with this Constitution. My honorable old daddy there [pointing to Mr. Singletary] won't think that I expect to be a Congress-man, and swallow up the liberties of the people. I never had any post, nor do I want one. But I don't think the worse of the Constitution because lawyers, and men of learning, and moneyed men, are fond of it.

Massachusetts Ratifying Convention,
January 25, 1788

Paul Revere, painting by John Singleton Copley, 1768–70. Gift of Joseph W., William B., and Edward H. R. Revere. Courtesy, Museum of Fine Arts, Boston

Should Artisans Support the Constitution?

Paul Revere, artisan, Federalist

Revere was on a committee of three artisans who drafted the following resolutions adopted at a meeting of 380 Boston artisans.

THAT, in the judgment of this body, the proposed frame of government, is well calculated to secure the liberties, protect the property, and guard the rights of the citizens of America; and it is our warmest wish and prayer that the same should be adopted by this commonwealth.

THAT, it is our opinion, if said constitution should be adopted by the United States of America, trade and navigation will revive and increase, employ and subsistence will be afforded to many of our townsmen, who are now suffering from want of the necessaries of life; that it will promote industry and morality; render us respectable as a nation; and procure us all the blessings to which we are entitled from the natural wealth of our country; our capacity for improvement, from our industry, our freedom and independence.

THAT it is the sense of this body, that if the proposed frame of government should be rejected, the small remains of commerce yet left us, will be annihilated, the various trades and handicrafts dependent thereon, must decay; our poor will be increased, and many of our worthy and skilful mechanicks compelled to seek employ and subsistence in strange lands.

Massachusetts Gazette, January 18, 1788

Thomas Paine, pro and con

I declare myself opposed to several matters in the Constitution particularly to the manner in which what is called the Executive is formed and to the long duration of the Senate. . . . I would have voted for it myself had I been in America or even for a worse, rather than have none, provided it contained the means of remedying its defects by the same appeal to the people by which it was to be established. . . . It was very well said by an anonymous writer in Philadelphia . . . that "thirteen staves and ne'er a hoop will not make a barrel," . . . any kind of hooping the barrel, however defectively executed would be better than none.

A Letter to George Washington (Philadelphia, 1796)

Thomas Paine, artist unknown, copied from the 1792 portrait by George Romney

How Democratic Is the House of Representatives?

Melancton Smith, Anti-Federalist

The idea that naturally suggests itself to our minds, when we speak of representatives, is, that they resemble those they represent. They should be a true picture of the people, possess a knowledge of their circumstances and their wants, sympathize in all their distresses, and be disposed to seek their true interests. The knowledge necessary for the representative of a free people not only comprehends extensive political and commercial information, such as is acquired by men of refined education, who have leisure to attain to high degrees of improvement, but it should also comprehend that kind of acquaintance with the common concerns and occupations of the people, which men of the middling class of life, are, in general more competent to than those of a superior class. . . .

From these observations results this conclusion—that the number of representatives should be so large, as that, while it embraces the men of the first class, it should admit those of the middling class of life. I am convinced that this government is so constituted that the representatives will generally be composed of the first class in the community. . . . The great easily form associations; the poor and middling class form them with difficulty. . . . A substantial yeoman, of sense and discernment, will hardly ever be chosen. From these remarks, it appears that the government will fall into the hands of the few and the great. This will be a government of oppression.

New York State Ratifying Convention, June 21, 1788

Alexander Hamilton, Federalist

It is said to be necessary that all classes of citizens should have some of their own number in the representative body, in order that their feelings and interests may be the better understood and attended to. But we have seen that this will never happen under any arrangement that leaves the votes of the people free. Where this is the case, the representative body, with too few exceptions to have any influence on the spirit of the government, will be composed of landholders, merchants, and men of the learned professions. But where is the danger that the interests and feelings of the different classes of citizens will not be understood or attended to by these three descriptions of men? Will not the landholder know and feel whatever will promote or injure the interests of landed property? And will he not from his own interest in that species of property be sufficiently prone to resist every attempt to prejudice or incumber it? Will not the merchant understand and be disposed to cultivate as far as may be proper the interests of the mechanic and manufacturing arts to which his commerce is so nearly allied? Will not the man of the learned profession, who will feel a neutrality to the rivalships between the different branches of industry, be likely to prove an impartial arbiter between them, ready to promote either, so far as it shall appear to him conductive to the general interests of the society?

The Federalist, No. 35

Is the President a King?

"An Old Whig," Anti-Federalist

In the first place the office of President of the United States appears to me to be clothed with such powers as are dangerous. To be the fountain of all honors in the United States, commander in chief of the army, navy and militia, and with the power of making treaties and of granting pardons, and to be vested with an authority to put a negative upon all laws, unless two thirds of both houses shall persist in enacting it, and put their names down upon calling the yeas and neas for that purpose, is in reality to be a KING as much *a King as the King of Great Britain*, and a King too of the worst kind;— an elective King.

Philadelphia *Independent Gazetteer*,
November 1, 1787

Alexander Hamilton, engraving by W. S. Leney, 1810, after the painting by Ezra Ames

Alexander Hamilton, Federalist

The President of the United States would be an officer elected by the people for *four* years. The King of Great-Britain is a perpetual and *hereditary* prince. The one would be amenable to personal punishment and disgrace: The person of the other is sacred and inviolable. The one would have a *qualified* negative upon the acts of the legislative body: The other has an *absolute* negative. The one would have a right to command the military and naval forces of the nation: The other in addition to this right, possesses that of *declaring* war, and of *raising* and *regulating* fleets and armies by his own authority. The one would have a concurrent power with a branch of the Legislature in the formation of treaties: The other is the *sole possessor* of the power of making treaties.

The Federalist, No. 69

Mercy Otis Warren, Anti-Federalist

There is no provision by a bill of rights to guard against the dangerous encroachments of power in too many instances to be named. . . . We are told by a gentleman of too much virtue and real probity to suspect he has a design to deceive—"that the whole constitution is a declaration of rights,"—but mankind must think for themselves, and to many very judicious and discerning characters, the whole constitution with very few exceptions appears a perversion of the rights of particular states, and of private citizens. . . .

The rights of individuals ought to be the primary object of all government, and cannot be too securely guarded by the most explicit declarations in their favor. This has been the opinion of the Hampdens, the Pyms, and many other illustrious names, that have stood forth in defence of English liberties; and even the Italian master in politicks, the subtle and renounced Machiavel, acknowledges that no republic ever yet stood on a stable foundation without satisfying the common people.

The Columbian Patriot, Boston, 1788

Mercy Otis Warren, engraving from *The Women of the American Revolution,* vol. I, by Elizabeth F. Ellet, 1848

James Wilson, Federalist

In a government, consisting of enumerated powers, such as is proposed for the United states, a bill of rights would not only be unnecessary, but, in my humble judgment, highly imprudent. In all societies, there are many powers and rights, which cannot be particularly enumerated. A bill of rights annexed to a constitution, is an enumeration of the powers reserved. If we attempt an enumeration, every thing that is not enumerated, is presumed to be given. The consequence is, that an imperfect enumeration would throw all implied power into the scale of the government; and the rights of the people would be rendered incomplete. On the other hand; an imperfect enumeration of the powers of government, reserves all implied power to the people; and, by that means the constitution becomes incomplete; but of the two it is much safer to run the risk on the side of the constitution; for an omission in the enumeration of the power of government, is neither so dangerous, nor important, as an omission in the enumeration of the rights of the people.

Pennsylvania Ratifying Convention, December 4, 1787

Can the Federal Government Abolish Slavery?

Patrick Henry, Anti-Federalist

Among ten thousand *implied powers* which they may assume, they may, if we be engaged in war, liberate every one of your slaves if they please. And this must and will be done by men, a majority of whom have no common interest with you. They will, therefore, have no feeling of your interests. It has been repeatedly said here, that the great object of a national government was a national defence. . . . In this state there are two hundred and thirty-six thousand blacks, and there are many in several other states. But there are few or none in the Northern States; and yet, if the Northern States shall be of opinion that our slaves are numberless, they may call forth every national resource. May Congress not say, *that every black man* must fight? Did we not see a little of this in the last war? . . . Slavery is detested. We feel its fatal effects—we deplore it with all the pity of humanity. Let all these considerations, at some future period, press with full force on the minds of Congress. Let that urbanity, which I trust will distinguish America, and the necessity of national defence, —let all these things operate on their minds; they will search that paper, and see if they have power of manumission. And they have not, sir? Have they not power to provide for the general defence and welfare? May they not think that these call for the abolition of slavery? May they not pronounce all slaves free, and will they not be warranted by that power?

Virginia Ratifying Convention,
June 15, 1788

James Madison, Federalist

I was struck with surprise when I heard [Mr. Henry] express himself alarmed with respect to the emancipation of slaves. Let me ask, if they should even attempt it, if it will not be a usurpation of power. There is no power to warrant it, in that paper. If there be, I know it not. But why should it be done? Says the honorable gentleman, for the general welfare: it will infuse strength into our system. Can any member of this committee suppose that it will increase our strength? Can any one believe that the American councils will come into a measure which will strip them of their property, and discourage and alienate the affections of five thirteenths of the Union? Why was nothing of this sort aimed at before? I believe such an idea never entered into any American breast, nor do I believe it ever will enter into the heads of those gentlemen who substitute unsupported suspicions for reasons.

Virginia Ratifying Convention,
June 24, 1788

Is It a "Consolidated" or a "Mixed" Government?

Patrick Henry, engraving
by E. Wellmore,
nineteenth century, after
the painting by J. B.
Longacre

Patrick Henry, Anti-Federalist

That this is a consolidated government is demonstrably clear; and the danger of such a government is, to my mind, very striking. I have the highest veneration for those gentlemen; but sir, give me leave to demand, What right had they to say, *We the people*? My political curiosity, exclusive of my anxious solicitude for the public welfare, leads me to ask, Who authorized them to speak the language of, *We, the people*, instead of, *We, the states*? States are the characteristics and the soul of a confederation. If the states be not the agents of this compact, it must be one great, consolidated, national government, of the people of all the states.

If we admit this consolidated government, it will be because we like a great, splendid one. Some way or other we must be a great and mighty empire; we must have an army, and a navy, and a number of things. When the American spirit was in its youth, the language of America was different: liberty, sir, was then the primary object. . . . But now, sir, the American spirit, assisted by the ropes and chains of consolidation, is about to convert this country into a powerful and mighty empire. If you make the citizens of this country agree to become the subjects of one great consolidated empire of America, your government will not have sufficient energy to keep them together. Such a government is incompatible with the genius of republicanism. There will be no checks, no real balances, in this government. What can avail your specious, imaginary balances, your rope-dancing, chain-rattling, ridiculous ideal checks and contrivances?

Virginia Ratifying Convention,
June 2, 1788

James Madison,
engraving by W. R.
Jones, 1814, after the
painting by Gilbert
Stuart

James Madison, Federalist

Give me leave to say something of the nature of the government. . . . There are a number of opinions; but the principal question is, whether it be a federal or consolidated government. In order to judge properly of the question before us, we must consider it minutely in its principal parts. I conceive myself that it is of a mixed nature; it is in a manner unprecedented; we cannot find one express example in the experience of the world. It stands by itself. In some respects it is a government of a federal nature; in others it is of a consolidated nature. . . .

The members to the national House of Representatives are to be chosen by the people at large, in proportion to the numbers in the respective districts. When we come to the Senate, its members are elected by the states in their equal and political capacity. But had the government been completely consolidated, the Senate would have been chosen by the people in their individual capacity, in the same manner as the members of the other house. Thus it is of a complicated nature; and this complication, I trust, will be found to exclude the evils of absolute consolidation, as well as of a mere confederacy. If Virginia was separated from all the states, her power and authority would extend to all cases: in like manner, were all powers vested in the general government, it would be a consolidated government; but the powers of the federal government are enumerated; it can only operate in certain cases; it has legislative powers on defined and limited objects, beyond which it cannot extend its jurisdiction.

Virginia Ratifying Convention,
June 6, 1788

Silences in the Sources

The winners usually write history; the losers often lose a second time, in the history books as well as in history. So it was with the great debate over ratifying the Constitution. The Federalists won the political battle. The losers, the anti-Federalists, were so strong they helped shape the final outcome by forcing amendments to the Constitution that became the Bill of Rights. But until recently, history has usually been written with a Federalist bias.

Part of the problem is that the historical record favored the Federalists. *The Federalist*, the essays written by Madison, Hamilton, and Jay commonly referred to as the "Federalist Papers," became the classic commentary on the Constitution. The Chicago Historical Society was proud to buy a copy of the first edition. The anti-Federalist leaders were not of a single mind and produced no such collection of essays. Instead they wrote numerous articles and pamphlets, no one of which became a collector's item.

Only in recent decades, as scholars have come to consider the anti-Federalists worthy of further analysis, have they begun to assemble and republish the anti-Federalist writings. There is now a five-volume collection entitled *The Anti-Federalist Papers.* Scholars completing *The Documentary History of the Ratification of the Constitution* at the University of Wisconsin are assembling state by state the entire debate over the Constitution, collecting letters, newspapers, handbills, pamphlets, and speeches. When this project is completed we will have a much better sense what the man in the street or the man in a country tavern thought about the Constitution in 1787–88. It may also contribute to the ongoing reinterpretation of the Constitution. At the end of the twentieth century such anti-Federalist ideas as restricting the powers of the presidency and limiting terms of congressmen so they will be forced to "return to the people" take on a new meaning.

Of all the writings in the battles over ratifying the *Constitution*, The Federalist *alone has come to be regarded as the classic commentary on the document.*

At the time, the essays were the work of partisan political writers, a collection of eighty-five articles published first in the newspapers and then in book form. The chief authors were Alexander Hamilton and James Madison, with John Jay contributing only five essays. When bound volumes of the essays were ready in the spring of 1788, they were rushed off to influence delegates in the pivotal states, Virginia and New York, whose conventions met in the early summer. The essays became a debater's handbook in the conventions.

Everything about the venture was political. The authors called the series The Federalist *to disguise their argument for a national government as opposed to a confederation. They used the pseudonym Publius after Publius Valerius, the Roman leader who established a state republic and who was honored in Rome by the name Publicola, which meant "people-lover." And they wrote, Madison recalled, "in haste . . . in order to get through the subject while the Constitution was before the public."*

John and Archibald McLean, New York printers, printed only five hundred bound copies, and when the debates were over they still had copies left. It would be many years before the partisan polemic would be transformed into a classic.

The Federalist, *by James Madison, Alexander Hamilton, and John Jay, 1788*

The Bill of Rights

In 1789 the first Congress passed the first amendments to the Constitution, later known as the Bill of Rights. To satisfy opponents of the Constitution, James Madison shepherded seventeen proposals through the House of Representatives, which were then presented to the Senate. The Senate reduced them to twelve, a committee of the House and Senate rewrote them, and Congress submitted them to the states for ratification.

The first two of the twelve proposed amendments failed in the states. The first would have increased the number of representatives in the House, a point much desired by opponents to the Constitution, who feared that the House was not large enough to represent the people. The second would have limited the power of Congress to increase its own salaries.

On December 15, 1791, the necessary three-fourths of the state legislatures ratified the remaining ten amendments. In this volume of the *Journal of the Senate* are the official amendments agreed to by the Senate and House, in the language now in the Constitution.

The Third Article (today the First Amendment) protected freedom of religion; freedom of speech, press, and assembly; and the right to petition, all of which the framers of the Bill of Rights considered indispensable to the functioning of a free government.

The Fourth and Fifth articles (now the Second and Third amendments) protected the right of the people to a militia. These articles calmed their deep fears of a standing army encroaching on private rights—an issue that had come to a head in the Revolution at the time of the Boston Massacre.

The Sixth through the Tenth articles (now the Fourth through Eighth amendments) guaranteed what can be summed up as due process of the law for the accused. An individual's rights were protected at every stage of his or her encounter with the law. A citizen had the right to know the charges against him, the right to a speedy trial by jury, the right to a lawyer, the right to bail, the right not to testify against himself, the right to be free of "cruel and unusual punishments," and the right not to be tried twice for the same offense. All these legal rights were considered necessary to protect the individual in the exercise of his political rights.

The final two articles, the Eleventh and the Twelfth (now the Ninth and Tenth amendments) protected all other rights "retained by the people" even if they were not enumerated, and reserved to the states all powers not specifically prohibited to them. They were "safety" amendments.

These ten amendments, while they did not satisfy the opponents of the Constitution who wanted much more fundamental structural changes, helped overcome common fears. In time they won broad support as a fundamental part of the Constitution. Later generations would extend their protections still further, often after bitter controversies.

Opposite: The Bill of Rights, from the *Journal of the First Session of the Senate of the United States of America*, 1789

The Conventions of a Number of the States having, at the Time of their adopting the Constitution, expressed a Desire, in order to prevent misconstruction or abuse of its Powers, that further declaratory and restrictive Clauses should be added: And as extending the Ground of public Confidence in the Government, will best insure the beneficent Ends of its Institution—

RESOLVED, by the Senate and House of Representatives of the United States of America in Congress assembled, two thirds of both Houses concurring, That the following Articles be proposed to the Legislatures of the several States, as Amendments to the Constitution of the United States, all or any of which Articles, when ratified by three fourths of the said Legislatures, to be valid to all intents and purposes, as part of the said Constitution—Viz.

Articles in addition to, and amendment of, the Constitution of the United States of America, proposed by Congress, and ratified by the Legislatures of the several States, pursuant to the fifth Article of the original Constitution.

ARTICLE the FIRST.

After the first enumeration, required by the first Article of the Constitution, there shall be one Representative for every thirty thousand, until the number shall amount to one hundred; after which the proportion shall be so regulated by Congress, that there shall be not less than one hundred Representatives, nor less than one Representative for every forty thousand persons, until the number of Representatives shall amount to two hundred; after which the proportion shall be so regulated by Congress, that there shall not be less than two hundred Representatives, nor more than one Representative for every fifty thousand persons.

ARTICLE the SECOND.

No law, varying the compensation for the services of the Senators and Representatives, shall take effect, until an election of Representatives shall have intervened.

ARTICLE the THIRD.

Congress shall make no law respecting an establishment of religion, or prohibiting the free exercise thereof, or abridging the freedom of speech, or of the press, or the right of the people peaceably to assemble, and to petition the Government for a redress of grievances.

ARTICLE the FOURTH.

A well regulated militia, being necessary to the security of a free State, the right of the people to keep and bear arms, shall not be infringed.

ARTICLE the FIFTH.

No soldier shall, in time of peace, be quartered in any house, without the consent of the owner, nor in time of war, but in a manner to be prescribed by law.

ARTICLE the SIXTH.

The right of the people to be secure in their persons, houses, papers, and effects, against unreasonable searches and seizures, shall not be violated, and no warrants shall issue, but upon probable cause, supported by oath or affirmation, and particularly describing the place to be searched, and the persons or things to be seized.

ARTICLE the SEVENTH.

No person shall be held to answer for a capital, or otherwise infamous crime, unless on a presentment or indictment of a Grand Jury, except in cases arising in the land or naval forces, or in the militia, when in actual service in time of war or public danger; nor shall any person be subject for the same offence to be twice put in jeopardy of life or limb; nor shall be compelled in any criminal case, to be a witness against himself, nor be deprived of life, liberty or property, without due process of law; nor shall private property be taken for public use without just compensation.

ARTICLE the EIGHTH.

In all criminal prosecutions the accused shall enjoy the right to a speedy and public trial by an impartial Jury of the State and District wherein the crime shall have been committed, which District shall have been previously ascertained by law; and to be informed of the nature and cause of the accusation, to be confronted with the witnesses against him, to have compulsory process for obtaining witnesses in his favor, and to have the assistance of counsel for his defence.

ARTICLE the NINTH.

In suits at common law, where the value in controversy shall exceed twenty dollars, the right of trial by Jury shall be preserved, and no fact, tried by a Jury, shall be otherwise re-examined in any court of the United States, than according to the rules of the common law.

ARTICLE the TENTH.

Excessive bail shall not be required, nor excessive fines imposed, nor cruel and unusual punishments inflicted.

ARTICLE the ELEVENTH.

The enumeration in the Constitution, of certain rights, shall not be construed to deny or disparage others retained by the people.

ARTICLE the TWELFTH.

The powers not delegated to the United States by the Constitution, nor prohibited by it to the States, are reserved to the States respectively, or to the people.

FREDERICK AUGUSTUS MUHLENBERG,
SPEAKER OF THE HOUSE OF REPRESENTATIVES.

JOHN ADAMS, VICE-PRESIDENT OF THE UNITED STATES, AND PRESIDENT OF THE SENATE.

Attest.
JOHN BECKLEY, *Clerk of the House of Representatives.*
SAMUEL A. OTIS, *Secretary of the Senate.*

The Republic in Action

Opposite: Stephens's
Philadelphia Directory for
1796

6

Only capital letters set off George Washington's name and occupation from those of fellow citizens in this Philadelphia city directory. Philadelphia was the nation's temporary capital from 1790 to 1800, and Washington's home and office at 190 High Street was a far cry from a royal palace.

The directory was an alphabetical arrangement of the "names, occupations and places of abode of the citizens." The names and occupations on the page on which Washington is listed tell us much about the nation's largest city, which had a population of forty-two thousand in 1790 and sixty thousand in 1800.

It was a port city based on maritime commerce (William Watson, sea captain; Stephen Watts, mariner; Joseph Way, pilot). Most of its working citizens, like most of the men listed on this page, were skilled craftsmen, some of whom owned their own shops, some of whom worked for others (Charles Watson, "taylor"; Thomas Watson, grocer; Jacob, Joseph, and Samuel Wayne, all carpenters). Most would have been in the "middling" class. At the top of the social ladder would be a "gentleman," who would have lived off his income without working (Joseph Watkins), and a merchant (John Watson); at the bottom a "labourer" (Cesar Warrington) and a chimney sweeper (Thomas Watson).

Only a narrow range of trades were open to women. Women listed in the directory usually were widows; some were single, and others were wives with a trade of their own: Mary Warren, "school-mistress"; Sarah Wartman, "widow, boarding-house"; Mary Waters, "widow, doctoress"; Margaret Watson, "millener"; Arabella Watson, "widow, seamstress."

"All men are created equal" did not mean that all men achieved social and economic equality. In Philadelphia in 1800 less than 1 percent of the population owned as much wealth as the 75 percent at the bottom. But listing all inhabitants alphabetically suggests that people regarded themselves as equal before the law—as citizens.

Warren Mary, school-mistress, Shipherds court.
Warrington Cesar, labourer, 73, So. Fifth st.
Wartman Sarah, widow, boarding-house, 15, Branch st.
Warts John, sea-captain, near 19, Vernon st.
WASHINGTON GEORGE, PRESIDENT of the UNITED STATES, 190, High Street.
Wastlie John, skin-dresser, 53, So. Fifth St.
Waterman Jesse, school-master, 28, North alley.
Waters Mary, widow, doctoress, Willings alley.
Waters Nathaniel, scrivener, 52, Walnut st.
Waters Patrick, currier, Merediths court.
Waters Thomas, labourer, 150, Spruce st.
Watkins John, shoemaker, Cedar st. bet. 13 & 21.
Watkins Joseph, gentleman, 121, Arch st.
Watkins Thomas, brush-maker, 13, Strawberry st.
Watkins William, tobacconist, 166, So. Water st.
Watman Adam, tavern-keeper, 240, No. Second st.
Watman George, butcher, Beach st.
Watson Arabella, widow, seamstress, German st.
Watson Charles C. taylor, 24, So. Fourth st.
Watson John, merchant, 254, Market st.
Watson Margaret, milener, 177, South Second st.
Watson Mary, widow near 84, No. Eighth st.
Watson Thomas, grocer, 48, Lombard st.
Watson Thomas, chimney sweeper, Old Fourth st.
Watson William, coachmaker, Black horse alley.
Watson William, sea-captain, 58, Artillery lane, bet. Front & Second st.
Watts Stephen, mariner, near 98, So. Fifth st.
Watts William, grocer, 8, Moravian alley.
Watt Samuel, merchant, 5, So. Front st.
Way Andrew, taylor, 1, Quarry st.
Way George, coachmaker, 152, Arch st.
Way Joseph, pilot, 481, South Front st.
Way Nicholas, M. D. 83, So. Second st.
Wayne Jacob, carpenter & chairmaker, 164 & 166 No. Front st.
Wayne Joseph, carpenter, South Front st. near Mead alley.
Wayne Samuel, house-carpenter, 17, Keys alley.
Wayne Thomas, cooper, 481, South Front st.
Weasley John, cooper, 386, No. Front st.
Weatherby Margaret, widow, midwife, Strawberry lane.
Weatherall Benjamin, tin man & coppersmith, 187, Market st.
Weatherer Alexander, fruiterer, 93, No. Front

R

From 1789 to 1820 Americans set in motion the first modern republic to govern an extensive territory. A republic, the revolutionary generation agreed, meant a representative, constitutional government whose authority rested ultimately on popular elections. About how democratic a republic should be, they disagreed.

The Federalists, in power until 1801, were led by George Washington, John Adams, and Alexander Hamilton. They believed that rulers should be men of property and gentility. Once elected they should be free to make decisions on the basis of their own wisdom. Many "high-toned" Federalists scorned democracy as rule by "the rabble."

Another wing of the revolutionary generation, in the tradition of Thomas Paine, favored the vigorous expression of popular opinion through democratic societies, elections, and a vigilant press. Led by James Madison, Thomas Jefferson, and Albert Gallatin, they formed the first opposition party, the Republicans, which some called the Democratic-Republicans. Rulers, in Jefferson's view, should be drawn from men of "talent and virtue," whatever their origin or occupation. In 1801 the Republicans triumphed.

Whatever their differences, Federalists and Republicans shared a vision of a republic of white men. They presumed women would be represented by the male heads of their households. Slaves were not citizens; free blacks were second-class citizens. And as the republic expanded, it would displace, not incorporate, the American Indian peoples.

Setting a Republican Style

The republic demanded a republican style. Americans had rejected monarchy, where the king appeared in splendor amid the pomp and ceremony of a royal court. Thomas Paine had observed that this style was meant to overawe the populace. But what was the proper style for a republican president?

How for example should Congress address the president? Vice-President John Adams, convinced that a title was necessary to maintain the dignity of the office, favored "His Highness." The more democratic House of Representatives won out with "The President of the United States" rather than "His elective Highness." As vice-president, Adams beat a hasty retreat from his attempts to give a "high tone" to the presidency after some senators poked fun at him, suggesting the title for him of "His Rotundity." How should the president address the people? "My friends and Fellow citizens" was George Washington's choice. Should the president's likeness appear on coins? This smacked of monarchy. A woman personifying liberty was chosen instead.

Clothes were another test. George Washington and John Adams in their quest for dignity favored elegant dress for the chief executive. Their administrations set what that age considered a "high tone." Yet it was not nearly as high as some in their party favored. What they wore was a far cry from the royal ermine of King George III. Even so, in the eyes of many common people, their style was too aristocratic.

Thomas Jefferson moved much further toward republican simplicity when he became president in 1801. George Washington traveled in public in a handsome coach. Jefferson walked to his own inauguration and shocked the British ambassador by receiving him in carpet slippers. His was a Democratic-Republican style.

This image of George Washington, which Edward Savage made from an oil portrait he painted in 1792, became the most widely known image of Washington as president, surpassing in popularity the wartime image of Washington as general.

Washington was now the civilian, no longer the soldier, dressed not in a uniform but in an elegant yet austere black velvet suit, which appears to be the same suit he wore at his second inauguration. His hand is on a map of a plan for the city of Washington, to be built on the Potomac River. Washington the president is portrayed as a man of dignity and wisdom, a man above political parties or sectional interests, looking to the future of the United States.

George Washington, Esq., mezzotint by Edward Savage, 1793

In 1789, at his first inauguration, Washington wore a suit of brown Connecticut cloth to encourage American manufactures. For his second inauguration he apparently no longer felt the need to make this symbolic gesture, for he chose this suit of black French velvet, cut in a dignified, yet simple, republican style.

This suit came to the Chicago Historical Society in 1920 with authentication. It was exhibited for many years, and when its condition deteriorated, a replica was made by a Chicago clothing manufacturer.

Suit worn by George Washington at his second inauguration, 1793

In monarchical societies the king always appeared in public in glorious apparel to bedazzle the populace with his majesty. Official painters were expected to spread the image. This painting was copied from the original done by Allan Ramsay, the official court painter, about 1767.

George III, painting by Frederick Dudley Wallon, c. 1894

Suits worn by John
Adams, c. 1780

John Adams, the son of a Massachusetts yeoman and shoemaker, was anything but an aristocrat in his bearing. He was a New England Yankee. Although he had gone to Harvard and become a lawyer, he loved to return to his home in rural Braintree, Massachusetts, as farmer John.

But his political conviction that the people had to "venerate persons in authority" led him to support whatever would lend an aura of dignity to high office: a title, elegant clothing, and appearing in public in a coach with four horses.

These suits are evidence of his own taste in official garb. He very likely wore the dark plum-colored velvet suit in England when he was received in court by the king after the peace treaty. John Singleton Copley painted Adams in this suit in London in 1783. The light suit, ecru in color and made of lighter-weight silk and cotton cloth, may have been intended for warmer seasons.

Each suit has three pieces: a full-skirted coat with pleated back, knee-length breeches, and a long-waisted waistcoat, ancestor of the modern vest. With the suits Adams wore a wig, another indispensable sign of status for a gentleman. Adams tied his own hair in a ponytail that hung down the back, leaving a hair stain on the light-colored suit. In the 1790s, when it became the republican style to go wigless, Adams was content to abandon his wig.

Republican Principles in Every Home

After serving two terms as president, George Washington, aware that he was establishing precedents, refused to run for a third term and issued an address to Americans calling them "My friends and Fellow citizens." In what was later named his "Farewell Address," Washington expressed his overriding concern for preserving American independence. He saw dangers to national union from foreign influences, sectional divisions, and political parties. He warned especially against the danger of the country becoming a slave to "an habitual hatred" of any foreign nation or of succumbing to "overgrown military establishments" at home.

John Adams, elected to the presidency over Thomas Jefferson in 1797 in the first contested presidential election, faced a country bitterly divided between Federalists and Republicans. As president Adams sanctioned both an undeclared war with France and the Alien and Sedition Laws, used to suppress his opponents at home. After one term he was defeated for reelection by Jefferson. Always independent-minded, Adams was proud that he had broken from the "high" Federalists to make peace with France. But he left the presidency a disappointed man.

Thomas Jefferson viewed his election in 1801 as a vindication of the "spirit of 1776." In his inaugural address he set down the "sacred principles" of a democratic republicanism "that though the will of the majority is in all cases to prevail, that will, to be rightful, must be reasonable: that the minority possess their equal rights, which equal law must protect, and to violate would be oppression."

Americans brought into their homes the principles the first presidents set down as sacred. Slogans on commemorative bowls and pitchers, called "Liverpool pitchers," popularized these principles. Jefferson's inaugural address, printed on silk, could be mounted on the wall.

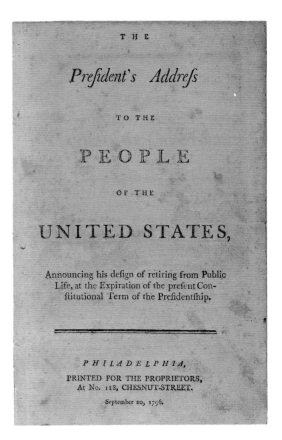

A first printing of
George Washington's
"Farewell Address,"
September 20, 1796

Liverpool pitchers were manufactured in British potteries for the American market. American agents told the manufacturers what slogans and pictures would sell and probably sent them engravings to copy. These prints were transferred to the pitchers in the firing process. The pitchers were used to pour water into wash basins (this was an age before running water), to decorate a mantel over the fireplace, or perhaps to pour milk, cider, or beer.

The slogans hark back to the Revolution:
Success to AMERICA whose MILITIA is
better than Standing ARMIES,
May its Citizens Emulate Soldiers And its
Soldiers HEROES
While Justice is the Throne to which we are
bound to bend
Our Countrys Rights and Laws we ever will
defend.
Sacred to the memory of G. Washington,
who emancipated America from slavery and
founded a republic upon such just and
equitable principles that it will serve
as a model.

Pitcher, English, c. 1800

The slogans are "PEACE PLENTY and
INDEPENDENCE" and "Spring."

Pitcher, English, c. 1800

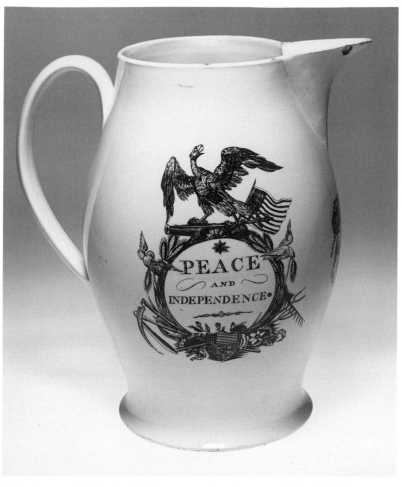

The slogan on the death of Washington is: "Wash-
ington in Glory," "America in Tears," "PEACE /
AND / INDEPENDENCE." "E. Pluribus Unum."

Pitcher, English, c. 1800

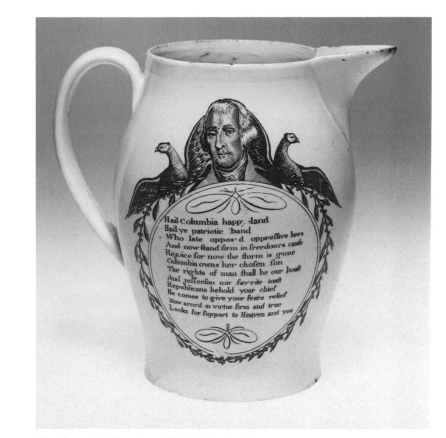

Broadside, inaugural
address of President
Thomas Jefferson,
printed on silk, 1801

*The slogan is Jeffersonian: "Hail Columbia happy
land. . . . The rights of man shall be our boast / And
Jefferson our favorite toast."*

Pitcher, English, c. 1800

"The will of the majority is to prevail"

The American Revolution and the debates over the Constitution gave large numbers of Americans a sense of their own citizenship. There was a quickening of popular participation in politics. The states lowered property qualifications for suffrage, as the Constitution allowed. More men qualified to vote and more of them voted. Politicians appealed to the citizenry through broadsides, political cartoons, and especially newspapers.

The framers of the Constitution, the Federalists, were not friends to political parties, condemning them as "factions." But James Madison broke with the Federalists to join Thomas Jefferson to lead the first opposition political party.

National leaders were still drawn from men of wealth and standing in society. But new self-made and self-educated men appeared, drawn mainly to the Democratic-Republicans. Some of them made politics their career instead of their avocation.

When the Federalists became a party, their basis of support was among the merchant elites, commercial farmers, and a section of the southern planters. John Adams boasted it was the party of the "education, the talents, the virtues and the property of the country." By 1800 the Democratic-Republicans had won over most of the farmers, most of the city artisans, and a segment of the merchants. Their presidents were Virginia planters: Thomas Jefferson, James Madison, and James Monroe.

The two parties did not survive the period. The Federalists disappeared, rejected by the voters, and after the Democratic-Republicans dominated national politics from 1801 to 1825, divisions developed among them, laying the basis for new parties.

A Free Press

In 1790 there were 90 newspapers in the country; by 1810 there were almost 240, an index of the growing interest in politics in the new nation. Although many papers were avowedly Federalist or Republican, some printers tried to be independent or at least to appear so. The typical paper was four tabloid-sized pages, often displaying advertisements on the first and last pages and teeming with political "intelligence" and articles of opinion on the inside. In the large cities daily papers were common.

The slogan on the masthead of this staunchly
Democratic-Republican paper glorifies mankind in
the spirit of the Enlightenment.

The Herald of Liberty,
Washington, Pennsyl-
vania, March 18, 1799

Northern Sentinel,
Burlington, Vermont,
October 28, 1814

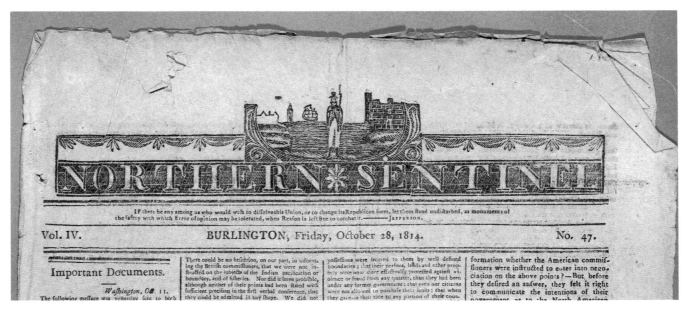

The masthead of this paper features a quotation on
freedom of opinion from Jefferson's inaugural address.

The New-York Journal,
& Patriotic Register,
August 21, 1793

One of the country's leading Republican papers, the
Journal *came out three times a week, then daily.*

Der Friedens Bothe,
Bucks County, Pennsyl-
vania, March 14, 1816

This German-language paper, whose title translates
"The Messenger of Peace," presented itself as
"independent in politics."

Boston Gazette, March 17, 1814

A Federalist paper bitterly opposed to the War of 1812, the Gazette *was one of the first papers to run cartoons, this one a plea for the Federalist ticket and "No Embargo, No War, No Conscription, No Direct Taxes."*

A printer might try to get a newspaper going by posting a broadside like this one, which asks for subscriptions at "two dollars per annum." Henry Willcocks launched his paper in Winchester, Virginia, but did not stay with it very long. He moved to York, Pennsylvania, to found the Pennsylvania Herald, which he published from 1789 to 1791, then went to a nearby town to publish the Lancaster Journal, which ran from 1791 to 1796. In small country towns, newspapers and editors came and went.

Printing and circulating broadsides like this one, by which Loyd Dorsey announces to his fellow citizens that he is a candidate for that state's General Assembly, was the old way of electioneering. In the new way members of a party got together in a caucus or committee and selected a candidate who identified himself with a party label. Newspapers and broadsides then publicized the "ticket."

Broadside proposing a new weekly newspaper, *The Virginia Gazette, and Hobb's Hole Advertiser,* January 1, 1787

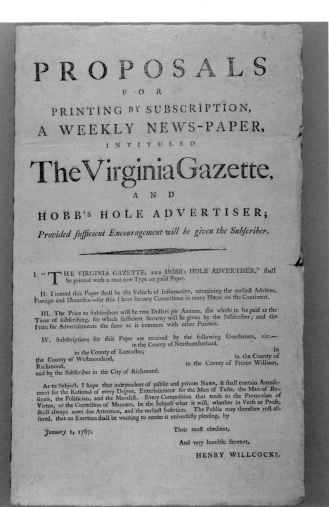

PROPOSALS

FOR

PRINTING BY SUBSCRIPTION,

A WEEKLY NEWS-PAPER,

INTITULED

The Virginia Gazette,

AND

HOBB's HOLE ADVERTISER;

Provided sufficient Encouragement will be given the Subscriber.

I. "THE VIRGINIA GAZETTE, AND HOBB's HOLE ADVERTISER," shall be printed with a neat new Type on good Paper.

II. I intend this Paper shall be the Vehicle of Information, containing the earliest Advices, Foreign and Domestic—for this I have literary Connections in many Places on the Continent.

III. The Price to Subscribers will be two Dollars per Annum, the whole to be paid at the Time of subscribing; for which sufficient Security will be given the Subscriber; and the Price for Advertisements the same as is common with other Printers.

IV. Subscriptions for this Paper are received by the following Gentlemen, viz.—
in the County of Northumberland,
in the County of Lancaster;
the County of Westmoreland,   in the County of
Richmond,   in the County of Prince William,
and by the Subscriber in the City of Richmond.

As to Subject, I hope that independent of public and private News, it shall contain Amusement for the Rational of every Degree, Entertainment for the Man of Taste, the Man of Business, the Politician, and the Moralist. Every Composition that tends to the Promotion of Virtue, or the Correction of Manners, be the Subject what it will, whether in Verse or Prose, shall always meet due Attention, and the earliest Insertion. The Public may therefore rest assured, that no Exertion shall be wanting to render it universally pleasing, by

January 1, 1787.   Their most obedient,

And very humble Servant,

HENRY WILLCOCKS.

To the Citizens of Anne-Arundel county.

THERE being two vacancies in the representation of this county to the GENERAL ASSEMBLY of MARYLAND, by the appointment of John F. Mercer and Edward Hall, Esquires, to other offices, I am induced to offer myself as a candidate to fill one of those vacancies. Should I meet with your approbation and support, by having your votes, (which I respectfully solicit,) at the ensuing election that will take place on MONDAY the 23d inst. I assure you that nothing on my part shall be wanting to advance your interests.

I am, my fellow-citizens,

With much respect,

Your obedient Servant,

LOYD DORSEY.

November 12, 1801.

Broadside "To the Citizens of Anne-Arundel county," November 12, 1801

The GERRY-MANDER: or, ESSEX SOUTH DISTRICT formed into a MONSTER!!

To gerrymander *is to reshape voting districts to give unfair advantage to one party in elections. The term, which first appeared in this cartoon, is an amalgam of Elbridge Gerry, the Republican governor of Massachusetts, and the word* salamander. *The Republican majority in Essex County, Massachusetts, realigned the voting district so that Republicans would outnumber Federalists. This cartoon adds fangs, wings, and claws to a map of the voting district, which was apportioned more fairly the following year.*

The Gerry-Mander,
broadside with woodcut,
by Elkanah Tisdale,
Boston, 1812

"The minority possess their equal rights"

The First Amendment to the Constitution provided that "Congress shall make no law . . . abridging the freedom of speech, or of the press." Federalists and Democratic-Republicans disagreed in defining how far freedom of speech was protected.

In 1798 Federalists, in an effort to suppress their Democratic-Republican opponents, passed the Sedition Law, which decreed that "if any person shall print, utter or publish . . . any false scandalous and malicious writing . . . against the government of the United States . . . or the President," the person was subject to a fine of up to two thousand dollars and a prison term of up to two years. Federalists indicted some twenty-five Jeffersonian editors and political leaders and jailed ten of them.

Congressional Pugilists,
artist unknown, 1798

Congressman Matthew Lyon was one of the principal targets of the Sedition Law. This cartoon ridicules the fracas between Lyon and Roger Griswold, a Connecticut Federalist. A few days before this event Griswold had insulted Lyon on the floor of Congress by raising an old discredited charge of cowardice in the Revolution. Lyon spat in his face. Federalists moved to expel Lyon from Congress, but their motion failed.

In this scene, Griswold is attacking Lyon with his cane while Lyon defends himself with tongs from the fireplace. The cartoonist mocks both men as well as the congressmen who cheer them on or laugh. This incident took place in February 1798; in July the Federalist majority passed the Sedition Act, under which they would send Lyon to jail.

Matthew Lyon

Matthew Lyon (1749–1822) was a self-made man, typical of the new men who rose in the more open political system of the young nation. Born in Ireland, he came to this country at fifteen, an impoverished indentured servant. He prospered in frontier Vermont, where he eventually became the owner of an iron foundry and the publisher of a newspaper.

During the Revolution he fought at Saratoga and at Fort Ticonderoga. He supported a democratic constitution for Vermont, written in the spirit of Thomas Paine. In 1797, on his fourth try, he was elected to Congress as a Democratic-Republican.

Aristocratic Federalists in Congress ridiculed Lyon as a "wild Irishman" of lowly origins who lacked "American blood." In 1798, after failing to expel him from the House, they indicted him under the Sedition Law for criticizing President Adams's foreign policy. Count One in the indictment was a passage by Lyon implying that the administration of John Adams showed "a continual grasp for power, an unbounded thirst for ridiculous pomp, foolish adulation or selfish avarice."

A Federalist judge sentenced him to four months in prison and levied a one-thousand-dollar fine. Lyon claimed the Sedition Law was unconstitutional. His constituents agreed, reelecting him to Congress from jail. While in Congress he witnessed the lapse of the Sedition Law. Soon after, Lyon moved west to frontier Kentucky to begin a second career in business and politics.

Jefferson, in his inaugural address of 1801, warned that after banishing "religious intolerance . . . we have yet gained little if we countenance a political intolerance as despotic, as wicked and as capable of as bitter and bloody persecutions." The minority "possess their equal rights." As president he freed political prisoners and let the Sedition Law lapse.

"If there be any among us who would wish to dissolve the Union or to change its republican form," he wrote, "let them stand undisturbed as monuments of the safety with which error of opinion may be tolerated where reason is left free to combat it."

In 1798, when the Federalist-sponsored Sedition Law made it a crime to criticize the president, Republicans argued that opinions should not be the subject of legislation. In 1804 Republicans in New York brought the Federalist editor Harry Croswell to trial, convicting him under the libel law for his political accusations against President Jefferson. Alexander Hamilton (who had defended the Sedition Law) appealed Croswell's case to the state supreme court.

In his plea, reprinted in this pamphlet, Hamilton argues that the jury should be allowed to judge the truth or falsity of an accusation. The court divided evenly, and the following year the New York legislature enacted a law permitting the truth of a charge to be introduced in libel cases, a precedent-setting victory for freedom of the press.

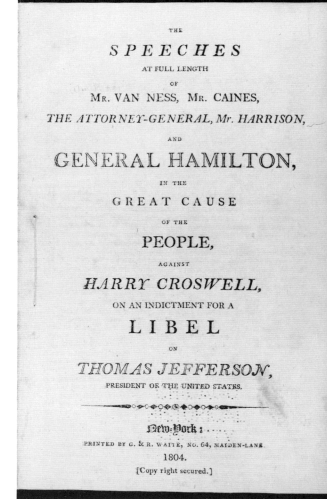

THE

SPEECHES

AT FULL LENGTH

OF

Mr. VAN NESS, Mr. CAINES,

THE ATTORNEY-GENERAL, Mr. HARRISON,

AND

GENERAL HAMILTON,

IN THE

GREAT CAUSE

OF THE

PEOPLE,

AGAINST

HARRY CROSWELL,

ON AN INDICTMENT FOR A

LIBEL

ON

THOMAS JEFFERSON,

PRESIDENT OF THE UNITED STATES.

New-York :

PRINTED BY G. & R. WAITE, NO. 64, MAIDEN-LANE.

1804.

[Copy right secured.]

Speeches in the People's Case against Harry Croswell for Libel on Thomas Jefferson, 1804

W hat role should government play "to promote the general Welfare," which the Preamble to the Constitution sets forth as one of the aims of the new government?

The economy boomed in the 1790s and early 1800s. Farmers opened new lands for cotton and corn. Merchants traded in world markets. Shipbuilders and artisans thrived. The first American factories opened, and new inventions pointed to the future: Eli Whitney's cotton gin, Oliver Evans's steam engine, Robert Fulton's steamboat.

Thomas Jefferson mirrored the changing thinking of many Americans toward the economy. To him it was a fundamental axiom that "those who labour in the earth are the chosen people of God. . . . Corruption of morals in the mass of cultivators is a phenomenon of which no age nor nation has furnished an example. . . . Dependence begets subservience and venality [and] . . . suffocates the germ of virtue." In his inaugural address in 1801 he stated his belief in the "encouragement of agriculture and of commerce as its handmaid."

At first Jefferson was hostile to factory production, fearful of creating a class of dependent, propertyless workers: "Let our workshops remain in Europe." But by 1816, sobered by the War of 1812, he wrote, "We must now place the manufacturer by the side of the agriculturalist."

Jefferson became enthusiastic about state governments' playing a leading role in building the means of communication and transportation: roads, canals, and improved waterways. In the first quarter of the nineteenth century the country began to build such a network, the sinews of a national economy.

A plain-looking Liverpool pitcher expressed the Jeffersonian agrarian ideal with the following verse:

Let the Wealthy & Great
Roll in Splendor & State
I envy them not I declare it
I eat my own Lamb
My own Chickens & Ham
I shear my own Fleece & I wear it
I have Lawns I have Bowers
I have Fruits I have Flowers
The Lark is my morning alarmer
So jolly Boys now
Here's God speed the Plough
Long Life & success to
the Farmer.

Pitcher, English, 1800

Twenty-five-year-old Samuel Hopkins was awarded the first patent for developing a new process of leaching wood ashes to produce pearl and potash—ingredients used in making soap.

First patent granted by the United States government, issued to Samuel Hopkins, July 31, 1790

Broadside "Addressed to the Friends of American Manufactures," 1816

The War of 1812 proved that factory manufacturing was needed to sustain American independence. This broadside publishes an exchange of letters between Benjamin Austin, a manufacturer and leader of Boston's Republicans, and Thomas Jefferson. Jefferson writes: "To be independent, for the comforts of life— we must fabricate them ourselves—we must now place the manufacturer by the side of the agriculturalist. . . . Experience has taught me that manufacturers are now as necessary to our independence as to our comfort."

Eli Whitney patented his cotton gin in 1794. Even though it was widely adopted, enabling slaveholders to expand cotton culture across the South, it never made him rich. Four years later, disgusted and in debt, he wrote to his brother: "I am as poor as a rat." Whitney spent the next decade designing and manufacturing muskets with interchangeable parts for the government, with the support of Jefferson, who was always interested in promoting inventions.

Eli Whitney, engraving by David C. Hinman, c. 1847

When Bass Otis painted the original of this portrait from life in 1816, Jefferson was seventy-three and in retirement at Monticello. His friends thought it a poor likeness, but it was clear that the former president was still of vigorous mind and at peace with himself. This is a copy of the original by an unknown artist.

Thomas Jefferson, artist unknown, after original by Bass Otis, nineteenth century

Dear Sir Monticello Sep. 25. 22.

Your favor of Aug. 8 has been duly recieved, and I thank you for the pamphlet inclosed on the subject of canals. the plan it proposes is great, and I sincerely wish it may be prosecuted with success. I hope these states will prove to the world how much more it will contribute to it's happiness to lay out the contributions of the people in opening canals for communication and irrigation, making good roads, erecting public buildings for science and the arts &c than in slaughtering men, burning their houses, and wasting their lands. I sincerely wish you may find constant employment in this system of improvement, and derive the due reward to your merits for the useful services you may render in improving your native state. accept the assurances of my great esteem and respect.

Th: Jefferson

Mr. Mills.

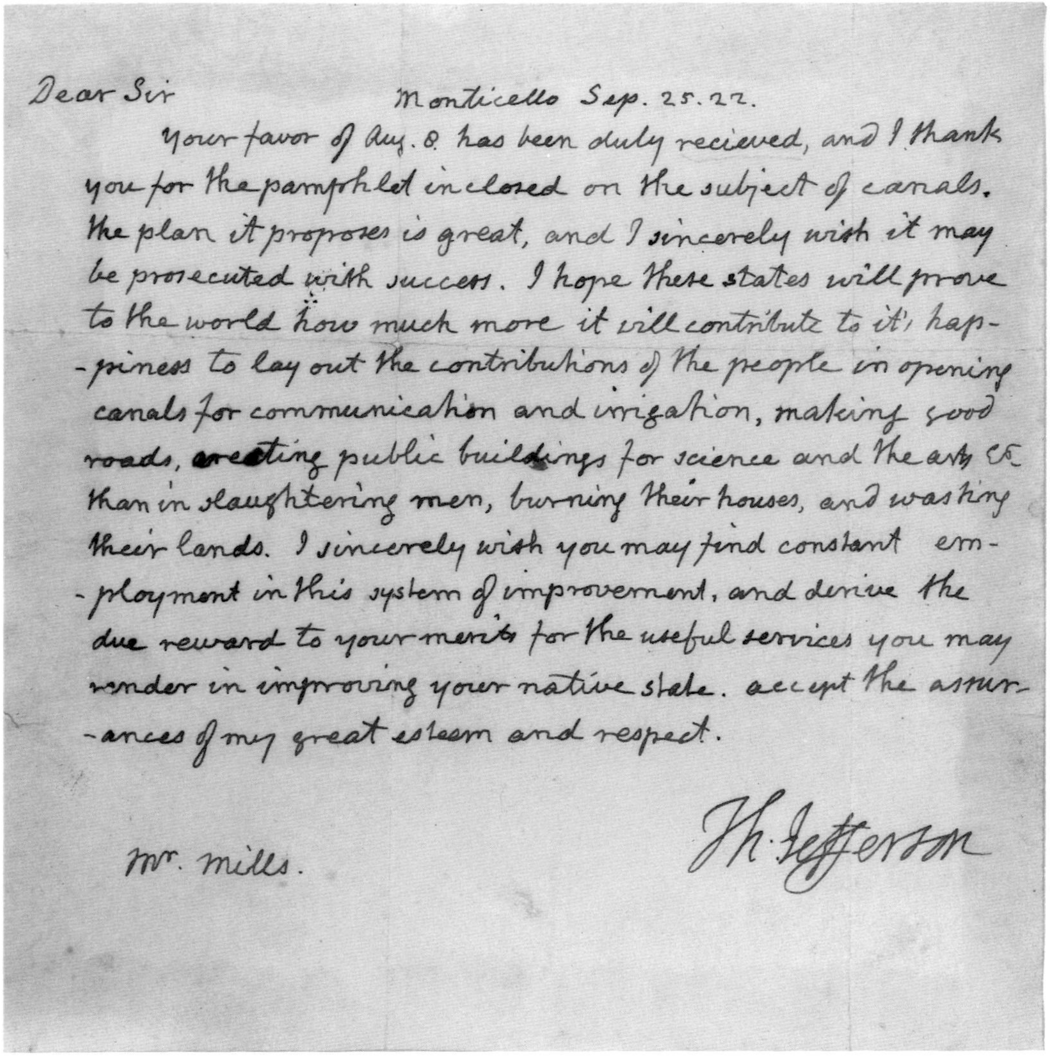

Letter from Thomas Jefferson to Robert Mills, September 25, 1822

In this rare, unpublished letter, Jefferson eloquently sums up his passion for peace and his priorities for government. The occasion was a letter from Robert Mills, whom Jefferson had adopted as a protégé in 1803. Mills, the "state engineer and architect" of South Carolina, had sent Jefferson a pamphlet outlining his plan for spending the $100,000 a year that the state had appropriated for roads, rivers, and canals. This was Jefferson's enthusiastic reply.

Dear Sir Monticello Sep. 25. 22.

Your favor of Aug. 8 has been duly recieved, and I thank you for the pamphlet inclosed on the subject of canals. The plan it proposes is great, and I sincerely wish it may be prosecuted with success. I hope these states will prove to the world how much more it will contribute to its' happiness to lay out the contributions of the people in opening canals for communication and irrigation, making good roads, erecting public buildings for science and the arts etc. than in slaughtering men, burning their houses, and wasting their lands. I sincerely wish you may find constant employment in this system of improvement, and derive the due reward to your merits for the useful services you may render in improving your native state. accept the assurances for my great esteem and respect.

Th. Jefferson

Mr. Mills.

Advertisement for stage-coaches from *The New-York Journal, & Patriotic Register*, August 21, 1793

Lower Stage Office, No. 50, Cortlandt ſtreet
NEW LINE DISPATCH,

SETS out every day (Satur-days excepted) at three o'clock in the after-noon, and arrives at Philadelphia the next day about the ſame hour.

The proprietors of this line aſſure their friends, and the public, that every attention ſhall be paid to the accommodating them in the moſt agreeable manner.

No more than ſeven paſſengers will be admitted in this line, except by the expreſs deſire of the company—At their uſual prices of 4 dollars, and an allowance of 14lb of baggage, free of expence. ✝✝✝ The proprietors will not be accountable for any baggage conveyed in the line.

A genteel *carriage*, and four good *horſes*, will be ſtarted at any hour, moſt ſuitable to the com-pany, and proceed as they pleaſe.

N. B. Extra ſtages and expreſſes will be for-warded at any hour, by   J. H. BUTMAN,

For WARD, LYON, PAGE, & Co.

New York, April 6, 1793.   56 2aw. 1y.

Mail bags were carried by stagecoaches that had established regular lines from city to city, advertising their routes in the newspapers.

The United States established a postal system in 1782. Mail was packed in coarse bags like this carpet bag made from a heavy woven material.

Mail bag, c. 1800

This chart of the distances between American cities is unusual testimony to the transportation system in existence by 1815. Printed on cotton, this souvenir is something like the mileage chart on a modern American road atlas or map. At the right all the postal towns are numbered. At the left is a table presenting the mileage between towns.

Bandanna, "A Geographical View of all the Post Towns in the United States of America," Glasgow, Scotland, 1815

Women in the New Republic

Did the "rights of man" extend to women of the new republic? Some women clearly thought so. But Americans generally did not, despite women's active participation in the Revolution.

Votes measured the "will of the majority" of men. Women were expected to cheer at public festivities and to sing songs urging men on to patriotism, but they were not full citizens. When women married, control over their property passed to their husbands. Divorce was rare.

In education, however, women made strides toward equality. Middle-class men and women agreed that the education of females was essential for the future of the republic. Republican mothers should be educated in order to rear their sons as republican citizens and their daughters as mothers of the next generation of citizens.

In the early 1800s, more elementary schools were opened to girls. At the secondary level some private male academies opened "ladies' departments." And hundreds of "female academies" were founded. As levels of literacy for women began to approach those of men, a generation of formally educated middle-class women appeared, mothers and grandmothers of women who in the 1840s would raise anew the issue of the rights of women.

Lansingburgh Academy.

TWO quarters have expired, since the Public were apprised of the improving prospects of this flourishing Seminary. In order to secure every solid advantage, and at the same time to avoid every speculative experiment, the Trustees have adopted, in this institution, an arrangement which has been successfully tested by some of the most respectable academies in the United States.— These advantages are secured by *separating the departments* of education. The Academy now presents to Students pursuing Classical Studies, the benefits of an Academy *exclusively Classical*; and to Students pursuing English Studies, the benefits of an Academy *exclusively English*. The Trustees have the satisfaction to acknowledge that this arrangement has fully realised their expectations. They have been encouraged by its success, to institute an additional department, for Young Ladies; and contemplate, as soon as circumstances will admit, to establish a school exclusively for the younger classes in English.

The Academy for Young Gentlemen is at present divided into two departments, and the Students are arranged into two select Schools, the Classical and the Commercial School, according to the ultimate design of their education; but they are transferred from one to the other, according to their immediate requirements.

The *Classical Department* consists of Students in the Latin, Greek and English Classics, including all the branches introductory to a college education, or to the study of the learned professions. The study of the ancient Languages is accompanied by the auxiliary studies of ancient Geography and History, sufficiently to understand the allusions to the classical antiquities, and to comprehend the spirit of the classical authors. Every Student pursuing Classical Studies continues his English Studies; and by the connexion between the Classical and Commercial Departments, his progress in the Classics is facilitated by a concurrent course of English.

The *Commercial Department* comprises *strictly* all Students in pursuit of a comprehensive mercantile education, or who are preparing to enter on active business, and *generally* all Students in pursuit of a solid English education; including, together with the subordinate branches, scientific Penmanship, reduced to practice—Book-keeping, by single and double entry, in theory and in practice—History, Political Economy, and the higher branches of Mathematics, embracing Geometry, Trigonometry, Algebra, Navigation, Surveying, &c. The progress of the Commercial as well as the Classical Student is facilitated by the cooperation of the two departments, where their objects of education coincide.

The *Ladies' Department* comprises all the studies of the other two departments which are usually pursued by young Ladies, together with other branches belonging exclusively to female education; among which are—fine Needle-work, Drawing, Painting on velvet, silk and paper, with various other kinds of fancy work.

By thus dividing the departments, the Trustees have aimed to secure more capable and efficient instruction, and by separating the schools and simplifying the studies of the youth, to ensure their more perfect classification, and more productive industry. In pursuance of this arrangement, aided by a generous subscription, they have erected in the same vicinity two commodious buildings, to be occupied as a classical and commercial Academy, and capable of accommodating all the schools. Besides the recitation chambers, there is a chapel-hall, equal to the accommodation of all the Students, in their weekly and quarterly exercises. It is believed that no academy in the state has incurred an equal expence in fitting and furnishing the apartments for study. To consult both the industry and health of the Student, he is separated at a suitable distance from others, and accommodated with a chair and a desk, fitted for sitting or standing.

The Preceptors are well qualified, by education and experience, for the duties of their respective stations. They have been for several years employed as teachers in this institution, and have given entire satisfaction to all whose children have been intrusted to their care.

As intellectual and moral education should ever be united in the same system, a uniform and efficient discipline will be maintained, and Students will receive attention to their improvement in manners and morals, as well as to their progress in science and literature. They will be required to practice a strict observance of the Lord's day, and a regular attendance on public worship.

RATES OF TUITION.

For the Latin and Greek Classics, and the common studies in Colleges, including History, Philosophy, Political Economy, Chemistry, Geometry, Navigation and Surveying, (per quarter), $5 00

For the common Academic Studies, comprising Grammar, Rhetoric, Geography, Penmanship, Arithmetic and Book-keeping, $4 00

Reading, Writing, common Arithmetic, Murray's Grammar abridg'd, and Cumming's small Geography, $3 00

There are two vacations in a year, each continuing two weeks: The first commences on the Saturday preceding Christmas, and the second on the Saturday preceding the 4th of July. Board may be had in good families, from $1.25 to $2 per week.

By order of the Trustees,

SAMUEL BLATCHFORD, *President.*

E. W. WALBRIDGE, *Clerk.* September 1, 1821.

Broadside, Lansingburgh Academy, New York, 1821

By 1821, the Lansingburgh Academy, a private secondary school for boys in upstate New York, had opened a "Ladies' Department." In the "Classical Department" students could learn Latin, Greek, and the English classics in preparation for college. In the "Commercial Department" they could learn bookkeeping, history, political economy, and mathematics. Thus, young women could take academic courses as well as exclusively female subjects such as fine needlework.

In 1792 Mary Wollstonecraft's Vindication of the Rights of Women, *a clarion call for women's rights in England, was reprinted in several American cities. Excerpts of the book appeared in* The Lady's Magazine, *published in Philadelphia. As a frontispiece to its bound volume the magazine ran this allegorical image. A woman identified as the "Genius of the Ladies Magazine" is kneeling in front of "Liberty," the symbol of America, presenting a petition titled "The Rights of Woman." She is accompanied by the "Genius of Emulation." At their feet in the foreground are symbols of the arts, science, and literature—knowledge that they seek. Other magazines, addressed as this one is to "the fair daughters of Columbia," appeared elsewhere in the 1790s with articles by and for women.*

Frontispiece from *The Lady's Magazine and Repository of Entertaining Knowledge*, vol. I, 1792

By tradition women were expected to express their support for the nation's new leaders at ceremonial functions. In Trenton, New Jersey, in 1789, as President-elect Washington made his way to New York, the first capital, the triumphal arch bore the motto, "The Hero who Defended the Mothers will Protect the Daughters." Women were not expected to play an active role in public affairs as they had done in the Revolution.

Women were expected to sing patriotic songs when the country went to war, as it did in the undeclared naval battle with France in 1798–99 under President John Adams. In this song, "Columbia's Fair Daughters" were supposed to "bless with their charms" men who took up arms. "Inspired by your President, Sweethearts and Wives" will hail triumphant heroes.

"The Ladies Patriotic Song," 1799

THE
YOUNG LADY's
ACCIDENCE:
OR,
A SHORT AND EASY
INTRODUCTION
TO
ENGLISH GRAMMAR.

Deſigned principally for the uſe of young Learners, more eſpecially thoſe of the FAIR SEX, though proper for either.

BY CALEB BINGHAM, A. M.
Author of the CHILD's COMPANION, AMERICAN PRECEPTOR, and COLUMBIAN ORATOR.

"Delightful taſk! to rear the tender thought,
"To teach the young idea how to ſhoot,---"

THE *FOURTEENTH* EDITION.

Publiſhed according to Act of Congreſs.

BOSTON:
PRINTED BY *E. LINCOLN*,
For the AUTHOR, No. 44, Cornhill.
1803.

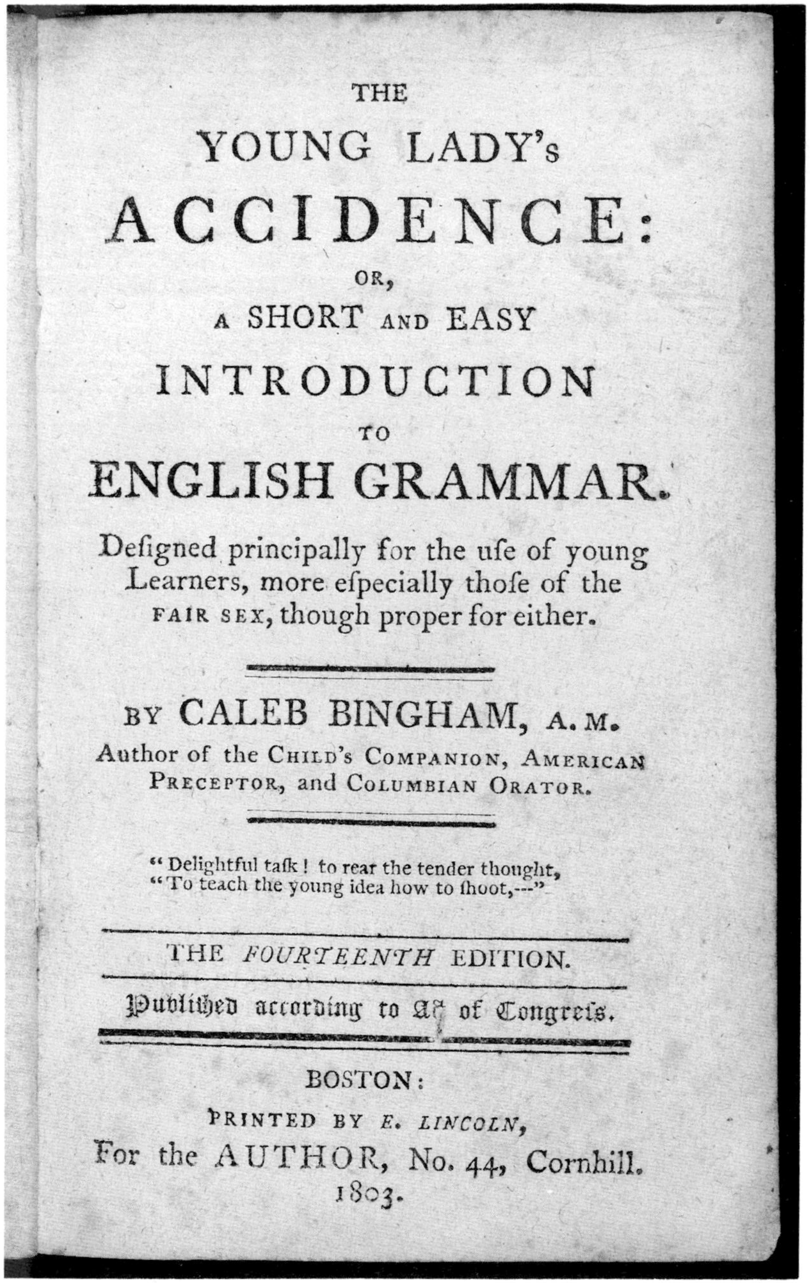

Title page from *The Young Lady's Accidence: or, a Short and Easy Introduction to English Grammar*, by Caleb Bingham, 1803

The growing recognition of the need to educate women led to the publication of textbooks principally for girls. In content most differed little from textbooks for boys, and The Young Lady's Accidence *proclaimed itself proper for "young learners" of either sex.*

Emma Willard was an innovative educator and probably the first female author of textbooks in America. Willard used images that would interest children, such as animals and the common objects in a country store, to teach about the countries of the world.

Besides this book pictured on the right, Willard wrote a "universal" geography, a history of the United States, and a world history. In 1819 she published a plea to the New York legislature "for improving female education" by founding schools for girls. She was the founder of the Troy Female Academy in New York.

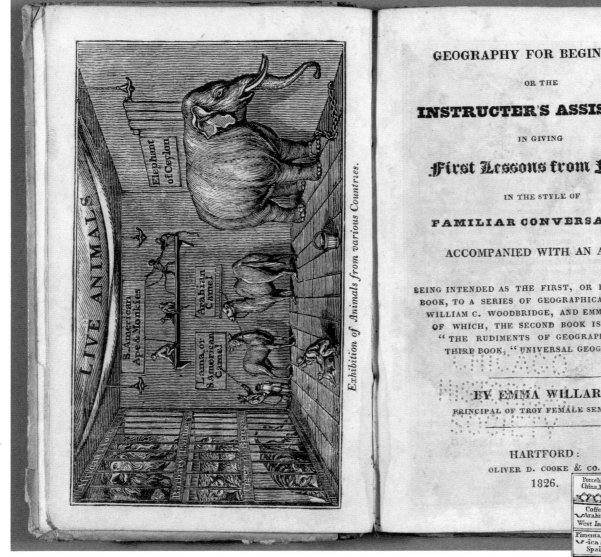

GEOGRAPHY FOR BEGINNERS:

OR THE

INSTRUCTER'S ASSISTANT,

IN GIVING

First Lessons from Maps,

IN THE STYLE OF

FAMILIAR CONVERSATION.

ACCOMPANIED WITH AN ATLAS.

BEING INTENDED AS THE FIRST, OR INTRODUCTORY
BOOK, TO A SERIES OF GEOGRAPHICAL WORKS, BY
WILLIAM C. WOODBRIDGE, AND EMMA WILLARD;
OF WHICH, THE SECOND BOOK IS ENTITLED
"THE RUDIMENTS OF GEOGRAPHY," THE
THIRD BOOK, "UNIVERSAL GEOGRAPHY."

BY EMMA WILLARD,

PRINCIPAL OF TROY FEMALE SEMINARY.

HARTFORD:

OLIVER D. COOKE & CO.

1826.

Title page and illustration from *Geography for Beginners*, by Emma Willard, 1826

Country Store, exhibiting the Productions of Various Countries.

Arithmetic notebook belonging to Elizabeth Braswell, 1819

This painted tin box held bottles of ink and small books.

Although mathematics was excluded from the female curriculum at some coeducational academies, girls were instructed in basic arithmetic along with reading, spelling, penmanship, and geography.

Workbox taken to school by Maria Erwin, c. 1785

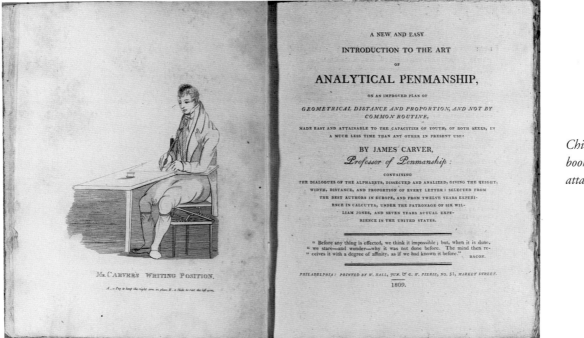

A NEW AND EASY

INTRODUCTION TO THE ART

OF

ANALYTICAL PENMANSHIP,

ON AN IMPROVED PLAN OF

GEOMETRICAL DISTANCE AND PROPORTION, AND NOT BY COMMON ROUTINE,

MADE EASY AND ATTAINABLE TO THE CAPACITIES OF YOUTH, OF BOTH SEXES, IN
A MUCH LESS TIME THAN ANY OTHER IN PRESENT USE:

BY JAMES CARVER,

Professor of Penmanship:

CONTAINING

THE DIALOGUES OF THE ALPHABETS, DISSECTED AND ANALIZED, GIVING THE HEIGHT,
WIDTH, DISTANCE, AND PROPORTION OF EVERY LETTER: SELECTED FROM
THE BEST AUTHORS IN EUROPE, AND FROM TWELVE YEARS EXPERI-
ENCE IN CALCUTTA, UNDER THE PATRONAGE OF SIR WIL-
LIAM JONES; AND SEVEN YEARS ACTUAL EXPE-
RIENCE IN THE UNITED STATES.

"Before any thing is effected, we think it impossible; but, when it is done,
"we stare—and wonder—why it was not done before. The mind then re-
"ceives it with a degree of affinity, as if we had known it before."
BACON.

PHILADELPHIA: PRINTED BY W. HALL, JUN. & G. W. PIERIE, NO. 51, MARKET STREET.

1809.

MR. CARVER'S WRITING POSITION.

Children practiced penmanship with the help of books like this one that made handwriting "easy and attainable to the capacities of youth, of both sexes."

Title page and foldout from *A New and Easy Introduction to the Art of Analytical Penmanship,* by James Carver, 1809

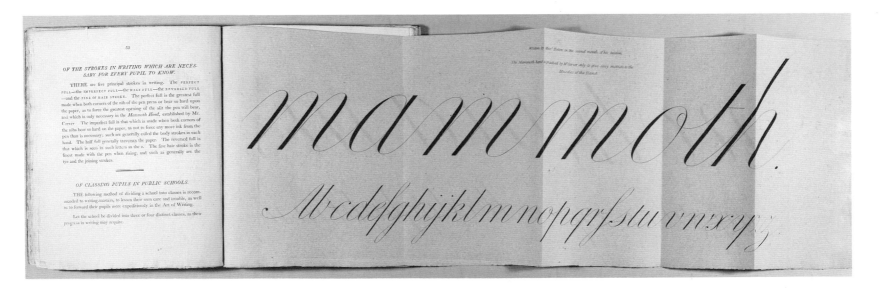

African Americans: Free and Unfree

Neither the Declaration of Independence nor the Constitution and Bill of Rights abolished slavery. The census of 1790 counted almost seven hundred thousand slaves; by 1820 they numbered 1.5 million.

After the Revolution some slave owners from the upper South, like Robert Carter and George Washington, provided for the gradual emancipation of their slaves. All northern states acted to free slaves within their borders, by constitution, law, or court case. But Congress did no more than stop the importation of new slaves in 1808, and slavery continued to spread.

Slaves still demonstrated the same hunger for freedom that they had shown during the war. Hannah, a Virginia slave faced with the prospect of manumission, beseeched her owner to sell her a loom so that she could continue her weaving trade as a free person. Arch, identified by his Maryland master as a "handsome Negro lad about twenty years of age," took the only course open to thousands of young male slaves—he ran away.

Free black life was transformed as the number of freedmen and women grew from a few thousand before the war to about fifty-nine thousand in 1790 and a quarter of a million in 1820. In eastern cities, African Americans formed communities with their own churches, schools, and fraternal societies. But for white America, the issues raised during the Revolution of abolishing slavery and achieving equality for free blacks was not on the political agenda and would not be raised until the next generation.

Broadside, act of the New Jersey General Assembly for the gradual abolition of slavery, February 15, 1804

New Jersey, the last northern state to abolish slavery, enacted a plan to gradually free the children born to slaves in that state. Under its provisions every child born to a slave after the Fourth of July 1804 would become emancipated at age twenty-five if male, twenty-one if female.

SCHEDULE

OF THE

WHOLE NUMBER OF PERSONS

WITHIN THE SEVERAL DISTRICTS OF THE UNITED STATES,

ACCORDING TO AN ACT "PROVIDING FOR THE

ENUMERATION OF THE INHABITANTS OF

THE UNITED STATES," PASSED

MARCH THE 1st, 1790.

	DISTRICTS.	Free white Males of sixteen years and upwards, including Heads of Families.	Free white Males under sixteen years.	Free white Females, including heads of families.	All other free Persons.	Slaves.	Total.
2 . 2 2	*VERMONT,	22,435	22,328	40,505	252	16	85,539
4 4 3	NEW-HAMPSHIRE,	36,086	34,851	70,160	630	158	141,885
13 13 11	{ MAINE,	24,384	24,748	46,870	538	none.	96,540
	{ MASSACHUSETTS,	95,453	87,289	190,582	5,463	none.	378,787
2 1 1	RHODE-ISLAND,	16,019	15,799	32,652	3,407	948	68,825
6 6 5	CONNECTICUT,	60,523	54,403	117,448	2,808	2,764	237,946
9 9 8	NEW-YORK,	83,700	78,122	152,320	4,654	21,324	340,120
5 5 4	NEW-JERSEY,	45,251	41,416	83,287	2,762	11,453	184,139
12 12 10	PENNSYLVANIA,	110,788	106,948	206,363	6,537	3,737	434,373
1 1 1	DELAWARE,	11,783	12,143	22,384	3,899	8,887	59,094
8 7 6	MARYLAND,	55,915	51,339	101,395	8,043	103,036	319,728
18 18 15	{ VIRGINIA,	110,936	116,135	215,046	12,866	292,627	747,610
2 1 1	{ KENTUCKY,	15,154	17,057	28,922	114	12,430	73,677
10 10 8	NORTH-CAROLINA,	69,988	77,506	140,710	4,975	100,572	393,751
6 6 5	SOUTH-CAROLINA,						
2 2 1	GEORGIA,	13,103	14,044	25,739	398	29,264	82,548

100 97 81		Free white Males of twenty-years and upwards, including Heads of Families.	Free Males under twenty-one years of age.	Free white Females, including heads of families.	All other free Persons.	Slaves.	Total.
	S. WESTERN TERRITORY,	6,271	10,277	15,365	361	3,417	35,691
	N. WESTERN TERRITORY,						

Truly stated from the original Returns deposited in the Office of the Secretary of State.

TH: JEFFERSON.

This broadside summary of the first federal census, taken in 1790, shows the growth of the African American population, slave and free. Free white males and females are listed in the first three columns to the right of the list of states, or "Districts." Slaves are listed in column five. "All other persons" (column four) means free blacks, as well as some Indians. On this broadside addressed on the back to Mr. Rutherford in Philadelphia, someone added up and entered the total number of slaves at 687,216 and the total population at 3,864,602. The total number of free blacks comes to 59,466.

One purpose of the census was to apportion seats in Congress. The Constitution provided for one representative for every forty thousand persons, with each slave counting as "three-fifths of a person." The person scribbling in the left margin of this document, probably a politician, wanted to determine how many congressmen each state would have if the ratio were changed to one for thirty-four thousand or one for thirty-nine thousand. Six southern states could count their growing slave populations in determining their representation, which gave them a political advantage in Congress.

Schedule of the 1790 United States Census, Philadelphia, October 24, 1791

The unknown slave in Charleston who wore this metal tag, "Servant, 1812," was hired out and may have saved his portion of the wages to buy his own freedom. In large southern cities masters often hired out their slaves as porters, servants, artisans, and fruit vendors. In Charleston, to distinguish slaves who were hired out from runaways or free blacks, the city required slaves to wear metal tags indicating their occupation.

It was common to see newspaper advertisements and broadsides posted in public places, announcing rewards for runaway slaves. Arch was in many ways typical of runaways: he was male, young (and therefore without a wife and children), and he was of light skin. According to his master, he "talks sensible and artful, but if close examined is apt to tremble," which suggests he was fearful in the presence of masters and overseers. Because he was from Maryland, a border state, his prospects of escaping to a free state were good.

Slave-hiring badge issued for a servant in Charleston, South Carolina, made by John J. Lafar, 1812

Reward announced for Arch, a runaway slave from Maryland, 1791

THIRTY DOLLARS REWARD.

RAN away, on the 22d of August last, *a handsome Negro Lad*, named

ARCH,

ABOUT twenty years of age----the property of the Subscriber----of a yellow complexion, talks sensible and artful, but *if close examined is apt to tremble*; he is rather under the size of a man, active-made, with small legs, and has a ridge, or scar on the back of his neck. He had on and took with him, a new Russia-sheeting shirt, an old Irish linen, and an old country linen ditto, a pair of old black everlasting breeches, a pair of oznabrig trousers, and an old hat, though he probably will part from his cloaths, and procure others if an opportunity offers.

I live in Maryland, near Frederick-Town, and will pay the above Reward, if the said fellow be taken *Sixty* miles, or any further distance from home; or a *Half Dollar* per mile, for any distance under, in case he be secured in any goal, so that I get him again; and if brought home reasonable charges, by.

IGNATIOUS DAVIS.

Frederick-County, September 7, 1791.

Frederick-Town: Printed by JOHN WINTER.

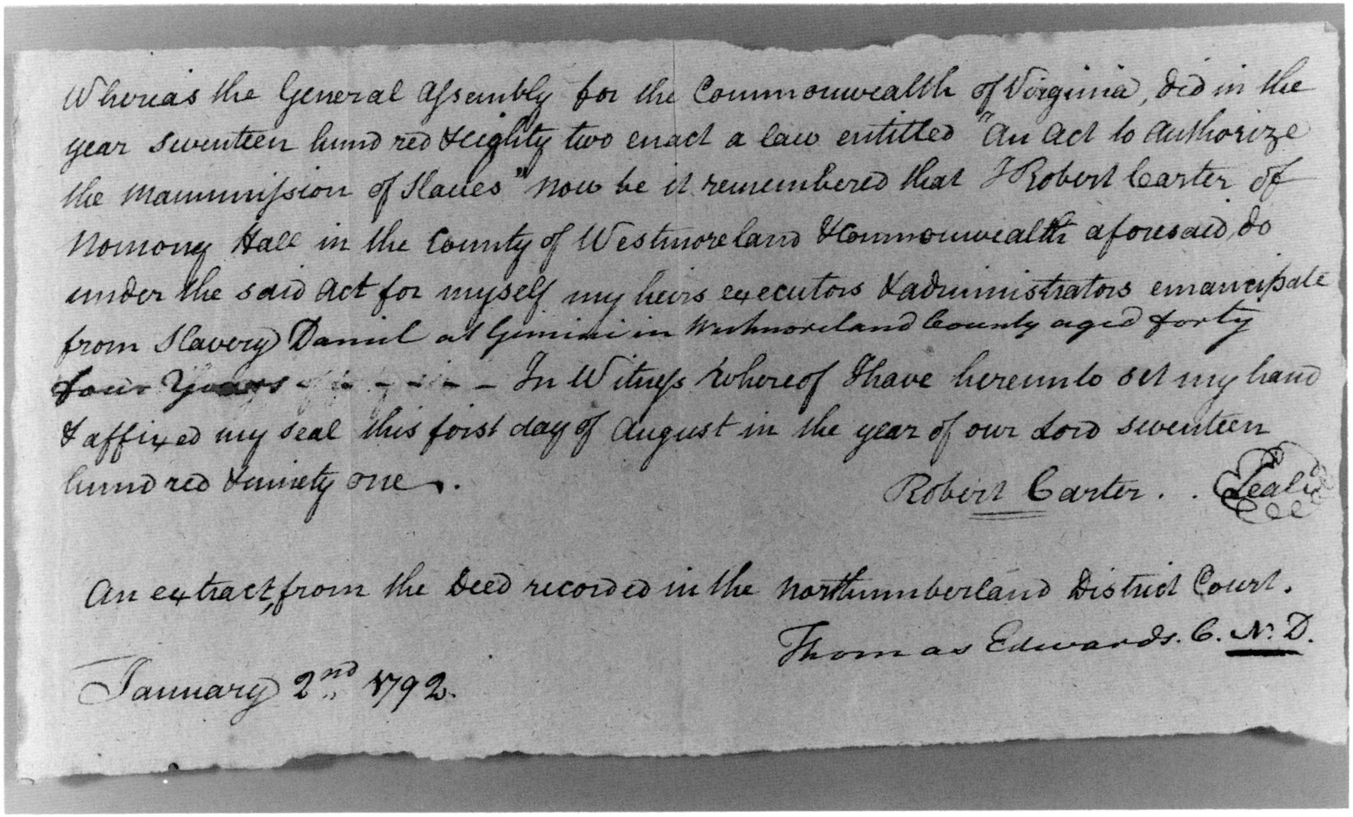

Whereas the General Assembly for the Commonwealth of Virginia, did in the year seventeen hundred & eighty two enact a law entitled "An Act to Authorize the Manumission of Slaves" now be it remembered that I Robert Carter of Nomony Hall in the County of Westmoreland & Commonwealth aforesaid do under the said Act for myself my heirs executors & administrators emancipate from Slavery Daniel at Gemini in Westmoreland County aged forty four years ~ ~ ~ ~ ~ In Witness whereof I have hereunto set my hand & affixed my seal this first day of August in the year of our Lord seventeen hundred & ninety one.

Robert Carter. [Seal]

An extract from the deed recorded in the Northumberland District Court.

Thomas Edwards. C. N. D.

January 2nd 1792.

Manumission certificate
of Daniel Wilson,
January 2, 1792

Manumission was a voluntary act by an individual slaveholder, freeing his or her own slaves. After the Revolution the Virginia and Maryland legislatures made it easier for an individual to manumit slaves. On August 1, 1791, Robert Carter of Nomony Hall, one of Virginia's largest slaveholders with 485 slaves on eighteen plantations, filed a deed indicating his intention to free his slaves gradually. He then freed his slaves in groups over a twenty-one-year period. By this certificate issued by the local court, Robert Carter freed Daniel Wilson, age forty-four, a slave living on Gemini, Carter's plantation in Westmoreland County, Virginia. The following year he freed Wilson's wife, Judith, age forty-eight.

Hannah Harris was a weaver on Leo, Robert
Carter's plantation in Loudoun County in the
Northern Neck of Virginia. She was one of nine
children of George Harris, the African American
foreman of Leo plantation, and his wife, Rachel. A
1789 inventory of slaves at Leo indicates she was
thirty-three, valued at fifty pounds if sold and at
seven pounds, ten shillings if hired out for the year, as
was often done with skilled slaves. The records do not
show whether she was married or had children.

In 1792, knowing she would be freed the next
year, Hannah, preparing for life after slavery, sent
this note to Carter.

Dear master Hannah beges [begs] one favour
that is to buy her loom that she know [now]
workes with and you will oblige her
migh[til]y from your Homble [humble]
Servant Hannah the wever

The note was endorsed on the back in Carter's handwriting: "5th Apr, 1792. Leo. Negro Hannah, weaver,
will be free Jany, 1793. She wants to buy her loom."

On February 28, 1793, Hannah Harris, now
thirty-seven, was among a group of twenty-seven
slaves to whom the local court issued certificates
of manumission. Between 1792 and 1800 her eight
sisters and brothers were also emancipated.

On large plantations owners often designated a
number of slave women to spin and weave textiles to
make clothes for the slaves and sacks for packing produce. On Leo plantation the inventory recorded a
weaving house, sixteen by sixteen feet, in which
Hannah likely worked. Several looms and half a
dozen spinning wheels could have been housed there.
As early as 1775 Robert Carter issued orders to grow
flax, which could be woven into a rough linen called
oznaburg.

Reading Hannah the Weaver's Note

Until the summer of 1991 Hannah was a mystery to us. We knew little more about her than what was in her note, which was found in a small collection of the business papers of Robert Carter in the Chicago Historical Society. This collection includes the certificates for five other freed slaves: Dinah, Hall, Judith, Daniel, and Primus.

Then, at the end of July 1991, the *New York Times* ran a front-page story on the two-hundredth-anniversary celebration of Carter filing his deed of emancipation. Among the speakers was John Barden, a historian writing his dissertation at Duke University on the emancipation of Carter's slaves. We wrote to Barden, who was as excited to find Hannah's note as we were to locate someone researching the Carter records in a score of libraries. He identified her family name as Harris, reported her age, and established the context of her manumission.

Mysteries still challenge us. What can we tell about Hannah from her note? Did she write it? In the South it was unusual for a slave to be allowed to learn how to read or write, but less so on Carter's plantations. The handwriting and spelling clearly suggest someone not used to writing. She may well have written it.

But what brought her to ask to buy her loom? One has to read between the lines. She began as a suppliant (she "beges one favour") and signed her name in a deferential form expected of slaves ("your Homble Servant"). But her tone was forceful ("you will oblige her migh[til]y").

Freedom was in the air; her brother Anthony and sister Keziah had already been freed, and she was about to be free. She did not ask for her loom as a gift; she offered to buy it, presumably paying for it with the money she would earn as a free person. She took it for granted that she had a right not only to her own labor but also to the means to survive as a free person.

Did Hannah get her loom? Carter's endorsement on the back gives no hint of his decision. Very likely she did, because Carter rented plots of land to other freed slaves, recognizing their need to sustain themselves.

What happened to Hannah Harris? No one knows for sure, but it is not difficult to imagine this strong woman with a skilled trade surviving. Perhaps as more descendants of the African Americans search for their roots, we will learn more about Hannah the weaver.

Captain Paul Cuffe, engraving by Mason and Maas, after a drawing by John Pole, 1812. Courtesy, The National Portrait Gallery, Smithsonian Institution

PORTRAIT OF AN AMERICAN

Paul Cuffe

In 1780 twenty-one-year-old Paul Cuffe (1759–1817) and other free African Americans of Dartmouth, Massachusetts, petitioned for exemption from taxes. As "poor despised black people," they were not allowed to vote, yet they had to pay taxes. Did the principles of the Revolution not apply to him, a seaman who had been a prisoner of war?

Thirty years later, when this silhouette drawing was made, Paul Cuffe was probably the richest African American in the United States. He is portrayed with his ship *Traveller*, one of several he owned. He owned property worth almost twenty thousand dollars. The son of an American Indian mother and an African-born father, he mastered the skills of seamanship and whaling while still in his teens. Step by step he built his own fleet.

But his success did not blind him to the despair of other free blacks. A devout Quaker, he saw in emigration to Africa a solution that would also bring Christianity to Africans. In 1815 he sailed the *Traveller*, carrying the first thirty-eight emigrants to Sierra Leone. Many former slaves who had fought with the British in the Revolution had migrated to this British colony from Nova Scotia.

Cuffe's goal was to create a refuge for oppressed American blacks. He believed slaves should be freed and have the choice of forming colonies either in America or in Africa. In Africa, Cuffe declared, blacks "might rise to be a people." Africa is "just such a country as we the people of Color stand in need of."

When Cuffe died in 1817 he was honored by funeral eulogies in the interracial Quaker meetinghouse and then buried in a segregated section of the Quaker cemetery.

The black men, women, and children listed on board the Nautilus *in 1821 were free African Americans who hoped to find in Africa the equality and opportunity denied them in the United States. Some, it is clear from the list, worked in skilled trades as carpenters and bricklayers, but others—three laborers, one seaman, one ship caulker—were in more lowly trades. All were either Baptist or Methodist.*

Paul Cuffe's efforts were focused on settling African Americans in Sierra Leone. The American Colonization Society, which sponsored the voyage of the Nautilus, *took over Cuffe's work and transported some freed slaves to Liberia. The Society had the support of liberal slaveholders like Jefferson and Madison who favored emancipation but opposed equality and therefore wanted to remove free blacks from the country. Most free African Americans hotly rejected the idea of emigration.*

List of emigrants leaving Norfolk, Virginia, for Liberia, Africa, on board the brig *Nautilus,* January 20, 1821

The Republic Moves West

This peace medal that the United States government gave to the chieftains of cooperating nations expressed the goals Americans sought for Indians. The medal was cast by the Philadelphia silversmith Joseph Richardson, Jr., whose father had made the silver armlet that the British bestowed on their allies in colonial days. On the front of the medal, George Washington extends the hand of peace to a chieftain who holds a peace pipe and casts down the tomahawk, symbol of war, at his feet. In the background two oxen pull a farmer's plow through cultivated fields.

The meaning would have been clear to Indians. The United States sought peace, but Washington, portrayed in uniform and wearing a sword, reminded them of American military power. On the back of the medal the eagle, symbol of American strength, holds the arrows of war in one claw, the olive branch in the other. One Indian chieftain to whom a medal was presented in 1794 caught the discrepancy between the Indian burying his hatchet and Washington bearing his sword. "Why does not the president bury his sword, too?" he asked.

Government policy encouraged Indians to abandon their way of life, in which men hunted and women grew crops, and to become yeoman farmers, each man tilling his own land. A "good" Indian, to the American government, was one who laid down his arms and became "civilized" by abandoning his traditional ways.

7

Silver peace medal (front and back), made by Joseph Richardson, Jr., 1793

In 1783 the acquisition from Britain of the area from the Appalachians west to the Mississippi doubled the size of the country. The United States claimed the lands that the Indian peoples had inhabited for thousands of years and had never ceded to the British or the Americans.

In the 1780s the government under the Articles of Confederation confronted three major issues for the area north and west of the Ohio River known as the Northwest Territory: establishing a government, devising a policy for the distribution of government-owned land, and dealing with the Indians. For its first quarter of a century the republic created by the Constitution of 1787 would struggle with these questions.

In the long run the solutions were a triumph for ordinary white people who aspired to land and self-government and a disaster for Indians who wanted to retain their independence, their ancestral lands, and their ways of life.

The Northwest Ordinance

With the Northwest Ordinance of 1787, Americans established the principle that these western territories would not be ruled as colonies, the way Britain had ruled them.

During and after the war thousands of settlers moved into the backcountry of the seaboard states. The first frontiersmen often squatted on land they did not have legal title to and raised demands for immediate statehood. Conservative easterners feared such democratic-minded pioneers as lawless and ignorant. Adopted as a compromise by the expiring Confederation Congress on July 13, the Northwest Ordinance governed the territory north and west of the Ohio River. The Ordinance made four historic guarantees.

It provided that new states would eventually enter the Union "on an equal footing with the original states," but only after they passed through several intermediate stages with a territorial legislature and an appointed governor. It promised that "schools and the means of education shall forever be encouraged" because "religion, morality and knowledge" are "necessary to good government and the happiness of mankind." It permitted "neither slavery nor involuntary servitude," the first time that the federal government had banned slavery anywhere. It promised that "the utmost good faith shall always be observed towards the Indians."

Slowly—over a longer period than settlers who believed in self-rule would have liked—new states established themselves from the original territories in the Northwest and entered the union: Ohio (1803); Indiana (1816); Illinois (1818); Michigan (1837); Wisconsin (1848); and Minnesota (1858). They formed a new kind of noncolonial empire, "an Empire for Liberty," Thomas Jefferson called it.

An ORDINANCE for the GOVERNMENT of the TERRITO-RY of the UNITED STATES, North-West of the RIVER OHIO.

BE IT ORDAINED by the United States in Congress assembled, That the said territory, for the purposes of temporary government, be one district; subject, however, to be divided into two districts, as future circumstances may, in the opinion of Congress, make it expedient.

Be it ordained by the authority aforesaid, That the estates both of resident and non-resident proprietors in the said territory, dying intestate, shall descend to, and be distributed among their children, and the descendants of a deceased child in equal parts; the descendants of a deceased child or grand-child, to take the share of their deceased parent in equal parts among them: And where there shall be no children or descendants, then in equal parts to the next of kin, in equal degree; and among collaterals, the children of a deceased brother or sister of the intestate, shall have in equal parts among them their deceased parents share; and there shall in no case be a distinction between kindred of the whole and half blood; saving in all cases to the widow of the intestate, her third part of the real estate for life, and one third part of the personal estate; and this law relative to descents and dower, shall remain in full force until altered by the legislature of the district.——— And until the governor and judges shall adopt laws as herein after mentioned, estates in the said territory may be devised or bequeathed by wills in writing, signed and sealed by him or her, in whom the estate may be, (being of full age) and attested by three witnesses;—and real estates may be conveyed by lease and release, or bargain and sale, signed, sealed, and delivered by the person being of full age, in whom the estate may be, and attested by two witnesses, provided such wills be duly proved, and such conveyances be acknowledged, or the execution thereof duly proved, and be recorded within one year after proper magistrates, courts, and registers shall be appointed for that purpose; and personal property may be transferred by delivery, saving, however, to the French and Canadian inhabitants, and other settlers of the Kaskaskies, Saint Vincent's, and the neighbouring villages, who have heretofore professed themselves citizens of Virginia, their laws and customs now in force among them, relative to the descent and conveyance of property.

Be it ordained by the authority aforesaid, That there shall be appointed from time to time, by Congress, a governor, whose commission shall continue in force for the term of three years, unless sooner revoked by Congress; he shall reside in the district, and have a freehold estate therein, in one thousand acres of land, while in the exercise of his office.

There shall be appointed from time to time, by Congress, a secretary, whose commission shall continue in force for four years, unless sooner revoked, he shall reside in the district, and have a freehold estate therein, in five hundred acres of land, while in the exercise of his office; it shall be his duty to keep and preserve the acts and laws passed by the legislature, and the public records of the district, and the proceedings of the governor in his executive department; and transmit authentic copies of such acts and proceedings, every six months, to the secretary of Congress: There shall also be appointed a court to consist of three judges, any two of whom to form a court, who shall have a common law jurisdiction, and reside in the district, and have each therein a freehold estate in five hundred acres of land, while in the exercise of their offices; and their commissions shall continue in force during good behaviour.

The governor and judges, or a majority of them, shall adopt and publish in the district, such laws of the original states, criminal and civil, as may be necessary, and best suited to the circumstances of the district, and report them to Congress, from time to time, which laws shall be in force in the district until the organization of the general assembly therein, unless disapproved of by Congress; but afterwards the legislature shall have authority to alter them as they shall think fit.

The governor for the time being, shall be commander in chief of the militia, appoint and commission all officers in the same, below the rank of general officers; all general officers shall be appointed and commissioned by Congress.

Previous to the organization of the general assembly, the governor shall appoint such magistrates and other civil officers, in each county or township, as he shall find necessary for the preservation of the peace and good order in the same: After the general assembly shall be organized, the powers and duties of magistrates and other civil officers shall be regulated and defined by the said assembly; but all magistrates and other civil officers, not herein otherwise directed, shall, during the continuance of this temporary government, be appointed by the governor.

For the prevention of crimes and injuries, the laws to be adopted or made shall have force in all parts of the district, and for the execution of process, criminal and civil, the governor shall make proper divisions thereof—and he shall proceed from time to time, as circumstances may require, to lay out the parts of the district in which the Indian titles shall have been extinguished, into counties and townships, subject, however, to such alterations as may thereafter be made by the legislature.

So soon as there shall be five thousand free male inhabitants, of full age, in the district, upon giving proof thereof to the governor, they shall receive authority, with time and place, to elect representatives from their counties or townships, to represent them in the general assembly; provided that for every five hundred free male inhabitants there shall be one representative, and so on progressively with the number of free male inhabitants, shall the right of representation increase, until the number of representatives shall amount to twenty-five, after which the number and proportion of representatives shall be regulated by the legislature; provided that no person be eligible or qualified to act as a representative, unless he shall have been a citizen of one of the United States three years and be a resident in the district, or unless he shall have resided in the district three years, and in either case shall likewise hold in his own right, in fee simple, two hundred acres of land within the same:—Provided also, that a freehold in fifty acres of land in the district, having been a citizen of one of the states, and being resident in the district; or the like freehold and two years residence in the district shall be necessary to qualify a man as an elector of a representative.

The representatives thus elected, shall serve for the term of two years, and in case of the death of a representative, or removal from office, the governor shall issue a writ to the county or township for which he was a member, to elect another in his stead, to serve for the residue of the term.

The general assembly, or legislature, shall consist of the governor, legislative council, and a house of representatives. The legislative council shall consist of five members, to continue in office five years, unless sooner removed by Congress, any three of whom to be a quorum, and the members of the council shall be nominated and appointed in the following manner, to wit: As soon as representatives shall be elected, the governor shall appoint a time and place for them to meet together, and when met, they shall nominate ten persons, residents in the district, and each possessed of a freehold in five hundred acres of land, and return their names to Congress; five of whom Congress shall appoint and commission to serve as aforesaid; and whenever a vacancy shall happen in the council, by death or removal from office, the house of representatives shall nominate two persons, qualified as aforesaid, for each vacancy, and return their names to Congress; one of whom Congress shall appoint and commission for the residue of the term; and every five years, four months at least before the expiration of the time of service of the members of council, the said house shall nominate ten persons, qualified as aforesaid, and return their names to Congress, five of whom Congress shall appoint and commission to serve as members of the council five years, unless sooner removed. And the governor, legislative council, and house of re-

After the Louisiana Purchase in 1803, President Jefferson dispatched Meriwether Lewis and William Clark to explore the new territory in advance of settlement. In addition to surveying the geography and geology of the region, they collected a large body of information about plant and animal life west of the Mississippi. Lewis and Clark were among the last white people to deal with Indians who were unaffected by white civilization, and their report is rich with detail about the diverse peoples they encountered.

Meriwether Lewis

Right: title page from *Travels in the Interior Parts of America,* by Captains Lewis and Clark, 1807. *Far right:* engraved portraits from *An Interesting Account of the Voyages and Travels of Captains Lewis and Clark,* compiled by William Fisher (Baltimore, 1812); *top:* Meriwether Lewis, *bottom:* William Clark

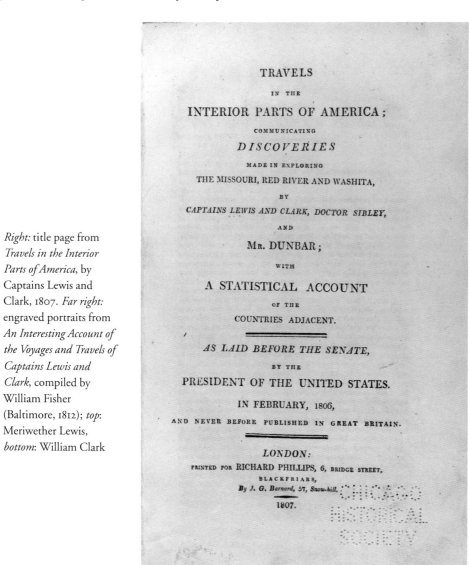

TRAVELS

IN THE

INTERIOR PARTS OF AMERICA;

COMMUNICATING

DISCOVERIES

MADE IN EXPLORING

THE MISSOURI, RED RIVER AND WASHITA,

BY

CAPTAINS LEWIS AND CLARK, DOCTOR SIBLEY,

AND

Mr. DUNBAR;

WITH

A STATISTICAL ACCOUNT

OF THE

COUNTRIES ADJACENT.

AS LAID BEFORE THE SENATE,

BY THE

PRESIDENT OF THE UNITED STATES.

IN FEBRUARY, 1806,

AND NEVER BEFORE PUBLISHED IN GREAT BRITAIN.

LONDON:

PRINTED FOR RICHARD PHILLIPS, 6, BRIDGE STREET,

BLACKFRIARS,

By J. G. Barnard, 57, Snow-hill.

1807.

William Clark

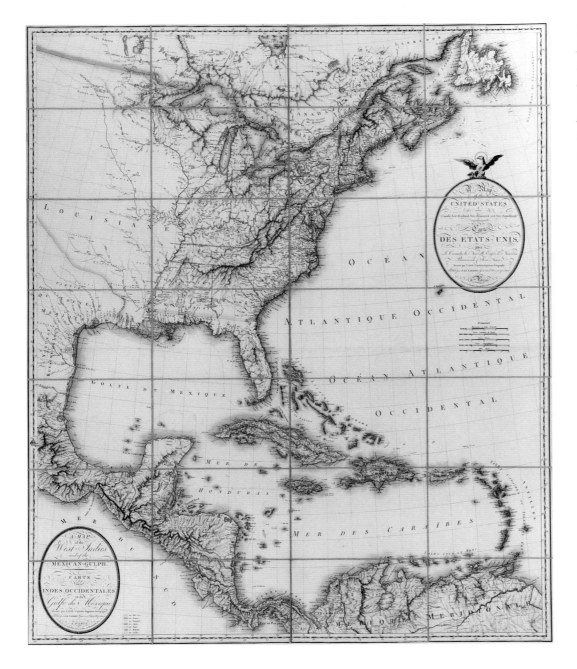

This map, published in France three years after the Louisiana Purchase, outlines the European powers' much-reduced American territories and the vastly expanded boundaries of the United States. It shows Ohio, which in 1803 had entered the Union as the seventeenth state, fully equal with the original thirteen states under the terms of the Northwest Ordinance.

A Map of the United States and Canada, New Scotland, New Brunswick, and New Foundland, published by P.A.F. Tardieu, 1806

Land for Settlers Writing from the western New York frontier in 1803, Uriah Chapman advised his grandson, a Connecticut schoolteacher, to go where "Land is yet Cheap" because "Geting On Land in Youth Generally makes young men the more Steady and makes the most Permant and Comfortable fortune." This desire to become independent by owning land drew people out of the East and the South, and from Europe.

In 1790 only one in twenty Americans lived beyond the Appalachians. In 1820 almost one in five, or two million, people lived in western states or territories. The land was not free, and pioneers acquired it in many ways. Some war veterans took bounty land promised them for military service, although most sold their certificates for cash. Other pioneers bought land from European or American companies. Most cash-poor immigrants could afford to buy federal land only after Congress amended the Land Ordinance of 1785 in the early 1800s, decreasing the size of the tracts and extending credit.

Uriah Chapman's grandson took his grandfather's advice and moved west to New York. After a few years he became ill and returned to Connecticut, where he died. How many settlers succeeded in the West is hard to measure. The dream, despite the harsh conditions of the frontier, beckoned tens of thousands to attempt the journey.

Left: Certificate for land due John Barnes, March 1, 1785

Right: Letter from Uriah Chapman to his grandson, Chapman Forseth, December 19, 1803

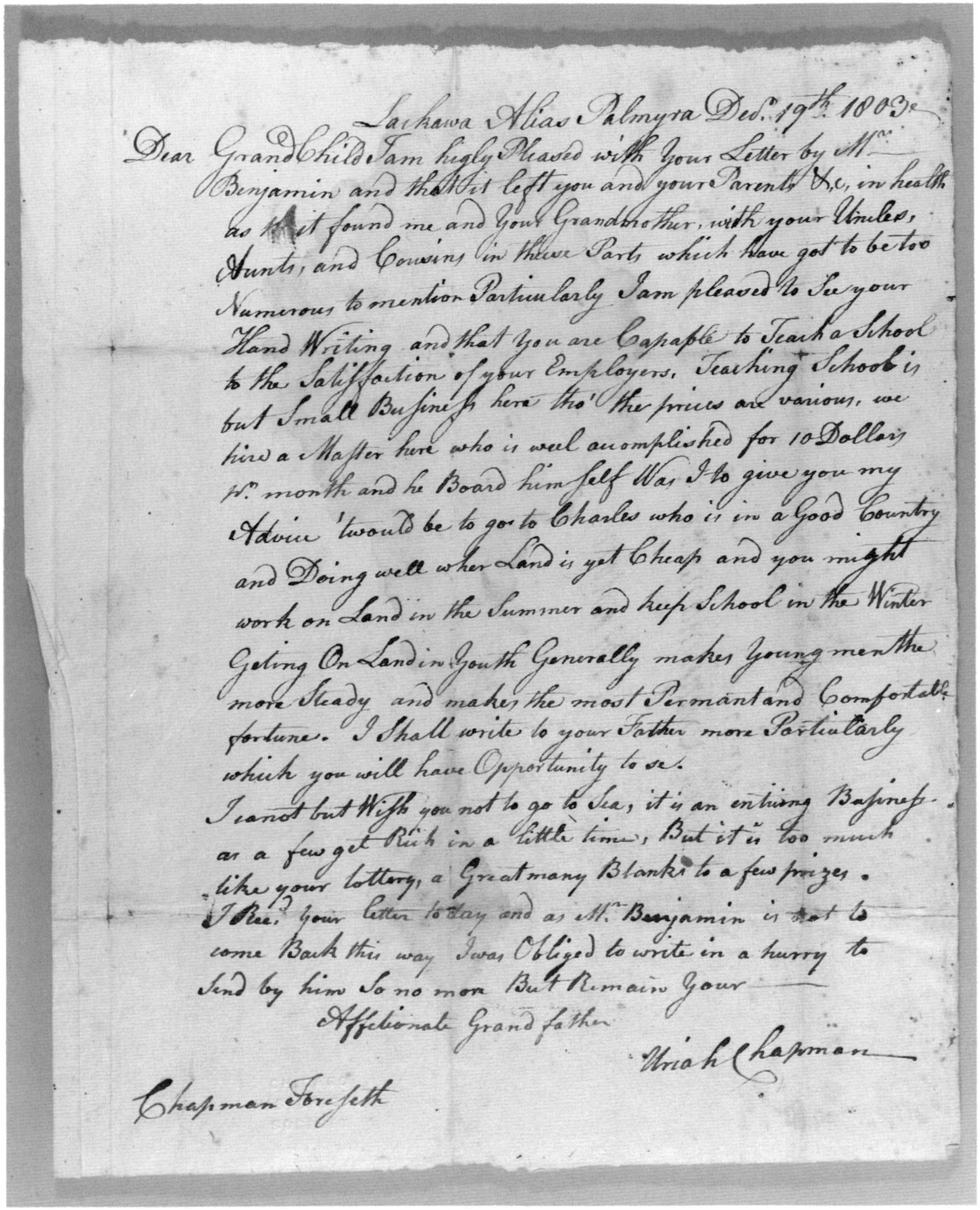

Lackawa Alias Palmyra Decr 19th 1803

Dear Grandchild

I am highly Pleased with your Letter by
Mr. Benjamin and that it left you and your
Parents etc. in health as it found me and your
Grandmother, with your Uncles, Aunts, and
Cousins in these Parts which have got to be
too Numerous to mention[.] Particularly I
am pleased to see your Hand Writing and
that you are Capable to Teach a School to the
satisfaction of your Employers. Teaching
School is but Small Business here tho' the
prices are various, we hire a Master here who
is weel [well] accomplished for 10 Dollars per
month and he Board himself[.] Was I to give
you my Advice 'twould be to go to Charles
who is in a Good Country and Doing well
wher Land is yet Cheap and you might work
on Land in the Summer and keep School in
the Winter. Geting On Land in Youth
Generally makes Young men the more Steady
and makes the most Permant and Comfortable fortune. I shall write to your Father
more Particularly which you will have
Opportunity to se.

I cannot but Wish you not to go to Sea,
it is an enticing Business as a few get Rich in
a little time, But it is too much like your lottery, a Great many Blanks to a few prizes. I
Recd your letter today and as Mr. Benjamin
is not to come Back this way I was Obliged to
write in a hurry to send by him So no more
But Remain Your

Affetionate Grandfather,

Uriah Chapman

Chapman Foreseth

Property lines in the East were usually irregular, defined by the contours of the land. In accordance with the Land Ordinance of 1785, surveyors imposed a rectangular pattern on the lands of the Northwest Territory in advance of settlement. This grid system, an enduring element of the midwestern landscape, divided public lands into townships of six square miles and established a standard of measurement for future land division.

Thomas Hutchins, official geographer of the United States, surveyed and platted five of the seven ranges of townships illustrated in this map of Ohio's southeastern border. He divided each township into thirty-six square sections, with each square-mile section equal to 640 acres.

Hutchins's grid system of townships became more useful as people were able to purchase smaller parcels of land. In the early 1800s farmers pressed for smaller land parcels of a quarter-section (160 acres) and for the extension of credit. As land was divided and subdivided, the boundaries of farms could be clearly identified on maps and in land transfer documents.

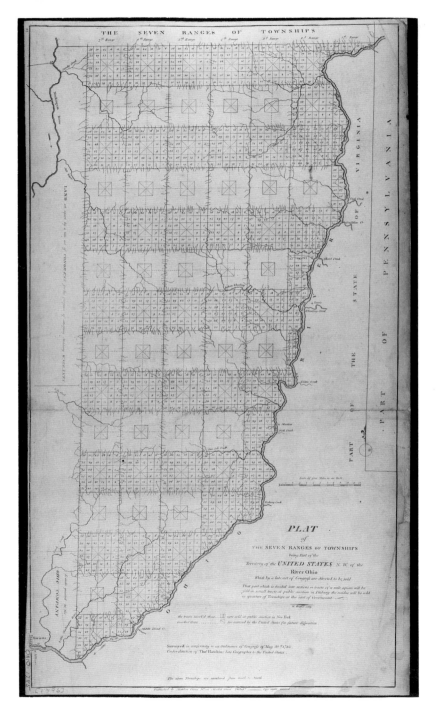

Plat of the Seven Ranges of Townships . . . N.W. of the River Ohio, published by Matthew Carey, 1796

After the War of 1812 the federal government set aside land in the Illinois territory for the land bounties promised to soldiers. Surveyors divided the land into ranges, sections, townships, and lots, as had been done earlier in Ohio. Veterans with warrants for land were then awarded specific tracts by lottery.

In this certificate the Commissioner of the Land Office, acting on behalf of President James Monroe, awarded John Transway, an infantry private, 160 acres southeast of section twenty of township four north in range nine west. Whether Transway settled his land or sold it to one of the speculators avidly buying up land bounties we do not know.

Military land grant issued to John Transway, November 5, 1817

Land companies bought and sold huge tracts of land from the federal government to sell to settlers or European businessmen. This French cartoon satirizes the frenzy with which American speculators bought and sold the land and duped European investors. The Scioto Company, which held an option on five million acres of federal land in the Ohio Territory, promoted land sales to the French. When the company collapsed, French investors were furious. The cartoon's caption expresses their outrage over the scandal: "Better to ensnare dupes, they draw up geographical maps, convert the rocky wastes into fertile plains, show roads cut through impassable cliffs, and offer shares in lands which do not belong to them."

Vente des deserts du Scioto, par des Anglo-americains

Le Citoien Mignard signale aujourdhui des Compagnies anglaises qui vendent des terres imaginaire dans les Etats unis; pour mieux luerrer les dupes, ils arrangent des Cartes geographiques, convertissent les rochers deserts en plaines fertiles, montrent des chemins fraies sur des roches inabordables, et pro- posent des actions pour des terreins qui ne leur appartiennent pas; l'ouvrage du C.en Mignard se vend 15 sols, et se trouve rue Taranne, N.o 24

A Paris, chez Depeuille, Rue des Mathurains St Jacques aux deux-Pilastres d'Or   *Extrait de l'ami des Loix N.o 836; Brumaire an 6.me*

Sale of the Deserts of Scioto by the Anglo-Americans, artist unknown, 1799

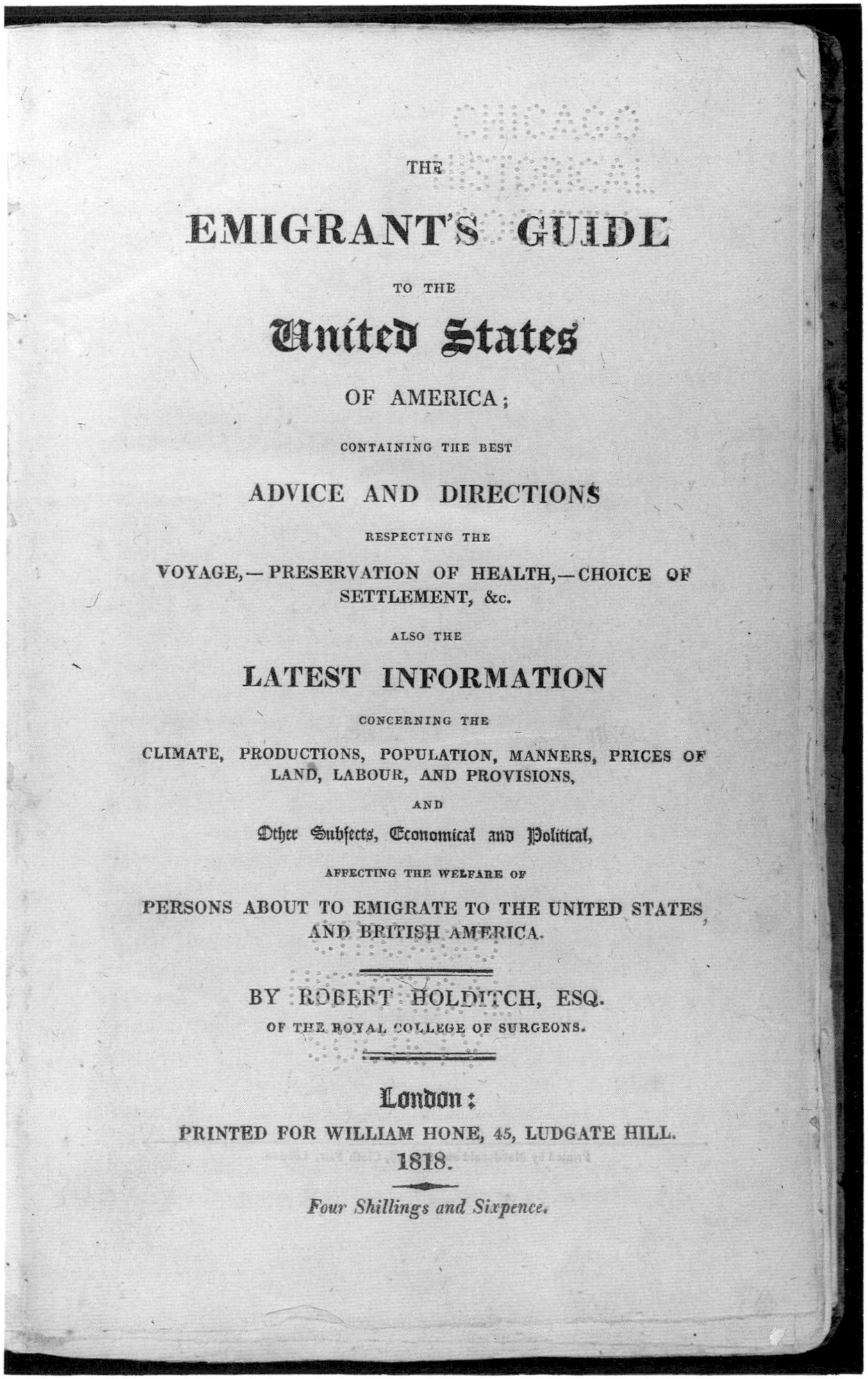

THE

EMIGRANT'S GUIDE

TO THE

United States

OF AMERICA;

CONTAINING THE BEST

ADVICE AND DIRECTIONS

RESPECTING THE

VOYAGE,—PRESERVATION OF HEALTH,—CHOICE OF
SETTLEMENT, &c.

ALSO THE

LATEST INFORMATION

CONCERNING THE

CLIMATE, PRODUCTIONS, POPULATION, MANNERS, PRICES OF
LAND, LABOUR, AND PROVISIONS,

AND

Other Subjects, Economical and Political,

AFFECTING THE WELFARE OF

PERSONS ABOUT TO EMIGRATE TO THE UNITED STATES
AND BRITISH AMERICA.

BY ROBERT HOLDITCH, ESQ.

OF THE ROYAL COLLEGE OF SURGEONS.

London:

PRINTED FOR WILLIAM HONE, 45, LUDGATE HILL.

1818.

Four Shillings and Sixpence.

Most migrants to the old Northwest came from the eastern United States. Large numbers came from the British Isles and some from Europe.

Aimed at British citizens who were considering a move to America, this guide offered "the latest information concerning the climate, productions, population, manners, prices of land, labour, and provisions." The author admonishes European emigrants for lingering too long in the eastern cities and encourages readers to "push out westward without delay," noting that "two dollars saved in Pennsylvania will purchase an acre of good land in the Illinois." Holditch suggests that emigrants bring with them clothing, razors, pocketknives, pencils, books, and good gunlocks, all scarce in the western territories.

Title page from *The Emigrant's Guide to the United States of America,* by Robert Holditch, 1818

The first settlers moving west had room only for the basic necessities: axes, guns, farm tools, kettles, and pans. But they also brought a few precious items that were reminders of the life they left behind.

Betsy Smith traveled in a covered wagon with her husband and children from western New York to Peru, Illinois. This teapot and cup and saucer are from a tea set that, according to family lore, was shipped by stagecoach from New York City to the family farm in Illinois.

The Pierce family brought with them this small chest on their journey from Vermont to Illinois in the early nineteenth century.

This "penny wooden" doll, distinguished by its wooden joints and a peg on top of its head, migrated west with an unknown little girl.

This pocket-size traveler's dictionary by John Melish includes detailed descriptions of counties and towns and a foldout map (below) with the latest roads. The directory highlights Ohio, Indiana, and Illinois, the new states, and the territories of the Old Northwest. The vast area west of the Mississippi River remained uncharted.

Opposite: English tea set, c. 1820; wooden box, c. 1800; wooden doll, c. 1818; pocket-size *Traveller's Directory through the United States,* by John Melish, 1818

Foldout map from *Traveller's Directory through the United States,* by John Melish, 1818

Danforth Armour

PORTRAIT OF AN AMERICAN

Danforth Armour (1799–1873) was the
third generation of Armours to farm
the land with a plow that was forged
for his grandfather in colonial days
by a village blacksmith. Danforth
was one of nine children reared
by John and Sarah Preston Armour
on their small farm near Union,
Connecticut.

By the early nineteenth century the
exodus from New England to the more fertile
soil of the West was under way. In 1819 the Armour family ventured to
Madison County, New York, and acquired land that had belonged to
the Oneida Indians. Using the family plow Danforth farmed about
one hundred acres near Stockbridge, growing grain and raising
livestock. He worked this farm almost forty years, rearing his own
family of six sons and two daughters.

Some of Danforth Armour's sons prospered on their own farms
in New York. Others left the family farm and made their way to
midwestern cities. Phillip Danforth Armour made his fortune in meat-
packing in Chicago. In the final years of his life, Danforth Armour
moved west once more, to northern Illinois.

Like other colonial plows, this plow was hewn from wood, either
ash or oak. Later the moldboard was sheathed with iron that had been
hammered on the local blacksmith's anvil. After 1837 midwestern
farmers could buy one of John Deere's new steel plows, strong enough
to break prairie sod.

In 1933 the Armour family plow broke ground for the
agricultural building at the Century of Progress Exposition in
Chicago, a fitting symbol of a farmer's world that had given way to an
industrial America.

Plow, c. 1760

Windsor Otis, an early settler in the timber-rich Western Reserve, worked the land with a team of oxen fitted to this yoke. The Western Reserve was five hundred thousand acres of wilderness in northern Ohio set aside for Connecticut citizens whose towns had been burned by the British during the Revolution.

VENERATE THE PLOUGH

Venerate the Plow, detail from "The Plan of a Farm Yard" in *Columbian Magazine*, October 1786. Courtesy, Newberry Library, Chicago

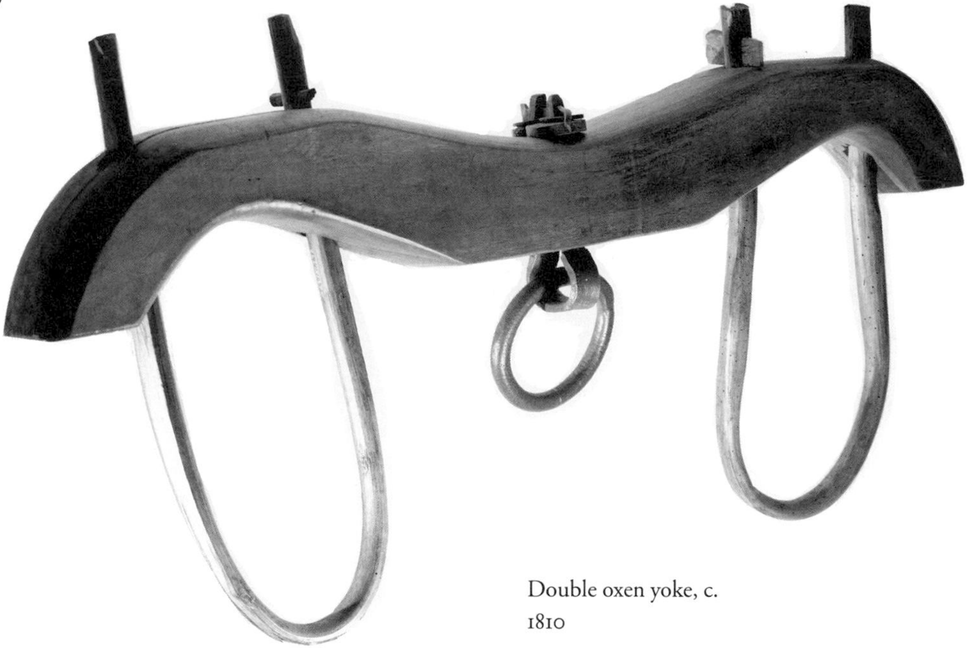

Double oxen yoke, c. 1810

Displacing the American Indians

For about ten thousand years, Indians inhabited the area surrounding the Great Lakes. By 1790 fourteen major nations, numbering about eighty thousand people, had divided the region along natural boundary lines. They grew crops in about three hundred villages that served as home bases for fishing trips and hunting or trading expeditions.

The promise of the Northwest Ordinance of 1787 that "the utmost good faith shall always be observed towards the Indians" was broken. American pressures on Indians were relentless: to cede lands, to convert to Christianity, to adopt horse and plow agriculture. Indians were divided in their response. Some ceded lands and moved on, but few adopted the white man's ways. Most resisted, joining in movements to revitalize Indian religions and ancestral ways.

In the Northwest Territory Indians twice formed confederacies to resist expansion. The United States fought two major wars to suppress massive Indian resistance: the first, in 1791–94; the second, in 1811–13. By 1820 American Indians had ceded almost all of the land of the Northwest Territory to the United States.

During the 1820s and 1830s James Otto Lewis painted more than eighty portraits of American Indians in the Great Lakes and Upper Mississippi region. Working under the patronage of Michigan's territorial governor, Lewis traveled to Indian settlements at Green Bay, Fond du Lac, and Prairie du Chien, where he sketched leaders of the Chippewa, Sioux, Potawatomi, Menominee, Fox and Sac, and Winnebago as they gathered at various treaty sessions.

Most of the Indian subjects sat for their portraits attired in ceremonial dress, and Lewis paid special attention to their faces and costumes. He completed most of his paintings in Detroit, where he perfected the sympathetic, dignified poses and colorful detailing that characterize his work. In 1835, Lewis's American Indian images reached a larger and more popular audience when they were issued as a collection of eighty colored lithographs, entitled Aboriginal Port Folio.

Chippeway Squaws at the Treaty of Fond du Lac, 1826, lithograph by F. Barincou for George Lehman and Peter S. Duval, after the painting by James Otto Lewis, 1835

The Pipe Dance and the Tomahawk Dance of the Chippeway tribe, lithograph by F. Barincou for George Lehman and Peter S. Duval, after the painting by James Otto Lewis, 1835, at the treaty of Prairie du Chien (Color Plate 14)

Symbolic of war as well as of peace, pipe tomahawks were popular trade items and functioned as both weapons and smoking implements. The Chippewas featured in Lewis's illustration are celebrating the peace treaty enacted at Prairie du Chien in 1825.

Pipe tomahawk head with reproduction stem, c. 1770

Sa-go-ye-wat-ha (Red Jacket), engraving by Mosely Danforth, date unknown

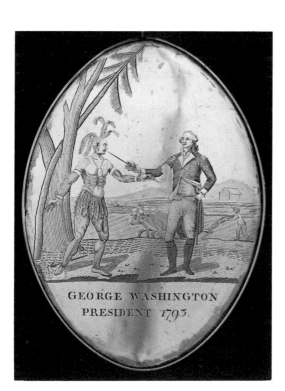

Silver peace medal (front), made by Joseph Richardson, Jr., 1793

Red Jacket, as chieftain of the Senecas, fought in different ways to maintain the independence and integrity of his people. The Senecas, one of the great Six Nations of the Iroquois, were relegated to a reservation in western New York in the 1790s. Red Jacket proudly resisted the efforts of Protestant missionaries to Christianize the Indians. In an oration to a missionary in 1805, he said: "Brother, Our seats [land] were once large and yours were small. You have now become a great people and we have scarcely a place left to spread our blankets. You have got our country, but are not satisfied; you want to force religion upon us. . . . Brother we do not wish to destroy your religion, or take it from you. We only want to enjoy our own." By the end of his life his own people had adopted Christianity and deserted him.

He was called "Red Jacket" because of the coat a British officer gave him during the Revolution when the Senecas fought as allies of the British. In 1792, to cultivate Red Jacket's friendship, government officials invited him to visit Philadelphia, where President Washington bestowed on him the peace medal he is shown wearing in this engraving.

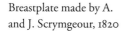

Breastplate made by A.
and J. Scrymgeour, 1820

Like the British during the colonial era, the United
States government bestowed silver medallions and
breastplates (or gorgets) on cooperating Indian
leaders.

Cataw, chief of the Ottawa nation in northwestern Michigan, received this breastplate from territorial governor Lewis Cass, very likely for Cataw's
loyalty to the United States during the War of 1812
and on the occasion of the Ottawa and Chippewa
ceding the Saint Martin Islands in Lake Huron in
1820.

On this breastplate, engraved by a New York silversmith, the Indian is holding a string of wampum
in his left hand and a calumet (or pipe of peace) in
his right. On the left, an American general in full
uniform offers the Indian more wampum, a medium
of exchange. Between them stands a bear. Above
them in a galaxy of stars soars an American eagle, a
symbol of the triumphant United States.

Murder of Jane McCrae by the Indians, artist and date unknown

Penn's Treaty with the Indians, 1682, painting by Benjamin West, c. 1771

Images of the American Indian: Merciless Scalpers and Noble Savages

All the images of Indians in this era were created by whites and conformed to different stereotypes of American Indians held by Europeans or Americans. They reflect hostile, fearful notions of the Indian as murderous scalper, romantic images of the noble savage, or the concept of the good Indian as one who abandoned traditional ways.

The painting (to the left) of the scalping of Jane McCrae in the Revolution reflects the traditional nightmares of the American Indian as a cruel and merciless savage who scalps innocent women. Indian leaders who organized resistance were depicted as villains. The cartoon of the killing of Tecumseh in the Battle of the Thames (p. 187) glorifies the American politicians who shot him.

The American Indian as noble savage, untainted by the corruptions of civilization, was long popular in England and Europe but not on the American frontier. Benjamin West's painting of the Lenape who made a peace treaty with William Penn was in this tradition. So was the British engraving of Joseph Brant, their ally, as a noble warrior in full Mohawk dress (p. 97).

American artists did not portray Indians as noble until the 1820s and 1830s, after American armies had defeated them in the Northwest. James Otto Lewis painted The Prophet in 1824, long after he and his brother Tecumseh had been crushed. As native Americans seemed to be vanishing in the old Northwest, the U.S. government commissioned Lewis to paint chieftains and other scenes of Indian life.

The stereotype of the good Indian, created in support of U.S. government policy, is embodied on the peace medal that the United States gave to American Indian nations who signed treaties with the government. The good American Indian was one who abandoned hunting for plowing and farming and surrendered to the Americans when defeated, a moment captured by the unknown artist who painted the signing of the Treaty of Greenville (p. 184).

These images in the white man's imagination—savage scalper, noble savage, or good Indian—were used by Americans to justify the conquest and subsequent degradation of Indian nations.

George Washington,

PRESIDENT of the

UNITED STATES of AMERICA,

To all to whom these Presents shall come:

KNOW YE, That the nation of Indians called the _Kaskaskias_ inhabiting the town of _Kaskaskia_

and other towns, villages ... _their persons, towns, villages, lands, hunting-_ grounds and other rights and property in the peace and under the protection of the United States of America: And all persons, citizens of the United States are hereby warned not to commit any injury, trespass or molestation whatever on the persons, lands, hunting-grounds, or other rights or property of the said Indians: And they and all others are in like manner forbidden to purchase, accept, agree or treat for, with the said Indians directly or indirectly, the title or occupation of any lands held or claimed by them; and I do hereby call upon all persons in authority under the United States, and all citizens thereof in their several capacities, to be aiding and assisting to the prosecution and punishment according to law of all persons who shall be found offending in the premises.

GIVEN under my Hand and the Seal of the United States this _____ day of _____ in the year of our Lord one thousand seven hundred and ninety-_____ and of the Independence of the United States of America the _seventeenth_.

Proclamation of protection for Kaskaskia Indians, May 7, 1793

When the United States made treaties in which Indian nations ceded land, it guaranteed them protection of the land not ceded. But intrusions by settlers were so common that the government printed a standard form warning citizens "not to commit any injury, trespass or molestation" and then filled in the blanks with the name of the nation and area that was off-limits to whites. This proclamation, signed by President Washington in 1793, protected the land of the Kaskaskias in central Illinois.

Such proclamations rarely worked. In 1796 Washington wrote in despair, "I believe scarcely any thing short of a Chinese Wall, or line of Troops will restrain Land Jobbers, and the Incroachment of Settlers, upon Indian Territory."

In 1794 Gen. Anthony Wayne led the victory over the Ohio Indian confederacy at the Battle of Fallen Timbers in northwestern Ohio. A year later, the two parties began treaty negotiations in Greenville, Ohio. An unknown artist, probably a soldier, painted this view of General Wayne conducting discussions with Little Turtle, chief of the Miamis. Tarhe the Crane, a Wyandot chief, is poised nearby holding a peace pipe. William Henry Harrison stands to the right of General Wayne, and, kneeling at left, another officer (possibly William Wells) acts as scribe and translator. This painting is the only extant image of the treaty sessions.

Indian Treaty of Greenville, artist unknown, 1795 (Color Plate 13)

First printing of the
Treaty of Greenville, 1795

(6)

P. fris La Fontaine.
Ant. Laffelle.
H. Laffelle.
Jn. Beau Bien.
David Jones, chaplain U. S. L.
Lewis Beufait.
R. Lachambre.
Jas. Pepen.
Baties Coutien.
P. Navarre.
Wm. Wells.
Jacques Laffelle.
M. Morin.
Bt. Sans Crainte.
Christopher Miller.
Robert Wilson.
Abraham x Williams.
Isaac x Zane.

Sworn Interpreters.

Delawares.

Kik-tha-we-nund, (or Anderfon.) x L. S.
Bu-kon-ge-helas, x L. S.
Pee-kee-lund, x L. S.
Welle-baw-kee-lund, x L. S.
Pee-kee-télé-mund, (or *Thomas Adams*.) x L. S.
Kifh-ko-pe-kund, (or *Captain Buffaloe*.) x L. S.
Ame-na-hehan, (or *Capt. Crow*.) x L. S.
Que-Shawk-fey, (or *George Wafhington*.) x L. S.
Wey-Win-quis, (or *Billy Sifcomb*.) x L. S.
Mofes, x L. S.

Shawanees.

Mif-qua-Coo-na-caw, (or *Red Pole*.) x L. S.
Cut-the-we-ka-faw, (or *Black Hoof*.) x L. S.
Kay-fe-wa-e-fe-kah, x L. S.
Wey-tha-pa-mat-tha, x L. S.
Nia-nym-fe-ka, x L. S.
Way-the-ah, (or *Long Shanks*.) x L. S.
Wey-a-pier-fen-waw, (or *Blue Jacket*.) x L. S.
Ne-que, taugh-aw, x L. S.
Hah-goo-fee-kaw, (or *Captain Reed*.) x L. S.

Ottowas.

Au-Goofh-away, x L. S.
Kee-No-fha-Meek, x L. S.
La Malice, x L. S.
Ma-chi-we-tah, x L. S.
Tho-wo-na-wa, x L. S.
Se-Caw. x L. S.

Chipewas.

Mafh-i-pi-nafh-i-wifh, (or *Bad Bird*.) x L. S.
Nah-fho-ga-fhe, (from lake Superior.) x L. S.
Ka-tha-wa-fung, x L. S.
Ma-fafs, x L. S.
Ne-me-kafs, (or *Little Thunder*.) x L. S.
Pe-fhaw-kay, (or *Young Ox*.) x L. S.
Nan-guey, x L. S.
Mee-ne-doh-gee-fogh, x L. S.
Pee-wan-fhe-me-nogh, x L. S.
Wey-me-gwas, x L. S.
Gob-ma-a-tick. x L. S.

Ottowas.

Che-go-Nickfka, (an Ottawa from Sandufky.) x L. S.

More than one thousand American Indians from a dozen nations convened for the treaty sessions in the summer of 1795. The list of ninety Indian leaders who were signers at Greenville appears on the last three pages of the government's official printing of the treaty.

As a result of this treaty the Indians gave up all their claims to southern Ohio. The United States government renounced its claim to the remaining Indian lands in the Northwest Territory but held onto sixteen specific tracts of land to be used for trading posts and military forts. Although the Treaty of Greenville recognized the rights of Indians to their land, settlers did not. After 1795, they moved into northern Ohio, Indiana, and Illinois in increasing numbers.

Indians were divided over the Treaty of Greenville. Among the Shawnees, for example, older chiefs, such as Black Hoof, Red Pole, and Blue Jacket, signed it, but younger chiefs, such as Tecumseh, did not. When American expansion again threatened the Shawnees, Tecumseh would organize military resistance.

Tens-qua-ta-wa, Shaw-nese Prophet, lithograph by F. Barincou for George Lehman and Peter S. Duval, after the painting by James Otto Lewis, 1835

The Prophet, brother of Tecumseh, led a movement to revitalize Indian religion that paved the way for Tecumseh's campaign to organize native peoples to resist the Americans by force. Lalawethikia, as he was originally called, lost his right eye in a childhood accident with an arrow. Never much of a hunter or a warrior, he sank into alcoholism, had religious visions, and emerged a crusader to restore the Shawnees and other nations of the Northwest to their ancestral ways.

As Tenskwatawa (The One That Opens the Door), he campaigned against alcohol as "the white man's poison," and against sexual promiscuity and violence. Urging American Indians to return to their traditional clothing, tools, and ceremonies, The Prophet held forth a vision of a golden age in which ancestral lands would be restored.

General Harrison, recognizing The Prophet's importance, defeated his followers at the Battle of Tippecanoe in 1811. He went on to destroy Prophets-town and with it the influence of The Prophet. This lithograph is based on a portrait that James Otto Lewis painted in Detroit in 1824.

Tecumseh

Tecumseh (1768–1813) was a Shawnee chieftain, tall and well-built, known as a bold orator and a compassionate warrior. He believed that American Indian lands were "the common property of the tribes," and that no one native people had a right to cede land "without the consent of all." He expressed his defiance eloquently: "The Great Spirit said he gave this great island [North America] to his red children. He placed the whites on the other side of the big water [the Atlantic]. They were not content with their own, but came to take ours from us. They have driven us from the sea to the lakes, we can go no farther."

Early in the 1800s, Tecumseh's brother Tenskwatawa, known as The Prophet, led a crusade among the Indians in the Northwest to revitalize their traditional ways, inspiring them to resist American expansion.

By 1810 Tecumseh had united Indians from many nations into one confederacy. Gen. William Henry Harrison attacked Prophets-town in 1811 at the Battle of Tippecanoe. In the War of 1812, Tecumseh had counted on military support from Great Britain, but it was inadequate. Harrison's army defeated the Indians and the British in 1813 at the Battle of the Thames in Canada, killing Tecumseh. In the eyes of his chief opponent, General Harrison, Tecumseh was "one of those uncommon geniuses which spring up occasionally to produce revolution."

"Sell a country?" asked Tecumseh. "Why not sell the air, the clouds and the great sea as well as the earth?"

Tecumseh, engraving from *Pictorial Field Book of the War of 1812*, by Benson Lossing, 1869

Plate 9
Sampler worked by
Susanna Lane, age 11,
1776

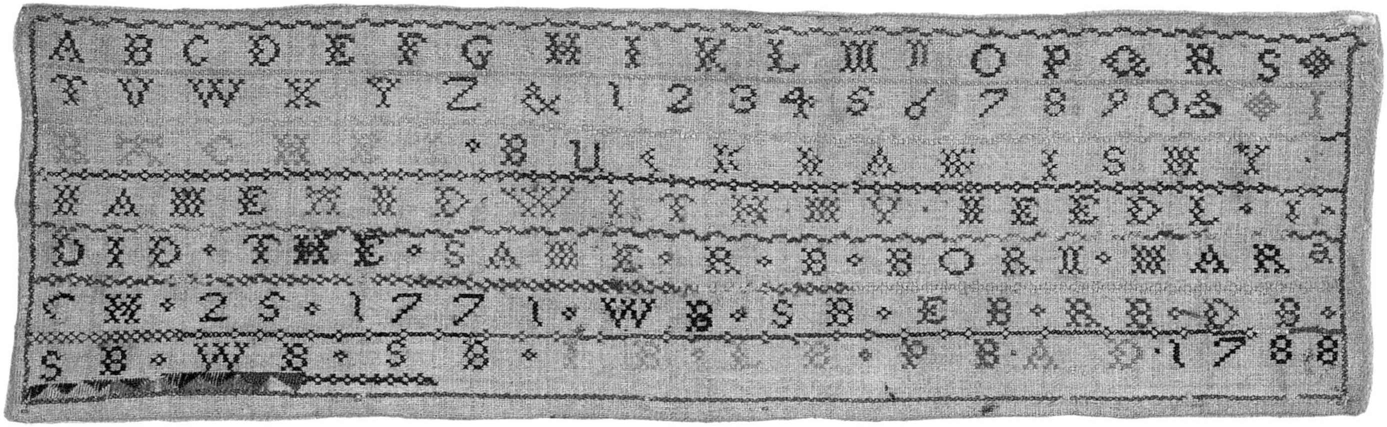

Plate 10
Sampler worked by Rachel Bucknam, age 17, 1788

Plate 11
Christening dress of
Joseph Williams

Plate 12
Woman's patchwork and
calico pocket, c. 1775

THE PIPE DANCE   and   THE TOMAHAWK DANCE

of the Chippeway tribe.

Painted at the treaty of Prairie du Chien 1825 by J. O. Lewis

Plate 15
Carved statue of George
Washington, artist
unknown, c 1830

UNDER ✫ MY ✫ WINGS ✫ EVERY ✫ THING ✫ PROSPERS

Plate 16
A View of New Orleans
taken from the Plantation
of Marigny, November
1803, by Boqueto de
Woieseri, 1803

Tecumseh's dream of a grand American Indian alliance ended with his death in 1813. This illustration of the warrior's final engagement at the Battle of the Thames originally appeared as the frontispiece for History of the Indian Wars, *by Henry Trumbull. Like many other writers of his generation, Trumbull presents a version of American history preoccupied with "the sufferings of the inhabitants of frontier settlements by the Savages."*

Col. Richard M. Johnson, who may have fired the fatal shot, takes center stage in the illustration. Tecumseh is depicted at the far right, armed with a spear and encouraging his warriors to attack. Johnson parlayed his reputation as a fearless slayer of Indians into a political career. Adopting the nickname "Old Tecumseh," he successfully campaigned for the vice-presidency in 1836 as Martin Van Buren's running mate using the slogan:

Rumpsey dumpsey, rumpsey dumpsey,
Colonel Johnson killed Tecumseh!

William Henry Harrison, victor in the Battle of Tippecanoe, was elected president in 1840 on the slogan "Tippecanoe and Tyler Too."

A View of Col. Johnson's Engagement with the Savages, engraving by Nathaniel Dearborn, from History of the Indian Wars, *1846*

Creating an American Culture

In colonial days there were few parades, but in the new nation, city mechanics and tradesmen paraded on many occasions to demonstrate pride in their crafts and in their republican citizenship. In 1788 they paraded to celebrate the new Constitution; each Fourth of July they paraded to celebrate Independence Day. This grand procession of the victuallers, as butchers were called, was an annual event in Philadelphia that took place in conjunction with White's Great Cattle Show.

In this 1821 scene some two hundred butchers dressed in top hats and gleaming white smocks (in contrast to the blood-soaked smocks of their everyday work) are rounding the corner on horseback. A brass band plays in one wagon, a prize cow perches on top of another wagon. A float behind them carries the same ship that was displayed in the 1788 parade celebrating the new Constitution. Artisans with their banners follow, grouped by trades in a two-mile-long procession. At the end of the festivities the prize cow was slaughtered and sold.

This lithograph was based on an original painting by Lewis Krimmel who, in other paintings, portrayed Philadelphia's common people participating in elections and celebrating the Fourth of July.

Opposite: White's Great Cattle Show, and Grand Procession of the Victuallers at Philadelphia, lithograph by Frederick Bourquin, c. 1845

8

Most of the distresses of our country have arisen from a belief that the American Revolution is over. This is so far from being the case that we have only finished the first act of the great drama. We have changed our forms of government, but it remains yet to effect a revolution in our principles, opinions and manners, so as to accommodate them to the forms of government we have adopted.

—BENJAMIN RUSH, 1786

Although the Revolution began to unify a diverse people, many Americans shared the opinion of Benjamin Rush, signer of the Declaration of Independence, leading physician, and reformer. Noah Webster advocated "a national language as well as a national government," producing a best-selling American speller and an American dictionary. John Adams called for works of history to provide a sense of a common past. Mercy Otis Warren and David Ramsay wrote the first histories of the Revolution, while veterans of the war wrote of their own experiences, sometimes with pride and sometimes with anger.

The new nation needed heroes and found its ideal in George Washington. Americans adopted symbols to express their aspirations: the stars and stripes for unity, the eagle for strength, a female goddess for liberty. After the War of 1812, a second war for independence, Albert Gallatin, a leading Democratic-Republican, could say "the people are more American, they feel and act more as a nation."

Here John Adams appears as he did in his ninetieth year. He died three years after this portrait was painted, on July 4, 1826, the fiftieth anniversary of American independence. Thomas Jefferson and Adams died the same day, hours apart, an event that struck many Americans with awe.

George P. A. Healy, who made this copy of the original by Gilbert Stuart, lived in Chicago from 1855 to 1865, where he painted more than five hundred portraits and historical subjects.

John Adams, by George P. A. Healy, 1860, after the portrait by Gilbert Stuart

In his retirement from the presidency, John Adams was alarmed with the "very extraordinary . . . Inattention" of Americans to the history of their own country. It was true that he was obsessed with the idea that his own role was overshadowed by the fame of Washington, Franklin, and Jefferson and that he was being discredited by the Federalists with whom he had broken. But he was also alarmed by the declining knowledge of American history, only one generation after the Revolution. In 1809, he summed up his complaints about the state of history in this letter to Joseph Ward, a fellow patriot. In another letter to Ward, he spoke of the "History of our country" as "getting full of Falsehoods." To Adams the indifference of his fellow Americans to their own history was "unaccountable."

Sir

I recd in season your interesting favor of the 10th of May: but have not had opportunity to acknowledge it till now.

There appears to me, to be a very extraordinary and unaccountable Inattention in our countrymen to the History of their own country. While every kind of Trifle from Europe is printed and scattered profusely in America our own original Historians are very much neglected. A copy of Dr. [Cotton] Mathers Magnalia is not to be purchased at any rate and is scarcely to be found. Yet this contains the greatest quantity of Materials relative to the first characters. Mr [Thomas] Princes chronology is rarely to be found. The second volume not at all. I never saw but one copy of it in all my life. [Jeremy] Belknaps and [George] Minots Labours are neglected. Dr. [Jonathan] Mayhews writings are forgotten. Samuel Adams and John Handcock are almost buried in oblivion. [William] Gordons [David] Ramseys, [John] Marshalls Histories appear to me to be Romances. And the funding system and the Banking systems seem to threaten a total Distruction of the Distinctions between virtue and vice.

Letter from John Adams to Joseph Ward, June 6, 1809

Symbols for a New Nation

What symbols should the new nation adopt? For 150 years Americans lived as a diverse people in thirteen colonies with little identity as a nation. In the revolutionary years and after, they chose most of the symbols that have since come to represent American ideals.

The flag adopted by the Continental Congress in 1777 symbolized unity. The alternate red and white stripes represented the thirteen states, the white stars on a field of blue "a new constellation," the Union. As the official seal, Congress chose the eagle, symbol of strength, under the motto "E Pluribus Unum," or "One Out of Many." And to personify America the country adopted a classically garbed maiden, Columbia. The stars and stripes, the eagle, and Columbia appeared in endless combinations—signs of American aspiration for unity, strength, and liberty.

The Eagle

Before adopting the eagle, Congress debated extensively on which symbol to select for the official seal of the United States. From the time of ancient Rome the eagle had been a traditional symbol of imperial strength. Benjamin Franklin was disappointed; the eagle was a "bird of bad moral character," a bird of prey "like those among men who live by sharping and robbing." He would have preferred the turkey, a much more respectable bird and a true original of America.

The eagle was portrayed with one talon holding an olive branch, the traditional symbol of peace, and the other holding a quiver of arrows, a symbol of war. The eagle was probably the most popular of all American symbols; Americans carved it in wood, embroidered it on needlework, and painted or drew it on everything imaginable.

Side chair probably
made by Samuel
McIntire in Salem,
Massachusetts, c. 1800

Carved eagle originally
affixed to the stern of a
ship, artist unknown,
c. 1820

Federal mirror, c. 1810

Empire sofa made in western Pennsylvania, c. 1830

The Flag

Americans fought the war with Britain under a great variety of flags. Each state, each militia regiment, each state's navy seemed to have its own flag. The rattlesnake flag with the slogan "Don't Tread on Me" was popular, as were different versions of the Liberty Tree or Pine Tree flag. The need for a uniform flag was first felt at sea as a means to identify American ships.

In 1777 Congress adopted a flag for the navy. The army followed suit slowly. For decades after the war no strict rules existed about how the stars should be arranged, and as new states entered the Union, more stripes and more stars were added.

Not until 1824 did Congress adopt the form that has since become familiar: thirteen red and white bars, and stars equal to the number of states. No official flag code governed the display of the flag until 1942, and no law punished physical mistreatment of the flag until 1968.

A pledge of allegiance to the flag was first proposed in 1892, but it was not adopted by Congress until 1942. In the early years of the young nation loyalty to American symbols was given freely by most citizens and did not require the coercion of laws.

A Concord, New Hampshire, furniture maker expressed his pride in the new nation by making this drum and adorning it with the American flag.

Field drum made by
Porter Blanchard, c. 1815

Americans owe their national anthem to the War of 1812. On the night of September 13, 1812, a lawyer named Francis Scott Key boarded a British ship to arrange for the release of an American prisoner. While he was on board, the British shelled Fort McHenry, near the city of Baltimore, Maryland. The fort resisted capture, and in the "dawn's early light" of September 14, the sight of the American flag waving from its ramparts inspired Key's lyrics. The tune to which Francis Scott Key fit his lyrics, "Anaecreon in Heaven," was a popular British drinking song. The song with Key's lyrics was sung throughout the nineteenth century, but Congress did not adopt it as the national anthem until 1931.

A View of the Bombardment of Fort McHenry, aquatint by John Bower, c. 1815

A beautiful American Indian princess is the symbol of North America in the cartouche from Mitchell's map (map appears on p. 3). She wears a headdress of feathers, and behind her grow stalks of corn, the grain whose cultivation was perfected by Indians.

Cartouche from *A Map of the British and French Dominions in North America*, by John Mitchell (London, 1755)

Liberty

From the time of the earliest explorations European artists depicted America, like the other continents, as a female and usually as an Indian maiden or princess. The symbol for Great Britain was Britannia, a woman holding a military shield with the British flag.

Colonial artists and engravers used these symbols more and more as Americans became more conscious of their separate identity. Paul Revere, for example, used both. In the revolutionary era Britannia and the Indian princess evolved into a symbol of the new country, a classically garbed maiden variously named the Goddess of Liberty, Liberty, or Columbia, the feminized version of Columbus.

Liberty commonly appeared holding a pike topped with a liberty cap. The liberty cap, popular first in the American and then in the French Revolution, was derived from the Phrygian cap bestowed upon a slave in ancient Rome when he was made a free person. In time Liberty appeared with the eagle and the flag. When the Statue of Liberty was erected in New York Harbor in 1886, it continued the long tradition of a woman as the symbol of American freedom.

Five-dollar coin, 1803

The female Liberty often appeared on American coins. Here she wears a liberty cap.

In this engraving for the masthead of Boston's patriot newspaper, Paul Revere depicted a female figure, Britannia, with the shield of Britain at her side. With her left hand she holds a spear with a liberty cap; with her right she opens a cage and frees a bird that flies toward the Boston skyline in the background. By 1775 Revere modified this image and changed Britannia to Minerva, the Roman goddess of wisdom.

Paul Revere engraving,
Boston Gazette, 1770

Women dominate this portrayal of the country, which has the subtitle, "An allegorical representation of the United States denoting their Independence and Prosperity." The central figure seated to the right is a plumed goddess, "the Genius of America." Minerva, the goddess of wisdom, guides her. George Washington, the flag, and the shield of the United States all represent independence.

The symbols of prosperity abound. Ceres, the Roman goddess of agriculture, sits to the left holding a sheaf of wheat amid the tools of farming. To her left, a woman spins on the porch of her cottage.

Mercury, the sole male, messenger to the Roman gods, stands amid bales and barrels of goods that the ships in the harbor will export to foreign markets. A cornucopia, or horn of plenty, rests at America's feet, overflowing with fruits and vegetables.

America Guided by Wisdom, engraving by Benjamin Turner, c. 1815, after a drawing by John Baralet

AMERICA GUIDED BY WISDOM:
An Allegorical representation of the United States, denoting their Independence and prosperity.

Yankee Doodle

In colonial days "Yankee" was a derisive term for New Englanders. British military bands mocked patriots by playing the nonsense song "Yankee Doodle." After several British defeats in 1775 Americans flung the song back at the British as if to say, "See what the Yankees you made fun of can do." "Yankee Doodle" became the most popular song of the Revolution.

Yankee-Doodle, or the American Satan, engraving by Joseph Wright, c. 1778

In this puzzling engraving, published in London about 1778, the artist depicts "Yankee Doodle, or the American Satan" as a young man dressed in plain clothing, standing with his hands in his pockets. He is not very satanic at all. Joseph Wright, the engraver, was American born, and his intention seems to have been to evoke sympathy for the Americans.

Brother Jonathan was another nickname for Americans. After the Revolution, this character appeared in stage plays as a rustic country bumpkin. American cartoonists first depicted the United States as Brother Jonathan during the War of 1812. The character is shown ramming the victory of Admiral Perry on Lake Erie down the throat of John Bull, symbol of Great Britain. In the 1820s and 1830s, Brother Jonathan evolved into Uncle Sam.

Brother Jonathan Administering a Salutary Cordial to John Bull, engraving by Amos Doolittle, 1813

An American Language

"Our honor requires us to have a system of our own, in language as well as government," wrote Noah Webster, a Connecticut lawyer turned teacher. He devoted his life to the cause of the American language: its spelling, its grammar, and its pronunciation. Before Webster there was no officially correct American way to spell (and hence the great variety of spellings in earlier writing). Webster's guiding principle was that the "general custom is the rule of speaking"; language, that is, must be guided by "the same republican principles as American civil constitutions."

The traditional long or tailed s was going out of style, and Webster had forgotten to include it in the alphabet in his speller. In this letter he asks his publisher to insert the old s "on the line with the short s." Proud that his new speller was moving ahead of its competitors, he looked forward to the first edition of his dictionary, which he hoped would "awaken a little American Spirit."

Letter from Noah Webster to his publishers, January 3, 1806

Noah Webster, engraving, artist unknown, c. 1867, after the portrait by Alonzo Chappel

The "blue-backed speller" originally appeared as part of a trilogy with a "grammar" and a "reader." A runaway best-seller second only to the Bible, the speller sold eighty million copies in Webster's lifetime. Webster abandoned many British forms of spelling; for example, he changed favour *to* favor, centre *to* center, *and* defence *to* defense. *With the publication of the speller came the phrase "Webster says" to settle any argument about the spelling or meaning of a word.*

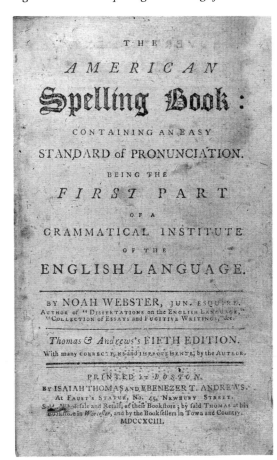

Title page from *The American Spelling Book,* by Noah Webster, 1793

AN

AMERICAN DICTIONARY

OF THE

ENGLISH LANGUAGE:

INTENDED TO EXHIBIT,

I. THE ORIGIN, AFFINITIES AND PRIMARY SIGNIFICATION OF ENGLISH WORDS, AS FAR AS THEY HAVE BEEN ASCERTAINED.
II. THE GENUINE ORTHOGRAPHY AND PRONUNCIATION OF WORDS, ACCORDING TO GENERAL USAGE, OR TO JUST PRINCIPLES OF ANALOGY.
III. ACCURATE AND DISCRIMINATING DEFINITIONS, WITH NUMEROUS AUTHORITIES AND ILLUSTRATIONS.

TO WHICH ARE PREFIXED,

AN INTRODUCTORY DISSERTATION

ON THE

ORIGIN, HISTORY AND CONNECTION OF THE

LANGUAGES OF WESTERN ASIA AND OF EUROPE,

AND A CONCISE GRAMMAR

OF THE

ENGLISH LANGUAGE.

BY NOAH WEBSTER, LL. D.

IN TWO VOLUMES.
VOL. I.

He that wishes to be counted among the benefactors of posterity, must add, by his own toil, to the acquisitions of his ancestors.—*Rambler.*

NEW YORK:
PUBLISHED BY S. CONVERSE.
PRINTED BY HEZEKIAH HOWE—NEW HAVEN.
1828.

Title page and detail from *An American Dictionary of the English Language,* by Noah Webster, 1828

pipes, and for poles to support palan
The smaller stalks are used for w
sticks, flutes, &c.

BAMBOO'ZLE, *v. t.* To confound;
ceive; to play low tricks. [*A low wo*
                                    Arbu

BAMBOO'ZLER, *n.* A cheat; one
plays low tricks.   *Arbu*

BAN, *n.* [Sax. *bannan, abannan,* t
claim; It. *bando,* a proclamation; S
Port. *bando;* Fr. *ban;* Arm. *ban;* I

In 1828, almost thirty years after Webster's schoolbooks first appeared, his efforts to establish a standard American language culminated with the publication of a much expanded and widely recognized American dictionary. Webster added many new American words such as applesauce, bamboozle, bullfrog, chowder, handy, *and* skunk.

George Washington Becomes a Legend

This wooden statue of Washington, three feet high, was probably made by an American early in the nineteenth century and, like a wooden "cigar store Indian," might have stood outside a shop on a busy street.

I n his own lifetime George Washington was a hero: the general indispensable for victory in war; the statesman who returned from his Virginia plantation to preside over the Constitutional Convention; the first president, who guided the country through the shoals of foreign wars and domestic politics.

He was a hero fit for a republic: he had not become a Cromwell or a Napoleon, a dictator, as some had feared. He rejected offers to become an American king; as president he refused to accept an imperial presidency, staying within the strict boundaries of the Constitution and retiring to private life after two terms.

In his own lifetime Washington accepted praise cautiously; he saw hero worship as a potential danger to a republic. John Adams spoke for many when he condemned the "superstitious veneration" and "idolotrous worship" of Washington. He respected him, he said, "as a man, not as a deity." But Americans needed a unifying hero, and Washington was a cement that bound them together.

When Washington died in 1799, he was portrayed in mourning pictures as "the father of his country," rising from his tomb to eternal glory. Parson Mason Weems, in his best-selling biography, turned Washington into a paragon of all virtues. Others used his image to sell their commercial products and to bless their political causes. Somehow the real hero survived all legends.

In an age when both men and women sniffed tobacco in the form of snuff, this fancy box would have been used to hold the finely powdered tobacco. Especially after his death, Washington's likeness was used on everything from cast-iron stoves to chocolate candy molds.

Carved statue of George Washington, artist unknown, c. 1830 (Color Plate 15)

Snuff box with miniature of George Washington, c. 1800

Mourning piece for
George Washington,
stipple and line engraving by Enoch G. Gridley,
c. 1800, after a design by
John Coles, Jr.

In this picture, distributed shortly after Washington's death in 1799, a soldier of the Continental line weeps for his former commander in chief, while Columbia, the female symbol of America, sits, her head bowed in grief. Washington's face is copied from the square-jawed portrait by Gilbert Stuart, which would become the standard Washington image.

Manufacturers of Liverpool pottery quickly capitalized on the market for Washington memorabilia. On this pitcher, Washington ascends from his tomb to heaven, supported by Father Time and an angel. Accompanied by the liberty cap, an eagle, and the shield of America, Columbia mourns, while, to the right, in a dubious piece of wishful thinking, an American Indian is depicted in sorrow.

Commemorative creamware pitcher, English, c. 1800

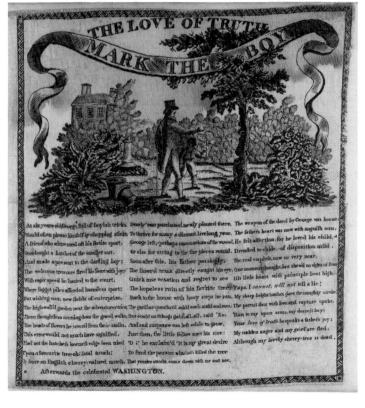

Title page from *The Life of George Washington*, by Mason Locke Weems (Philadelphia, 1820)

Parson Weems's biography of Washington exemplifies what John Adams had in mind about histories filled with "Falsehoods." Although Weems billed himself as the rector of the parish of Mount Vernon, he had never held such a position, nor could he, because the parish did not even exist. Weems had left the ministry years before, and he made his living peddling books through the countryside from his wagon. He knew what would sell, and he induced his publisher to produce his biography of Washington, which he said would earn them both "popularity and pence."

This is the twenty-third edition of a biography that first appeared in 1801 and went through more than eighty editions. Beginning in 1806, Weems added what he called on the title page his "curious anecdotes": Washington chopping down the cherry tree, Washington throwing a dollar across the Rappahannock River, Washington praying in the snow at Valley Forge. No evidence existed to support any of these tales.

Weems used Washington to teach virtues that would be "exemplary to his young countrymen." But by attempting to humanize Washington, he only made him more myth than man.

Of all Weems's anecdotes, none caught on like the cherry tree story, here printed in rhymed verse on a handkerchief that an enterprising British printer made for the American trade.

Memorial handkerchief, "The Love of Truth Mark the Boy," English, c. 1805

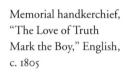

Like John Adams, many ordinary people were concerned with preserving for posterity their contributions to the Revolution. For them the Revolution had been the most important experience of their lives.

Veterans passed on their war exploits by telling stories to their children and grandchildren. Several hundred, like Andrew Sherburne or Ebenezer Fox, wrote their memoirs or allowed others to record them in "as told to" biographies. Tens of thousands set down their recollections in applications for a pension in response to an 1832 law that required them to give "a very full account" of their service.

Some former soldiers and seamen were so down and out they tried to capitalize on their moments of fame. Deborah Sampson Gannett, who had gone into battle as Robert Shurtleff, went on the lecture circuit; David Kennison offered himself as a museum exhibit in Chicago.

In the late 1830s, Abraham Lincoln observed that at the close of the Revolution "nearly every adult male had been a participator in some of its scenes." As a result "a living history was to be found in every family. . . . But those histories are gone. They can be read no more forever." Therefore the written accounts that survive are all the more valuable.

DEBORAH SAMPSON.
Published by H. Mann. 1797.

In 1782 Deborah Sampson, a twenty-two-year-old farm woman and a former indentured servant, donned a soldier's uniform, walked to a town where no one knew her, and enlisted in the Continental army under the name Robert Shurtleff. Stationed at West Point, she took part in hand-to-hand combat in which she was slashed on the forehead with a saber and later shot in the thigh with a musket ball. While she was in a hospital in Philadelphia with a fever, her real identity was discovered, and she was discharged from the army.

After the war she married Benjamin Gannett, a farmer of Sharon, Massachusetts, and they had three children. Herman Mann published a melodramatic biography of Sampson in 1797 and organized a speaking tour in which she lectured on her exploits.

When Sampson's war experience became known, her Baptist church expelled her, but the state of Massachusetts awarded her a pension. Paul Revere used his influence to get her a pension of four dollars a month from the United States. The pension was later raised to eight dollars, the same amount as for other veterans under the pension law of 1818. Sampson died poor in 1827 at the age of sixty-seven. A committee of Congress wrote, "The whole of the American Revolution furnished no other single example of female heroism." But whether other women also served in secret is almost impossible to know.

Frontispiece from the 1866 reprint of *The Female Review*, by Herman Mann, originally published in 1797

Illustration from *The Adventures of Ebenezer Fox in the Revolutionary War*, 1848

Title page from *Memoirs of Andrew Sherburne*, 1828

At the age of seventy-five Ebenezer Fox recorded his exciting adventures as a sailor during the Revolution. As an apprentice to a barber near Boston in 1776, Fox felt "the spirit of insubordination" in the air and, along with other boys, thought "we had wrongs to be redressed." His book tells of battles, capture, and escape during his three years at sea. Toward the end of his life he served as postmaster in Roxbury, Massachusetts. In this picture drawn for the book, Fox and another youth are questioned outside a tavern by a group of people who were curious about two obvious runaway apprentices.

Andrew Sherburne wrote a bitter autobiography. At the age of thirteen he sailed out of Portsmouth, New Hampshire, on a privateer in the hope of making his fortune. He was captured three times and suffered horrors in three British prisons, his health broken for life. For his service the government paid him in depreciated currency worth less than ten dollars. In 1818 it began to pay him a pension of eight dollars a month, but then tangled up the payments in red tape.

Unable to do hard manual labor, Sherburne made a paltry living as a clerk, a teacher, and finally as a part-time Baptist preacher. He struggled on the frontier in Maine and then in Ohio. He went from one Baptist community to another, begging for his sustenance.

Finally, furious with a government he felt had betrayed him, he wrote the angry story of his life and peddled his book from village to village to support himself.

MEMOIRS

OF

ANDREW SHERBURNE:

A PENSIONER OF THE

NAVY OF THE REVOLUTION.

WRITTEN BY HIMSELF.

"They that go down to the sea in ships, that do business in great waters; they see the works of the LORD, and his wonders in the deep."
Psalmist.

WILLIAM WILLIAMS,

UTICA;

1828.

To Chicagoans in the 1840s, David Kennison was "the last surviving member" of the Boston Tea Party; he claimed to have participated in almost every important battle from Lexington to Yorktown. Kennison made an exhibit of himself and a vial of the famous tea at a museum on Lake Street, where he solicited donations to support himself. Chicagoans thought he was 115 years old when they gave him a hero's funeral in 1852.

In reality, he was about eighty-five when he died. He was about seven at the time of the Tea Party, and, in 1780, at seventeen he was rejected by the army as undersized. He was indeed a veteran, but of the War of 1812, in which he was wounded and for which he received a pension. A poor laborer, he worked on farms, moving from Maine to Vermont to New York and finally to Chicago in 1845. There he found an audience eager to embrace a living link to the Revolution.

Affidavit signed by David Kennison attesting to the authenticity of his "historic" tea, 1848

Box with tea that David Kennison claimed to have taken during the Boston Tea Party

The Last of the Boston Tea Party.

I have taken the Museum in this city, which I was obliged to do, in order to get a comfortable living, as my Pension is so small, it scarcely affords the comforts of life. If I live until the 17th day of November, I shall be One Hundred and Twelve years old, and I intend making a Donation Party on that day, at the Museum. As I have fought in several battles for my country, and have suffered more than any other man will have to suffer, I hope. I would not go through the wars, and suffer what I have, for ten worlds like this. Now all I can ask of this generous public is to call at the Museum on the 17th day of November which is my birth day, and donate to me all they may think I deserve.

I shall be happy to have all the traveling community call and see me at all times.   DAVID KENNISON.
  nov 8—3mp

Advertisement from *Chicago Daily Democrat,* November 6, 1848

Portrait of David Kennison, artist unknown

The Domestic Arts Flourish

Sampler worked by Eliza
McCoy, age 10, 1800

A woman "should reverence herself," wrote Judith Sargent Murray in the 1790s. The country's most outspoken advocate of female education held that women "should be enabled to procure for themselves the necessaries of life; independence should be placed within their grasp." The "necessaries of life" included skills to function in the domestic sphere. Domesticity was a vocation. Although more women were single by choice early in the nineteenth century than before the Revolution, a woman was still defined as daughter, wife, or mother. In every one of these roles, needlework was indispensable. Farm women were still responsible for almost every step in the preparation of textiles. City women were now able to purchase more cloth, but they still had to sew most of the family's clothing.

Women took pride in their accomplishments in the domestic arts. Samplers, personal examples of needlework, proliferated in the early nineteenth century and won recognition for girls and young women. In sewing circles women of all ages came together. Here, as in church groups and female academies, women formed the friendships that strengthened the bonds of womanhood.

Needlework, deportment, reading, and writing were the principal subjects of female education. Girls who attended female academies embroidered samplers as part of their formal instruction. Many other girls, those who did not have the benefit of attending formal schools, were educated in the homes of local sewing mistresses. There young girls began working with needles as soon as they were able to hold them.

Beginning with ABCs and short verses and advancing to stitching that featured more difficult poems and phrases, girls mastered the rudiments of reading and writing in tandem with working samplers. Simple or elaborate, a sampler revealed its maker's artistry and was evidence of her educational accomplishments. The rich variety of surviving needlework from the first decades of the new nation reflects a golden age for this domestic art.

Sometimes samplers reveal society's changing expectations of young girls. Mary Newhall on the "Family Register" (listing the ten children born to her parents from 1793 to 1812) stitched a verse glorifying needlework: "And by my parents was taught / Not to spend my time for naught." Mary Bartlett, in her verse sewn about the same time, "blest the maid" whose "useful hours . . . glide. / The book, the needle and the pen divide." In other words, useful work for her included not only sewing but reading and writing, a reflection of the expanded ideas of the skills many in the new republic thought a girl needed.

Sampler worked by
Mary Newhall, age 14,
1812

Sampler worked by
Mary Bartlett, age 11,
1810

PORTRAIT OF AN AMERICAN

Lucy Calmes Wight

An early settler of Galena, Illinois, Lucy Calmes Wight (1802–95) was one of the many women who brought the culture of the new republic to the West.

Well before the Revolution, the Calmes family emigrated from France and settled in the Shenandoah Valley of Virginia, where Lucy was born. Her family soon moved to Kentucky, and the sampler she embroidered there reveals her schoolgirl accomplishments.

As a young newlywed in 1821, Lucy moved with her husband, Augustus Wight, to the new state of Illinois. They settled in Galena, a boomtown near the Mississippi River, in the center of a lead mining district.

Lucy set up her home and reared three children while her husband worked as a government supervisor for the mines. When she sat for her portrait, wearing a lace bonnet she very likely made, the Wights were leading citizens of the town.

She extended her domestic sphere beyond the home into the community. She helped establish Galena's First Baptist Church and founded one of its temperance societies. In her keepsake box, Lucy Calmes Wight preserved the treasures of a life that linked the early republic to the modern age.

Lucy Calmes Wight, artist unknown, c. 1830

Sampler worked by Lucy Calmes, age 9, 1811

Sewing box, c. 1790

Recovering Women's Lives

Because women are so often defined by their roles as daughters, wives, and mothers, historians have difficulty uncovering facts and details about their lives. To gain clues about women's lives we must look at what they made and used.

Lucy Calmes Wight left no written materials, but at least three of her possessions survived: a sampler she worked as a girl, her keepsake box, and a portrait of her painted by an itinerant folk artist. These odds and ends of Lucy's life were buried in a collection of artifacts and papers that documents the men in her life—her father, her husband, and her son-in-law. At the time of its purchase in the early 1920s, the collection was deemed significant because of the associations each of these men had with greater historical events and figures. Like most women, Lucy was known by different names at different times in her life, another difficulty in recovering women's lives. Within the museum, her things were dispersed and catalogued under maiden and married names.

When nine-year-old Lucy Neville Calmes stitched her name in her sampler in 1811, she was the daughter of Henrietta Neville and Marquis Calmes IV. We know little about her mother, but we know that her father was a captain in the Revolution and a brigadier general in the War of 1812. The man Lucy married, Col. Augustus Wight, was one of the government's first mine supervisors in Galena. Although Lucy outlived him by almost fifty years, she was identified only as "Mrs. Augustus Wight" when her portrait appeared in an exhibition of primitive art in 1950. The hand-painted keepsake box was catalogued under her maiden name, while the portrait was listed under her husband's name.

Madison Y. Johnson, Lucy's son-in-law, was a railroad lawyer and businessman in Galena whose claim to fame was as a Democratic politician and Southern sympathizer imprisoned during the Civil War. Lucy survived her prominent son-in-law by five years, but when she died at the age of ninety-three, her obituary in the local newspaper noted that she had died at "the residence of Madison Y. Johnson."

Stitching together the scattered bits and pieces Lucy left enabled us to unite the girl with the woman. Her full life still eludes us.

Throughout her life, Lucy probably kept her lace caps, sewing supplies, letters, and other personal possessions in this hand-painted chest.

Keepsake box, c. 1818

A Republican Spirit Among Craftsmen

Artisans expressed pride in themselves as citizens and craftsmen. "By Hammer and Hand all arts do stand" was the motto of the General Society of Mechanics and Tradesmen of New York City. This was their way of saying that the artisans' manual skills were indispensable to society. Mechanics paraded regularly on patriotic holidays, proud of the part they and their ancestors had played in the Revolution.

For master artisans, the period after the Revolution was a golden age, a time to fulfill their aspirations for personal independence. A skilled master, working alongside his journeymen and apprentices, would make an elegant chair or silver teapot, taking pride in the product that bore his name or mark. Craftsmen often incorporated the symbols of the new nation into their creations. Eagles were carved on furniture as well as on ships' bows. The cornucopia, symbol of plenty, was molded on a silver bowl.

The golden age passed quickly. To compete in an expanding market, workshops became little factories. Duncan Phyfe, the famous furniture maker, employed so many journeymen that no one can be quite sure who made a chair that bears his name. To protect themselves and to preserve the liberties their fathers had won in the Revolution, journeymen formed the first American trade unions.

Pride of craft had deep roots for artisans. In Britain traditionally each trade had its own guild, and each guild had its own arms. No guilds operated in America, but it was common for master craftsmen and journeymen to put the arms of their trade on flags, membership certificates, or commemorative pottery.

Detail of certificate of New York Mechanick's Society, 1795. Courtesy, The Historical Society of Pennsylvania, Philadelphia

Bowl with the motto:
"The Shipwright's
Arms," English, c. 1825

Craftsmen took pride in the antiquity of their trades. This bowl, with its print of the shipwright's arms, has a sailor to the left and a shipwright to the right, surrounding a picture of Noah's Ark. By biblical tradition Noah was considered the first shipwright.

Pitcher with the mottos:
"The Merchant-Taylors
Arms" and "Concordia
Parae Res Crescunt,"
English, 1802

A journeyman tailor worked for a master for wages. A master who no longer worked in the shop but collected the goods made by journeymen called himself a "merchant taylor." This Liverpool pitcher made for the American market features the traditional English guild symbol for this trade.

Pitcher with picture of a
sailing ship labeled "The
William and Jane" and
the motto "Success to a
Good Calker" "Joseph
Chaney," English, c. 1810

A caulker was the skilled artisan who filled the seams of wooden ships to make them waterproof. This pitcher was made to order for Joseph Chaney, probably at the request of his fellow craftsmen, to wish him well in retirement.

Jabez Briggs

These pages from an unsigned diary, written February 1 to May 31, 1791, provide a rare glimpse into the life of a country artisan as worker, citizen, churchgoer, husband, and father.

On the basis of clues in the diary he can be identified as Jabez Briggs (1760–?) of Sutton, Worcester County, in central Massachusetts.

Briggs's main business was making and repairing wheels for farmers' carts. His typical entry in the winter months was: "Worked in the shop."

Like other country artisans, Briggs was also a farmer. By mid-April, as the ground thawed, he sowed flax, barley, and wheat. He recorded the chores he did for others and they for him—"neighboring," as it was called in New England.

Man, he might have said, does not live by bread alone but by every word that comes from the mouth of God. He attended church faithfully on Sunday, where he heard Ebenezer Lamson, Sutton's Baptist preacher, expound on passages from the Bible. Briggs recorded each week's chapter and verse in his diary. A good citizen, he attended town meetings the first week of every month.

Some days were special. On March 8 he recorded "This Day I am 31 Years Old." On May 11 he wrote elatedly, "Had a SON, Born half past two morning."

Jabez Briggs did not stay in Sutton. By 1800 he and his family had moved to western Massachusetts. Doubtless he made the journey in a cart on wheels of his own making.

Engraving from Edward Hazen, *The Panorama of Professions and Trades* (Philadelphia, 1837)

March	2	Worked in the shop.
	6	Heard E.L. from James 2:5 and Malachi 3rd:7th.
	7	Went to Town Meeting.
	8	Worked in the shop. This Day I am 31 Years Old. . . .
	13	Was absent from Ch-h [Church]
	14	Worked in the shop
	15	Do [ditto, i.e., worked in the shop] David Fitts had two Wheels. Jonah Titus had a Wh.
	16	Worked in the shop Marble, And. Bigelow had two Wheels
	17	Went to Worcester after the Papers etc. . . .
	20	Heard E.L. from Psalm 16.8. . . .
	22	Worked in the shop. Went to Town meeting. . . .
	24	Do [ditto] My Cow calved. . . .
	27	Heard E.L. from Luke 9th ch. 23 verse
	28	Worked in the shop. Sold my Oxen to Saml Wallis for £8 f8 . . .
April	1	Worked in the shop . . .
	3	A Remarkable eclipse of the sun Heard E L from
	4	Sundry. Went to Town Meeting. had some flaxseed of Fath. had 11 lb. ¼ of Cheese of Jon. Put. . . .
	6	Sundry. Cleaned my flaxseed
	7	Hewed some Timber for a school House—(a snow)
	8	Worked in the shop
	9	Hewed timber for a school House . . .
	15	Finished a Woolen Wheele for Mother. went to Father . . .
	17	Heard E L from St. John 4th 8.
	18	Sowed some flaxseed east of the House and seeded it Down . . .
	21	Went to Worcester etc.—Burrows had his Trial
	22	Sowed some Oats etc.
	23	Sowed Barley wheat before the Barn and hay seed
	24	Heard E L from St. Mathew 5th, 14 Verse . . .
	28	Abner Sibley Laid some brick in my Great Room fireplace
	29	Plowed some for planting asa Putnam worked for me . . .
May	1	Heard E L from Romans 3-4 Ephes. 6th-13. it was [?]
	2	Drawed out Dung. Stephen Putnam worked for me . . .
	6	Worked in the shop making a Cart Body
	8	Heard E L from 145–19—Betty Whitmore was buried
	9	finished my Cart Body . . .
	11	Had a SON, Born half past two morning Anne Batch[ellor] . . .
	15	Heard E L from Heb 12-28 . . .
	25	Went to Brother Newcombs got my Coat and Breeches . . .

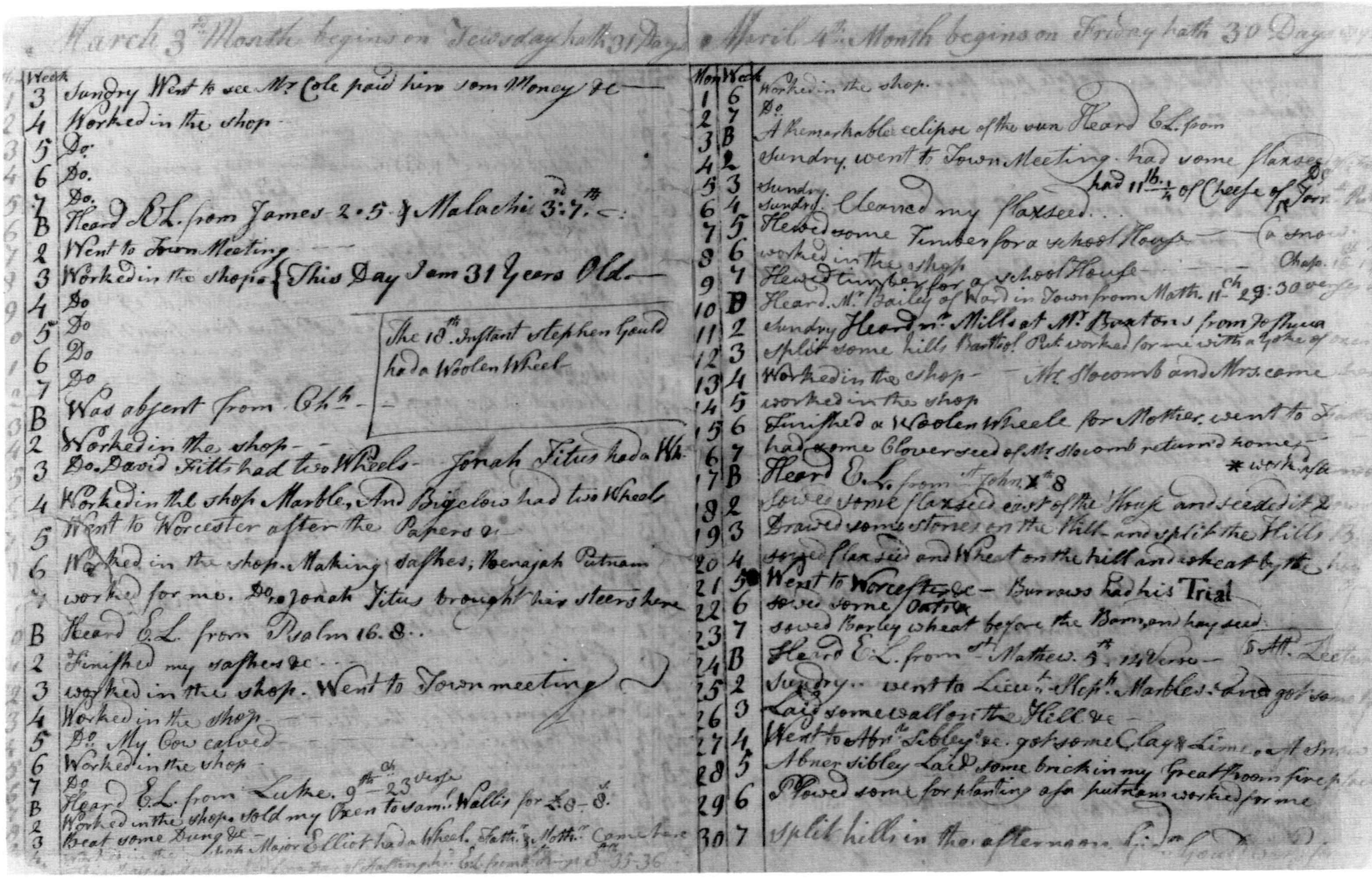

Diary of Jabez Briggs,
excerpts from entries
March through May 1791

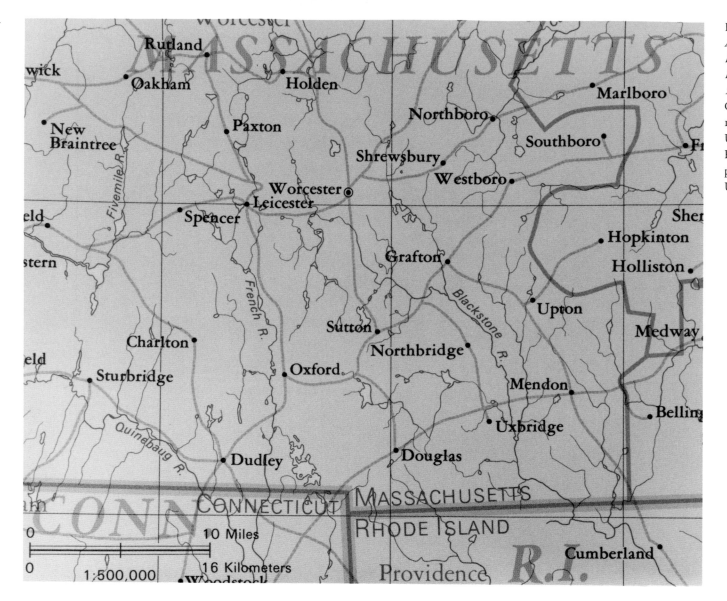

Detail from Map #3, *Atlas of Early American History: The Revolutionary Era, 1760–1790*, ed. Lester J. Cappon. Copyright © 1976 by Princeton University Press. Reproduced by permission of Princeton University Press

On the Trail of an Unknown Diarist

To identify Jabez Briggs of Sutton, Massachusetts, as the author of this diary, the historian and museum curator must play detective. The four-page diary in the Chicago Historical Society manuscript collections was without the name or the location of the writer.

Identifying the town came first. There were three clues. The author was a wheelwright and farmer and mentioned going to Worcester and back in one day. He listed the names of a dozen people for whom he worked or who worked for him, and identified the preacher he heard on Sundays as "E.L." Referring to an eighteenth-century map of Massachusetts, we drew a circle with Worcester at the center to encompass the towns within ten miles, which gave us the names of nine towns. We then turned to the 1790 federal census—the diary entries are all for 1791—to see in which of these towns we could locate some of the listed names. This turned out to be Sutton. We then confirmed Sutton by checking a list of Baptist ministers for Massachusetts, identifying "E.L." as Ebenezer Lamson, pastor of the Sutton Baptist Church.

Identifying the author was more difficult. The author provided one excellent clue: he noted the birth of his son for May 11, 1791. We then asked the present town clerk of Sutton to check birth records for 1791, which fortunately still exist. For May 11, 1791, the clerk reported the birth of James Briggs to Jabez and Lucy Briggs. We had found our man. The town's vital records then confirmed that Jabez Briggs had married Lucy Batchellor in 1787, and they had a daughter, Sylvia, in 1788. The Briggses were also listed in the census for Sutton for 1790 but not thereafter. The 1800 Massachusetts census located them in the western part of the state in Hampshire County. The rest of their lives must be left to others to reconstruct.

Wheelwright's mallet,
c. 1800

EPILOGUE

Nourishing the Tree of Liberty

This painting of New Orleans was completed in 1803, the year the United States acquired the vast Louisiana territory from France. This acquisition more than doubled the size of the nation. In the painting, the American flag flies in the port. The artist spread a banner carried by an eagle across the top of the painting. The motto, "Under My Wings Every Thing Prospers" expresses the optimism and nationalism of the American audience for whom he intended the picture.

Boqueto de Woieseri, the artist, described himself as a "designer, drawer, geographer, and engineer." He lived and worked in New Orleans for many years. In 1804 colored engravings of his painting, dedicated to President Thomas Jefferson, were sold in Philadelphia for ten dollars.

In negotiations with France, American leaders sought a port that would guarantee an outlet for ocean-bound produce from the West that came down the Mississippi River. The city portrayed in the painting is exactly that. In this busy seaport, ships fill the harbor.

When the United States took over the city in March 1804, a contemporary wrote that it had "about one thousand houses and eight thousand inhabitants including blacks and people of color." Who prospered under the eagle's wings? The merchants and plantation owners who lived in the elegant houses and walked down the broad promenade near the waterfront clearly prospered. The same could hardly be said of the slaves and "people of color" whom the artist depicted in the foreground going about their daily work.

From the beginning the Revolution held out promises. The Declaration of Independence of 1776, in justifying a revolution from Great Britain, proclaimed fundamental ideals: that "all men are created equal, that they are endowed by their Creator with certain unalienable Rights, that among these are Life, Liberty and the pursuit of Happiness" and that governments were founded on "the consent of the governed" to protect these "unalienable rights." Fifty years later, in the mid-1820s, what had the nation and ordinary people made of these ideals? To what extent had they been achieved?

It is difficult to answer almost any question about ordinary people. The evidence is often elusive. History tends to record the success stories of famous people.

We know what happened to General Washington; we do not know what happened to the two dozen farmers who signed the Tryon County, New York, militia list with their *X*s in 1775. We know what happened to Capt. John Paul Jones, but we do not know the fate of the seventy-nine ordinary seamen on the list who received prize money after the victory of *Bonhomme Richard* in 1779.

What happened, we should ask, to the two hundred thousand men who served in the army or the militia in the Revolution? We know that about twenty-five thousand died, and we assume that another twenty-five thousand were wounded. In 1818, when Congress passed the first general pension act, restricted to veterans "in the lowest grade of poverty," twenty thousand veterans applied, and eighteen thousand met this test. Two out of three of these veterans reported that they worked as laborers, worked as tenant farmers, or had no occupation. What happened to the twenty thousand or so women who, as laundresses, cooks, and nurses, served as an unofficial quartermaster corps and did not qualify for pensions?

How can we learn more about the meaning of the Revolution for ordinary people? By looking at the individuals whose lives we have attempted to flesh out in this book, we gain some good clues about others.

James Pike, Danforth Armour, Chapman Forseth, and Andrew Sherburne

If Americans were unfree, they aspired to freedom; if they were free, they sought the means to personal independence. In an economy of agriculture, commerce, and handicraft manufactures, independence was measured by owning land or becoming master of a trade or shop. For would-be farmers and artisans, the early decades of the new nation were, in many ways, a golden age.

The opening of new lands to settlement expanded the opportunities for farmers to acquire land. By 1820 almost two million people lived west of the Appalachian Mountains. The eleven states that had entered the Union since 1789 were frontier states: two in New England (Vermont and Maine), three in the Northwest (Ohio, Illinois, and Indiana), and six in the South—four east of the Mississippi (Kentucky, Tennessee, Mississippi, and Alabama), and two west of the Mississippi (Louisiana and Missouri). All of them were inhabited by men and women seeking a new life.

Farmers, wrote Thomas Jefferson, were "the chosen people of God if ever he had a chosen people." But the blessings of heaven rained unevenly. James Pike, who carved "The Liberty Tree" on his powder horn, made a go of it as a farmer in New Hampshire. Danforth Armour, owner of the wooden plow his forebears used to till the rocky soil of Connecticut, moved to western New York, where he thrived. But Chapman Forseth, the Connecticut schoolteacher who took his grandfather's advice to go where land was "yet Cheap" and moved to New York, became ill and returned to Connecticut to die. Andrew Sherburne, who went to sea during the war and who wrote an angry autobiography at the end of his life, found the land he was entitled to in Ohio worthless, and he abandoned the frontier.

As commerce and manufacturing expanded there were more opportunities for some artisans, often at the expense of others. Paul Revere, silversmith and engraver, became the owner of a brass and copper factory with many employees. Duncan Phyfe, the furniture maker whose beautiful chairs adorned the homes of the rich, prospered, but the several scores of journeymen he employed to make the chairs found it harder to make the leap from wage earner to master. What happened to Jabez Briggs, the wheelwright, when he moved from Sutton to western Massachusetts is hard to say. No one has traced the careers of the artisans listed in the Philadelphia city directory on the same page with "George Washington, President" to find out who did well and who ended up in the poorhouse.

Paul Revere, Duncan Phyfe, and Jabez Briggs

Landed expansion, which brought opportunity to large numbers of free white farmers and artisans as well as merchants and plantation owners, was at the expense of people of color.

Independence for the United States from Great Britain meant that American Indians had to fight for their independence from the United States. Indians took different paths to survive.

Joseph Brant, Red Jacket, and Tecumseh

Joseph Brant, who was portrayed with the silver armlet that was bestowed upon him by his British allies, won land from the British for the Mohawks in Canada. Red Jacket, who was portrayed with the silver medal that was bestowed upon him by President Washington, saw the Senecas reduced to living on a reservation, and he was unsuccessful in resisting the efforts of missionaries to convert them to Protestantism.

Indians of the Northwest fought American armies to a standstill, fought again and lost, and fought once more. We cannot say what happened to the ninety chieftains who signed the Treaty of Greenville in 1795. Only a minority of American Indians willingly became the yeoman farmers that the peace medal idealized. The Prophet led his people in a cultural renaissance to resist the white people's ways. His brother Tecumseh led Indians in military resistance. Both were defeated. The nations that became "civilized," like the Cherokees in the South, fared no better. By the mid-1820s the United States moved toward a new and drastic solution to the American Indian problem: the removal of the eastern Indian nations to the vast expanses beyond the Mississippi.

Hannah Harris, Arch, and Paul Cuffe

For African Americans the expansion of white southern pioneers into the Mississippi valley meant the vast expansion of slavery. By 1820, 1.5 million slaves lived in the United States. Two hundred and fifty thousand had been moved from the Old South to the new western South, and one hundred thousand had been imported from Africa before the ban on the slave trade in 1807.

Slavery was banned in the Northwest and had all but disappeared in the Northeast. Phillis Wheatley lived to 1784, just long enough to see a black woman successfully sue to abolish slavery in Massachusetts. Hannah Harris, the weaver, obtained her freedom from Robert Carter in 1793. It would be satisfying to think that she got her loom, and that Arch, the runaway Maryland slave, made his escape to freedom in 1791. Hannah and Arch lived in the Upper South, but in the Deep South manumission was uncommon, and running away was far more difficult.

Free African Americans were only halfway free. Paul Cuffe had to fight for the principle of "no taxation without representation" in Massachusetts and, when he died, the richest African American in America, he was buried in a segregated section of a Quaker cemetery. Discrimination and segregation were common in the North. The names of the free black families who chose to take the ship *Nautilus* to Africa are a stark reminder of the unfulfilled ideal of equality.

The ideal of the Declaration for a government deriving its "just powers from the consent of the governed" was carried beyond the expectations of most framers of the Declaration. Government by "the consent of the governed" grew. The Constitution of 1787 established a republican government that allowed for the states to expand suffrage. The Bill of Rights put into the Constitution liberties that the people expanded in rejecting the Sedition Law. The guarantee of the Northwest Ordinance that new states would enter the Union on "an equal footing" with the old states was fulfilled.

The concept of consent of the governed broadened, as did the ideas of republicanism. The states expanded suffrage to include most male property holders, then male taxpayers, moving toward universal male suffrage. Equally important, men exercised their citizenship by voting, by participating in politics, and by expressing their ideas in newspapers. To the wheelwright Jabez Briggs, republicanism meant participating in the town meeting and attending the church of his choice. To Irish-born Matthew Lyon, a former indentured servant elected to Congress, republicanism meant the right to hold elected office—regardless of birth or class—and the right to freedom of speech and freedom of the press. To the butchers and other artisans who paraded in Philadelphia and other American cities on festival days, it meant the democratic ideal: "I am as good as any other man."

Thomas Paine, with his confidence in the common sense of the common people, would have been pleased. John Adams, with far less confidence, would have had mixed feelings.

Matthew Lyon and the Butchers of Philadelphia

Many women found their own voices in the revolutionary era. Deborah Sampson disguised herself as a man to fight in the war, but afterward she claimed a pension in her own name. Before the war Mercy Otis Warren hid behind a pseudonym in her political writings; in 1805 she published her three-volume history of the Revolution in her own name and was not afraid to criticize male leaders, such as John Adams.

Although male Americans expanded suffrage to include white men without property, they granted women only a second-class citizenship. John Adams would hear nothing of Abigail's plea to end the "tyranny" of husbands over their wives. But he agreed that in a republic, mothers who were responsible for educating their sons as citizens should be better educated.

Few paths were open to the girls who embroidered the beautiful samplers that grace these pages. They would have more years of schooling than their mothers, and some would become

Deborah Sampson Gannett,
Mercy Otis Warren,
Emma Willard, and
Lucy Calmes Wight

schoolteachers. Emma Willard became the founder of a "female academy" and the author of school textbooks. Poor girls became seamstresses in the cities or minders of looms in New England textile factories. Lucy Calmes Wight, who moved from Kentucky to Galena, Illinois, with her husband, typified the middle-class woman who flourished in the "domestic sphere."

In this generation, very few Americans saw the inconsistency of making the female goddess Liberty the symbol of the nation while denying the "rights of women."

The Promise of the Declaration

Thus half a century after 1776, the ideals of the Declaration had been won by some but not by others. Success for many white Americans was built on the conquest of American Indians and the expansion of slavery of African Americans. The majority of white male Americans defined citizenship to exclude both groups. And by defining the "public sphere" as male and the "domestic sphere" as female, they confined women to second-class citizenship.

Wherever the ideals of the Declaration were not achieved, they remained an incitement for others to fulfill them. In 1829 journeymen workers in New York City adopted their own declaration of independence, declaring that their employers "have robbed us of certain rights." On Cape Cod, when the Mashpee Indians faced physical removal by the state of Massachusetts, they argued that "we as a tribe will rule ourselves, and have a right to do so; for all men are born free and equal, says the Constitution of the country." When women met in Seneca Falls, New York, in 1848 at the first Women's Rights Convention, they worded their grievances in the language of the Declaration of Independence. "We hold these truths to be self-evident: that all men and women are created equal."

African Americans were heirs to this same ambiguous heritage. After the Revolution a prominent white Virginian observed that in 1775 runaway slaves who joined the British "fought for freedom merely as a good; now they also claim it as a right." In 1800 Gabriel and his fellow slave artisans plotted a slave insurrection in Richmond, Virginia, as did Denmark Vesey in 1820 in Charleston, South Carolina. In 1829 David Walker, a black leader, wrote, "See your Declaration, Americans. . . . Do you understand your own language?" In the years before the Civil War, the prominent black abolitionist Frederick Douglass asked: "What to the American slave is your 4th of July? . . . Are the great principles of political freedom and natural rights embodied in your Declaration of Independence extended to us?"

The Tree of Liberty that James Pike and Nathan Plummer had carved on their powder horns in the Revolution continued to grow. In 1786, Capt. Daniel Shays, a veteran of the Revolution, led a rebellion of Massachusetts debtor farmers, who feared losing their land. At that time, Thomas Jefferson reflected that "the tree of liberty must be refreshed from time to time with the blood of patriots and tyrants." When William C. Nell completed *The Colored Patriots of the American Revolution* (1855), the first book of its kind, he was convinced that the Revolution of 1776 "yet left the necessity for a second revolution . . . in favor of Universal Brotherhood." "Colored Patriots" were ready to become "Patriots of the Second Revolution" as they had been in the first Revolution. They hoped to "nourish the tree of liberty, that all may be enabled to pluck fruit from its bending branches."

Discovering the role ordinary people have played in nourishing the Tree of Liberty in the past is one way to keep it alive for the future.

The Tree of Liberty

For Further Reading

The following books and articles provide additional information on the subjects and themes of the book. Many are available in local libraries; many are in paperback editions.

General

Short Books

Countryman, Edward. *The American Revolution.* New York, 1985.

Henretta, James A., and Gregory H. Nobles. *Evolution and Revolution: American Society, 1600–1820.* Lexington, Mass., 1987.

Morgan, Edmund S. *The Birth of the Republic, 1763–89.* Chicago, 1956. Rev. ed. 1977.

Longer Accounts

Alden, John R. *A History of the American Revolution.* New York, 1989.

Jensen, Merrill. *The Founding of a Nation, 1763–1776.* New York, 1968.

Middlekauff, Robert. *The Glorious Cause: The American Revolution, 1763–1789.* New York, 1985.

Interpretations

Becker, Carl. *The Spirit of '76 and Other Essays.* New York, 1942.

Greene, Jack P., ed. *The American Revolution: Its Character and Limits.* New York, 1988.

Jameson, J. Franklin. *The American Revolution Considered as a Social Movement.* Princeton, N.J., 1940.

Kurtz, Stephen, and James Hutson, eds. *Essays on the American Revolution.* Chapel Hill, N.C., 1973.

Lemisch, Jesse. "The American Revolution Seen from the Bottom Up." In *Towards a New Past,* edited by Barton Bernstein. New York, 1968.

Wood, Gordon S. *The Radicalism of the American Revolution.* New York, 1992.

Young, Alfred F., ed. *The American Revolution: Explorations in the History of American Radicalism.* DeKalb, Ill., 1976.

——. *Beyond the American Revolution: Explorations in the History of American Radicalism.* Dekalb, Ill., 1993.

Encyclopedias and Atlases

Boater, Mark. *Encyclopedia of the American Revolution.* New York, 1974.

Cappon, Lester J. *Atlas of Early American History: The Revolutionary Era, 1760–1790.* Princeton, N.J., 1975.

Morris, Richard B., et al. *Encyclopedia of American History.* 6th ed. New York, 1982.

Original Sources

Commager, Henry S., ed. *Documents of American History.* 8th ed. New York, 1969.

Jensen, Merrill, ed. *English Historical Documents: American Colonial Documents to 1776.* New York, 1955.

——. *Tracts of the American Revolution, 1763–1776.* Indianapolis, 1967.

Morris, Richard, and Henry S. Commager, eds. *The Spirit of '76: The Story of the American Revolution as Told by Participants.* New York, 1976.

Illustrated Histories

American Heritage. *Book of the American Revolution*. New York, 1971.

——. *History of the Thirteen Colonies*. New York, 1967.

DePauw, Linda, and Conover Hunt. *Remember the Ladies: Women in America, 1750–1815*. New York, 1976.

Jones, Michael. *The Cartoon History of the American Revolution*. New York, 1975.

Josephy, Alvin. *American Heritage Book of the Indians*. New York, 1961.

Kaplan, Sidney, and Emma Nogrady Kaplan. *The Black Presence in the Era of the American Revolution*. Rev. ed. Amherst, Mass., 1989.

Songs of the Era

Brand, Oscar. *Songs of '76: A Folksinger's History of the Revolution*. New York, 1972.

Lawrence, Vera Brodsky. *Music for Patriots, Politicians and Presidents*. New York, 1975.

Moore, Frank, and Peter Decker, eds. *Songs and Ballads of the American Revolution*. 1856. Reprint. Salem, N.H., 1969.

Introduction: Remembering the American Revolution

Historical Scholarship

Fitzgerald, Francis. *America Revised: History Schoolbooks in the Twentieth Century*. Boston, 1980.

Kammen, Michael. *A Season of Youth: The American Revolution and the Historical Imagination*. New York, 1978.

Kerber, Linda K. "The Revolutionary Generation." In *The New American History*, edited by Eric Foner. Philadelphia, 1990.

History in Museums

Benson, Susan, Steven Brier, and Roy Rosenzweig, eds. *Presenting the Past: Essays on History and the Public*. Philadelphia, 1986.

Janzen, Mary E. "Collaborative Risk-Taking: Making 'We the People' at the Chicago Historical Society." *Journal of Popular Culture* 12:2 (1989): 67–77.

Leon, Warren, and Roy Rosenzweig, eds. *History Museums in the United States: A Critical Assessment*. Urbana, Ill., 1989.

Young, Alfred F. "An Historian as Museum Curator." *Perspectives: American Historical Association Newsletter* 26:7 (1988): 1, 4–6.

——. " 'Ordinary People' in Great Events: An American Museum Experience." *History Workshop* 32 (1991): 211–17.

Chapter 1: A Diverse and Aspiring People

Bailyn, Bernard. *Voyagers to the West: A Passage in the Peopling of America on the Eve of the Revolution*. New York, 1986.

Franklin, John Hope. *From Slavery to Freedom: A History of Negro Americans*. 5th ed. New York, 1979.

Hawke, David F. *Everyday Life in Early America*. New York, 1988.

Hofstadter, Richard. *America at 1750: A Social History*. New York, 1971.

Nash, Gary. *Red, White, and Black: The Peoples of Early America*. 3d ed. Englewood Cliffs, N.J., 1991.

——. *The Urban Crucible: Social Change, Political Consciousness, and the Origins of the American Revolution, 1690–1776*. Cambridge, Mass., 1979.

Smith, Barbara Clark. *After the Revolution: The Smithsonian History of Everyday Life in the Eighteenth Century*. New York, 1985.

Ulrich, Laurel T. *Good Wives: Image and Reality in the Lives of Women in Northern New England, 1650–1750*. New York, 1982.

——. *A Midwife's Tale: The Life of Martha Ballard, Based on Her Diary, 1775–1812*. New York, 1990.

Chapter 2: The Road to Revolution

Anthony, Katherine. *First Lady of the Revolution: The Life of Mercy Otis Warren*. New York, 1958.

Bowen, Catherine Drinker. *John Adams and the American Revolution*. Boston, 1949.

Chinard, Gilbert. *Honest John Adams*. Boston, 1933.

Forbes, Esther. *Paul Revere and the World He Lived In*. Boston, 1972.

Maier, Pauline. *The Old Revolutionaries: Political Lives in the Age of Samuel Adams*. New York, 1980.

Morgan, Edmund S., and Helen M. Morgan. *The Stamp Act Crisis: Prologue to Revolution*. Rev. ed. New York, 1963.

Schlesinger, Arthur M., Jr. *Prelude to Independence: The Newspaper War on Britain, 1764–1776*. New York, 1957.

Chapter 3: Declaring Independence

Becker, Carl. *The Declaration of Independence.* New York, 1922.

Foner, Eric. *Tom Paine and Revolutionary America.* New York, 1976.

Jensen, Merrill. *The American Revolution within America.* New York, 1974.

Malone, Dumas, Hirst Milhollen, and Milton Kaplan. *The Story of the Declaration of Independence.* New York, 1954.

Paine, Thomas. *Common Sense.* Philadelphia, 1776. (Many modern reprints are available.)

Wills, Garry. *Inventing America: Jefferson's Declaration of Independence.* New York, 1979.

Chapter 4: Winning the War

General

Flexner, James T. *Washington: The Indispensable Man.* Boston, 1974.

Higginbotham, Don C. *The War of American Independence.* New York, 1971.

Hoffman, Ronald, and Peter J. Albert, eds. *Arms and Independence: The Military Character of the American Revolution.* Charlottesville, Va., 1984.

Soldiers and Sailors

Gross, Robert. *The Minutemen and Their World.* New York, 1976.

Moore, Warren. *Weapons of the American Revolution.* New York, 1967.

Morison, Samuel Eliot. *John Paul Jones: A Sailor's Biography.* Boston, 1959.

Peterson, Harold. *The Book of the Continental Soldier.* Harrisburg, Pa., 1968.

Women

Ellet, Elizabeth F. *The Women of the American Revolution.* 3 vols. New York, 1848–50. Reprint. New York, 1969.

Hoffman, Ronald, and Peter J. Albert, eds. *Women in the Age of the American Revolution.* Charlottesville, Va., 1989.

Kerber, Linda K. *Women of the Republic: Intellect and Ideology in Revolutionary America.* Chapel Hill, N.C., 1980.

Norton, Mary Beth. *Liberty's Daughters: The Revolutionary Experience of American Women, 1750–1800.* Boston, 1980.

African Americans

Berlin, Ira, and Ronald Hoffman, eds. *Slavery and Freedom in the Age of the American Revolution.* Charlottesville, Va., 1986.

Mason, Julian, Jr., ed. *The Poems of Phillis Wheatley.* Chapel Hill, N.C., 1989.

Nell, William C. *The Colored Patriots of the American Revolution.* Boston, 1855. Reprint. New York, 1968.

Quarles, Benjamin. *The Negro in the American Revolution.* Chapel Hill, N.C., 1961.

Robinson, William H. *Phillis Wheatley and Her Writing.* New York, 1984.

American Indians

Graymont, Barbara. *The Iroquois in the American Revolution.* Syracuse, N.Y., 1972.

Hagan, William T. *American Indians.* Rev. ed. Chicago, 1979

Hoxie, Frederick, ed. *Indians in American History.* Arlington Heights, Ill., 1988.

Kelsay, Isabel Thompson. *Joseph Brant, 1743–1807: Man of Two Worlds.* Syracuse, N.Y., 1984.

Tanner, Helen H., ed. *Atlas of Great Lakes Indian History.* Norman, Okla., 1987.

Washburn, Wilcomb. *The Indian in America.* New York, 1975.

Chapter 5: The Constitution and Bill of Rights

Original Sources

Elliot, Jonathan. *The Debates in the Several State Conventions on the Adoption of the Federal Constitution. . . .* 5 vols. 1st ed. Washington, D.C., 1836.

Hamilton, Alexander, James Madison, and John Jay. *The Federalist.* New York, 1788. (Many modern reprints are available.)

Jensen, Merrill, et al., eds. *The Documentary History of the Ratification of the Constitution.* 9 vols. to date. Madison, Wis., 1976.–

Kaminski, John P., and Richard Leffler, eds. *Federalists and Anti-Federalists: The Debate over the Ratification of the Constitution.* Madison, Wis., 1989.

Storing, Herbert J., and Murray Dry, eds. *The Complete Anti-Federalist.* 7 vols. Chicago, 1981.

Historical Accounts

Brant, Irving. *The Bill of Rights: Its Origin and Meaning.* Indianapolis, 1965.

Goldwin, Robert A., and William A. Schambra, eds. *How Democratic Is the Constitution?* Washington, D.C., 1980.

Kammen, Michael. *A Machine That Would Go of Itself: The Constitution in American Culture.* New York, 1986.

Levy, Leonard W. *Emergence of a Free Press.* New York, 1985.

Morris, Richard B. *The Forging of the Union, 1781–1789.* New York, 1987.

Storing, Herbert J. *What the Anti-Federalists Were For: The Political Thought of the Opponents of the Constitution.* Chicago, 1981.

Wills, Garry. *Explaining America: The Federalist.* Garden City, N.Y., 1982.

Chapter 6: The Republic in Action

Austin, Aleine. *Matthew Lyon: "New Man" of the Democratic Revolution, 1749–1822.* University Park, Pa., 1980.

Cunliffe, Marcus. *The Nation Takes Shape, 1789–1837.* Chicago, 1960.

Lamont, Thomas. *Rise to Be a People: A Biography of Paul Cuffe.* Urbana, Ill., 1986.

Miller, John C. *The Federalist Era, 1789–1801.* New York, 1960.

Morgan, Edmund S. *The Meaning of Independence: John Adams, George Washington, Thomas Jefferson.* New York, 1978.

Peterson, Merrill D. *Adams and Jefferson: A Revolutionary Dialogue.* New York, 1978.

——. *Thomas Jefferson and the New Nation: A Biography.* New York, 1986.

Young, Alfred F. *The Democratic Republicans of New York: The Origins, 1763–1797.* Chapel Hill, N.C., 1967.

Chapter 7: The Republic Moves West

Land and Government

Buley, R. Carlyle. *The Old Northwest: Pioneer Period: 1815–1840.* 2 vols. Bloomington, Ind., 1950.

Horsman, Reginald. *The Frontier in the Formative Years, 1763–1815.* New York, 1970.

Liberty's Legacy: Our Celebration of the Northwest Ordinance and the United States Constitution. Columbus, Ohio, 1987.

Onuf, Peter S. *Statehood and Union: A History of the Northwest Ordinance.* Bloomington, Ind., 1987.

Pease, Theodore C. *The Story of Illinois.* Chicago, 1965.

Philbrick, Francis S. *The Rise of the West, 1754–1830.* New York, 1965.

American Indians

Berkhofer, Robert F., Jr. *The White Man's Indian: Images of the Indian from Columbus to the Present.* New York, 1979.

Dowd, Gregory Evans. *A Spirited Resistance: The North American Indian Struggle for Unity, 1745–1815.* Baltimore, 1992.

Drinnon, Richard. *Facing West: The Metaphysics of Indian Hating and Empire Building.* New York, 1980.

Edmunds, R. David. *Tecumseh and the Quest for Indian Leadership.* Boston, 1984.

——. *The Shawnee Prophet* [Tenskwatawa]. Lincoln, Nebr., 1983.

Wallace, Anthony F. C. *The Death and Rebirth of the Seneca.* New York, 1969.

Chapter 8: Creating an American Culture

Literature and the Arts

Ellis, Joseph J. *After the Revolution: Profiles of Early American Culture.* New York, 1981.

Silverman, Kenneth. *A Cultural History of the American Revolution.* New York, 1986.

Symbols for a New Nation

Fox, Nancy. *Liberties with Liberty: The Fascinating History of America's Proudest Symbol.* New York, 1986.

Furlong, William, and Byron McCandless. *So Proudly We Hail: The History of the United States Flag.* Washington, D.C., 1981.

Horwitz, Elinor Lander. *The Bird, the Banner, and Uncle Sam.* Philadelphia, 1976.

Mastai, Boleslaw, and Marie-Louise D'Otrange. *The Stars and Stripes.* New York, 1973.

Veterans Remember the Revolution

Dann, John C., ed. *The Revolution Remembered: Eyewitness Accounts of the War for Independence.* Chicago, 1980.

Overton, Albert G. "David Kennison and the Chicago Sting." Typescript in Chicago Historical Society Collection. 9 pages. 1976.

Young, Alfred F. "George Robert Twelves Hewes (1742–1840): A Boston Shoemaker and the Memory of the American Revolution." *William and Mary Quarterly* 38 (1981): 561–623.

George Washington Becomes a Legend

Cunliffe, Marcus. *George Washington, Man and Monument*. New York, 1958.

Schwartz, Barry. *George Washington: The Making of an American Symbol*. Ithaca, N.Y., 1987.

Wecter, Dixon. *The Hero in America: A Chronicle of Hero Worship*. New York, 1941.

Wick, Wendy. *George Washington, an American Icon: The Eighteenth-Century Graphic Portraits*. Washington, D.C., 1982.

Wills, Garry. *Cincinnatus: George Washington and the Enlightenment*. Garden City, N.Y., 1984.

The Domestic Arts Flourish

Ring, Betty. *Let Virtue Be a Guide to Thee: Needlework in the Education of Rhode Island Women, 1730–1830*. Providence, R.I., 1983.

Swan, Susan. *Plain and Fancy: American Women and Their Needlework, 1700–1850*. New York, 1977.

A Republican Spirit in the Crafts

Laurie, Bruce. *Artisans into Workers: Labor in Nineteenth-Century America*. New York, 1989.

Pugh, Ralph. "Rescuing an Early American Artisan Diarist from Anonymity" [Jabez Briggs]. *National Genealogical Society Quarterly* 78:1 (1990): 33–38.

Rorabaugh, W. J. *The Craft Apprentice from Franklin to the Machine Age in America*. New York, 1986.

Wilentz, Sean. *Chants Democratic: New York City and the Rise of the American Working Class, 1788–1850*. New York, 1986.

In most works of history the authors include a bibliography of the original or primary sources on which they based their research. This work is based on original sources found in the Chicago Historical Society and assembled for the exhibition, *We the People: Creating a New Nation, 1765–1820*. The checklist that follows includes all of the objects on exhibit, most of which have been incorporated into this book. Readers who want to envision an object more clearly can find here its dimensions and what it is made of. The catalogue number is to assist readers who want more information, which may be available in the Society's files.

A Diverse and Aspiring People

A Map of the British and French Dominions in North America, 1st edition, 3d impression
Map
by John Mitchell (London, 1755)
Ink on paper
54 x 7 1/2 in. (137 x 19 cm.)

Penn's Treaty with the Indians, 1682
Painting
by Benjamin West, c. 1771
Oil on panel
17 1/8 x 23 7/8 in. (43 x 61 cm.)
1948.10
Gift of Mrs. Emily Crane Chadbourne

Wampum
c. 1820
Shell, thread, silk, tobacco
15 in. (38 cm.)
x.1201

Indian apron
Great Lakes region, c. 1760
Buckskin, porcupine quills, silver, dyed deer-tail hairs, feathers
16 x 23 1/2 in. (41 x 60 cm.)
1920.702
The Charles F. Gunther Collection

A Narrative of the Life of Mrs. Mary Jemison
Book
by James E. Seaver (London: Howden, 1826)
Ink on paper
6 x 3 3/4 in. (15 x 9 cm.)

Paneling from Dickinson farmhouse
Salem County, New Jersey, 1754
Pine
104 1/2 x 173 in. (265 x 439 cm.)
1945.2
Gift of Mr. and Mrs. Joseph M. Cudahy

Artisan's half-apron
c. 1800
Leather
31 1/4 x 27 in. (79 x 69 cm.)
1968.590ab

Blacksmith's anvil
c. 1810
Iron, wood
18 3/4 x 11 in. diameter (48 x 28 cm.)
x.1468

Blacksmith's tools
c. 1810
Iron
Hoop tongs: 19 1/2 in. (50 cm.)
Hollow bit tongs: 22 1/2 in. (57 cm.)

Exhibition Checklist

Woman's pocket
c. 1775
Patchwork and calico
14 x 11 in. (36 x 28 cm.)
XA1588
Gift of Otto L. Schmidt

Woman's pocket
c. 1775
Patchwork and printed cotton
15 1/2 x 11 in. (39 x 28 cm.)
XA1527

Christening dress of Joseph Williams, born March 29, 1779
1779
Printed linen
28 in. shoulder to hem (71 cm.)
2380-27H
Gift of the estate of Anna P. Williams

Infant's dress
c. 1800
Striped cotton
28 1/2 in. (72 cm.)
B270
The Charles F. Gunther Collection

Doll
c. 1795
Wood, kid leather, linen
23 in. (58 cm.)
1952.47
Gift of Mrs. Barton S. Snow

Cradle
c. 1830
Pine
37 x 18 x 30 1/2 in. (94 x 46 x 77 cm.)
XA87

Chest
Dutch, 1660
Wood, iron
16 1/4 x 10 1/4 x 10 1/4 in. (41 x 26 x 26 cm.)
1920.884
The Charles F. Gunther Collection

Chair, inscribed "G. Keller 1784"
1784
Maple, walnut, reed
36 x 21 x 17 in. (91 x 53 x 43 cm.)
1938.102a
Gift of the estate of Carrie Ryerson

Farmer's sickle
c. 1820
Iron, wood
24 in. (61 cm.)
DA1933.27

Ledger book
Roderick Chyne's Maryland tavern, 1759–62
Ink on paper
12 5/8 x 7 5/8 in. (32 x 19 cm.)

Coins
Silver dollar, 1798
Penny, Vermont, 1787
x.1477
Penny, Vermont, 1786
x.1479
Penny, New Jersey, 1787
x.1480
"Fugio" cent, 1787

Pocket inkwell
c. 1815
Brass, glass, quill
4 1/4 x 1 1/8 x 3/4 in. (11 x 3 x 2 cm.)
1924.16abc
Gift of Helen W. Boyden

Pocket inkwell
c. 1815
Brass, glass, quill
4 3/8 x 1 1/8 x 3/4 in. (11 x 3 x 2 cm.)
1927.9abc
Gift of Mary Shinn Perry

Baby mug
English, 1808
Silver
2 in. (5 cm.)
1974.114
Gift of the estate of Elizabeth Price Welch

Child's porringer
c. 1810
Pewter
1 3/4 x 5 in. (4 x 13 cm.)
1937.45
Gift of Samuella Crosby

Child's porringer
c. 1790
Pewter
2 x 5 1/2 in. (5 x 14 cm.)
1920.382
The Charles F. Gunther Collection

Puzzle
English, c. 1820
Wood
1 7/8 in. square (5 cm.)
1957.239
Gift of Mrs. William T. Priestley and
Mrs. Morgan Reichner

A Little Pretty Pocket-Book, Intended for the Instruction and Amusement of Little Master Tommy and Pretty Miss Polly, **the 1st Worcester edition**
Book
by Isaiah Thomas, 1787
Wood covers, leather spine, ink on paper
4 1/4 x 2 1/2 in. (11 x 6 cm.)

Sampler
by Sally Maynard, age 10, 1786
Linen
9 1/2 x 7 in. (24 x 18 cm.)
x.1232

Sampler
by Polly Ran, 1798
Homespun
9 7/8 x 8 7/8 in. (25 x 23 cm.)
x.1234

Slave shackles
Date unknown
Iron
16 1/2 in. (42 cm.)
x.1461
9 1/2 in. (24 cm.)
x.1462

"A Division of the Negros made, and agreed to between Colo. George Lee, and the Brothers of the deceased Majr. Lawrence Washington"
Manuscript
December 10, 1754
Ink on paper
13 x 8 1/4 in. (33 x 21 cm.)

Indenture apprenticing Jaques Rapalje to William Faulkner to learn the "Brewing, Malting & Fining" of beer
Printed form, manuscript
August 1, 1768
Ink on paper, red wax seal
13 x 8 1/4 in. (33 x 21 cm.)

Sentence transporting Richard Golding "to his Majesty's Plantations in America"
Printed form, manuscript
June 19, 1772
Ink on paper
3 1/2 x 6 1/2 in. (9 x 17 cm.)
Gift of Amelia McLoughlin Hardin

Ephrata Cloister hymnal
Book
c. 1750
Canvas, ink on paper
8 1/8 x 6 3/4 x 1 3/8 in. (21 x 17 x 3 cm.)

Figurine of Madonna and child
French, c. 1750
Ceramic
10 1/4 in. (26 cm.)
1962.131
Gift of Mrs. O. P. Decker

Plate
Dutch, late 18th century
Ceramic
9 in. diameter (23 cm.)
1920.130
The Charles F. Gunther Collection

Plate
French, c. 1760
Ceramic
9 in. diameter (23 cm.)
1920.132
The Charles F. Gunther Collection

The Road to Revolution, 1765–75

George the III, King of Great Britain
Mezzotint after the portrait by J. Meyer
by James McCardle, 1761
Ink on paper
14 x 10 3/8 in. (36 x 26 cm.)
1937.31
Gift of Mr. Charles B. Pike

The Regulations Lately Made concerning the Colonies and the Taxes Imposed upon Them
Pamphlet
by George Grenville (London: J. Wilkie, 1765)
Ink on paper
8 1/4 x 5 1/4 in. (21 x 13 cm.)

Tax assessment list for Rowley, Massachusetts
Manuscript
1772
Ink on paper
6 1/2 x 8 in. (16 x 20 cm.)

Paper currency issued by colonial assemblies
1765–75
Ink on paper

Proclamation dismissing the General Assembly, issued by Cadwallader Colden, the royal lieutenant governor of New York
Manuscript
October 9, 1765
Ink on paper, wax seal
12 13/16 x 7 15/16 in. (32 x 20 cm.)

Order from Attwood Shute, the mayor of Philadelphia, to Sheriff James Coultas to convene the Grand Jury
Manuscript
by Attwood Shute, October 9, 1756
Ink on paper, attached seal
12 3/4 x 7 7/8 in. (32 x 20 cm.)

Letter from the Earl of Shelburne, British secretary of state, to Sir William Johnson, superintendent of Indian affairs
Manuscript
by Earl of Shelburne, June 20, 1767
Ink on paper
12 x 15 3/8 in. (30 x 39 cm.)

The Letters of Governor Hutchinson and Lieut. Governor Oliver, 2d ed.
Pamphlet
by Governor Hutchinson and Lieutenant Governor Oliver (London: J. Wilkie, 1774)
Ink on paper
8 1/4 x 5 1/4 in. (21 x 13 cm.)

Patriots Take Action

Typesetter's composing stick with reproduction type
c. 1780
Steel
7 5/8 x 1 5/8 in. (19 x 4 cm.)
1931.9
Gift of Benjamin F. Fergus

The Massachusetts Spy Or, American Oracle of Liberty, vol. v, no. 219
Newspaper, facsimile
Worcester, Massachusetts: Wednesday, May 3, 1775
Ink on paper
17 x 11 1/2 in. (43 x 29 cm.)

Dunlap's Pennsylvania Packet or, the General Advertiser, vol. v, no. 212
Newspaper
Philadelphia, Pennsylvania: Monday, November 13, 1775
Ink on paper
18 9/16 x 12 in. (47 x 30 cm.)

Sermon on Luke 4:18–19
Manuscript
by Isaiah Dunster, 1775
Ink on paper
6 x 7 1/2 in. (15 x 19 cm.)

Resolution by Boston merchants restricting the importation of British goods
Manuscript
August 1, 1768
Ink on paper
12 1/4 x 7 1/2 in. (31 x 19 cm.)

Poems, Dramatic and Miscellaneous
Book
by Mercy Otis Warren (Boston: I. Thomas & E. T. Andrews, 1790)
Ink on paper
7 1/8 x 4 1/4 in. (18 x 12 cm.)

The Bloody Massacre perpetrated in King Street, Boston on March 5th, 1770
Hand-colored engraving, 1st state
by Paul Revere, 1770
Ink on paper
10 3/8 x 9 in. (26 x 23 cm.)
1973.2
Gift of Mr. and Mrs. Theodore Tieken

Boston Massacre
Engraving, after the painting by Alonzo Chappel
by Alonzo Chappel, 1868
Ink on paper
5 3/8 x 7 1/4 in. (14 x 18 cm.)

The Bostonians in Distress
Mezzotint
by Philip Dawe, 1774
Ink on paper
13 5/8 x 9 1/4 in. (35 x 23 cm.)
1940.8
Gift of Charles B. Pike

Accounting of cash received from New York contributors for the relief of Boston's poor
Manuscript
1774–75
Ink on paper
8 1/8 x 14 3/4 in. (21 x 37 cm.)

The Destruction of Tea at Boston Harbor
Hand-colored lithograph
by Nathaniel Currier, 1846
7 5/8 x 12 3/8 in. (19 x 31 cm.)
1963.9
Gift of Mrs. Stuyvesant Peabody

Tea chest
English, c. 1775
Mahogany, tin
6 1/2 x 12 x 7 5/8 in. (17 x 30 x 19 cm.)
1944.80a-e
Gift of Dr. Leila E. Whitehead

Tea caddy
c. 1780
Tin
4 x 6 x 2 3/4 in. (10 x 15 x 7 cm.)
1958.123ab
Gift of Harriette Holt Borgeson

A New Method of Macarony Making
Mezzotint
Attributed to Philip Dawe, 1774
Ink on paper
13 1/2 x 9 7/8 in. (34 x 25 cm.)
Gift of Charles B. Pike

**The Bostonians Paying the Excise-man, or Tarring
& Feathering**
Mezzotint
Attributed to Philip Dawe, c. 1774
Ink on paper
13 3/4 x 9 7/8 in. (35 x 25 cm.)
1940.7
Gift of Charles B. Pike

The War Begins

Letter from John Jones to his "Loving Wife"
Manuscript
by John Jones, April 22, 1775
Ink on paper
7 1/2 x 12 3/8 in. (19 x 31 cm.)

Plate I: *The Battle of Lexington, April 19, 1775*
Hand-colored engraving
by Amos Doolittle, December 1775
Ink on paper
11 5/8 x 17 3/4 in. (30 x 45 cm.)
1973.1a
Gift of William McCormick Blair

Plate II: *A View of the Town of Concord*
Hand-colored engraving
by Amos Doolittle, December 1775
Ink on paper
11 5/8 x 17 3/4 in. (30 x 45 cm.)
1973.1b
Gift of William McCormick Blair

Plate III: *The Engagement at the North Bridge in
Concord*
Hand-colored engraving
by Amos Doolittle, December 1775
Ink on paper
11 5/8 x 17 3/4 in. (30 x 45 cm.)
1973.1c
Gift of William McCormick Blair

Plate IV: *A View of the South Part of Lexington*
Hand-colored engraving
by Amos Doolittle, December 1775
Ink on paper
11 5/8 x 17 3/4 in. (30 x 45 cm.)
1973.1d
Gift of William McCormick Blair

From Rebellion to Revolution

Common Sense
Pamphlet
by Thomas Paine (London: J. S. Jordan, 1791)
Ink on paper
8 3/16 x 4 1/2 in. (21 x 11 cm.)

Letter from James Cogswell to Joseph Ward
Manuscript
by James Cogswell, March 5, 1776
Ink on paper
8 1/4 x 5 7/8 in. (21 x 15 cm.)
Gift of Mrs. William T. Priestley and
Mrs. Morgan Reichner

Thomas Paine
Painting, after the 1792 painting by George
Romney
Artist unknown, date unknown
Oil on canvas
16 x 11 7/8 in. (41 x 30 cm.)
1933.43
Gift of the Thomas Paine Monument Association

Declaring Independence, 1776

*The Manner in which the American Colonies
Declared themselves Independant*
Engraving, after a drawing by Hamilton
by G. Noble, from Edward Barnard's *New, Comprehensive and Complete History of England*, 1783
Ink on paper
13 1/8 x 8 1/16 in. (33 x 20 cm.)

Legal notice announcing the Malden, Massachusetts, town meeting, "In His Majesty's Name"
Manuscript
February 19, 1773
Ink on paper
9 3/4 x 7 3/16 in. (25 x 18 cm.)

Legal notice announcing the Malden, Massachusetts, town meeting, "In the name of the Government and People of the Massachusetts State"
Manuscript
April 14, 1777
Ink on paper
12 1/2 x 7 1/2 in. (32 x 19 cm.)

Thomas Jefferson
Painting, after the painting by Bass Otis, 1815
Artist unknown, date unknown
Oil on canvas
36 1/2 x 28 1/2 in. (93 x 72 cm.)
1923.2
Gift of the Iroquois Club of Chicago

John Adams
Painting, after the painting by Gilbert Stuart by George P. A. Healy, 1860
Oil on canvas
30 1/4 x 25 1/4 in. (77 x 64 cm.)
1924.10
Gift of Mrs. Lysander Hill

Declaration of Independence, first printing, first state
Broadside
Printed by John Dunlap, Philadelphia, Pennsylvania, July 4, 1776
Ink on paper
18 1/2 x 14 11/16 in. (47 x 37 cm.)
1983.039.1
Gift of the Frederick Henry Prince Trusts

Pulling Down the Statue of George III
Engraving in line and stipple, after the painting by Johannes Oertel
by John McRae, c. 1860
Ink on paper
20 x 30 3/8 in. (51 x 77 cm.)
1920.803
The Charles F. Gunther Collection

Winning the War

Cartridge box
c. 1775
Leather, wood
7 x 8 x 3 in. (18 x 20 x 8 cm.)
1920.1730
The Charles F. Gunther Collection

Tinderbox with flint
c. 1775
Iron
5/8 x 2 1/2 x 1 1/2 in. (2 x 6 x 4 cm.)
1920.272ab
The Charles F. Gunther Collection

Canteen for water or rum
c. 1775
Wood
7 in. diameter (18 cm.)
x.1470

Drum
Date unknown
Wood, rope, leather
16 x 15 3/4 in. diameter (41 x 40 cm.)
1920.1653
The Charles F. Gunther Collection

Fife
Date unknown
Brass
13 x 5/8 in. diameter (33 x 2 cm.)
1926.155
Gift of Mr. Bradford Leadbeater

American long rifle, .52 caliber
c. 1780
Maple, brass
62 1/2 in. length (159 cm.)
1969.150
Gift of Charles R. Walgreen, Jr.

American long rifle, .52 caliber
c. 1780
Wood, brass
62 1/2 in. length (159 cm.)
1920.1652
The Charles F. Gunther Collection

New England fowler, .80 caliber
c. 1770
Walnut, iron, brass
59 1/2 in. length (151 cm.)
1920.1371
The Charles F. Gunther Collection

British-American musket, .75 caliber
c. 1775
Oak, tiger-striped
58 1/2 in. length (149 cm.)
1920.1390
The Charles F. Gunther Collection

Soldiers

Portrait & Uniform of An American General. A real representation of the Dress of An American Rifle-man, from Edward Barnard's *New, Comprehensive and Complete History of England*
Engraving
1783
Ink on paper
8 1/2 x 13 1/2 in. (22 x 34 cm.)

Roster of enlisted men, Tryon County, New York
Manuscript
July 16, 1775
Ink on paper
12 7/8 x 8 1/2 in. (33 x 22 cm.)

Act of the Connecticut General Assembly to fill the state's quota of soldiers for the Continental army
Broadside
February 21, 1781
Ink on paper
13 x 8 3/8 in. (33 x 21 cm.)

Certificate for land due John Barnes
Printed form, manuscript
March 1, 1785
Ink on paper
3 1/2 x 6 1/2 in. (9 x 17 cm.)

Powder horn
by James Pike, March 12, 1776
Cow horn, wood
14 1/4 in. (36 cm.)
1933.33
Gift of Charles B. Pike

Powder horn
by Ira West, September 1775
Cow horn, wood
15 1/2 in. (40 cm.)
1920.522
The Charles F. Gunther Collection

Powder horn
by Nathan Plummer, 1777
Cow horn, wood
14 3/4 in. (37 cm.)
1920.509
The Charles F. Gunther Collection

Powder horn
by Jonathan Dibble, 1775
Cow horn, wood
12 1/2 in. (32 cm.)
1920.510
The Charles F. Gunther Collection

The Home Front

Short swords
c. 1770
Steel, horn, iron, walnut
25 in. (63 cm.)
1920.1554
25 in. (63 cm.)
1920.833
25 in. (63 cm.)
1920.828
The Charles F. Gunther Collection

Bullet mold, .50 caliber
c. 1780
Brass
5 1/2 in. (14 cm.)
1951.430

Bullet mold
c. 1780
Steel
41 1/2 in. (105 cm.)
Gift of Emma C. Lauth

Kettle
Date unknown
Iron
6 1/2 x 9 in. (17 x 23 in.)

Ladle
c. 1780
Pewter, brass
17 in. (43 cm.)
1931.39
Gift of Otto L. Schmidt

Receipt for tools sent by Mark Bird to Col. Jonathan Mifflin at Valley Forge
Manuscript
December 22, 1777
Ink on paper
8 x 8 1/4 in. (20 x 21 cm.)

Act of the Connecticut General Assembly to procure flour and grain for the troops
Broadside
October 2, 1779
Ink on paper
16 3/4 x 13 1/8 in. (43 x 33 cm.)

Scale of Depreciation, Agreeable to an Act of the (now) Commonwealth of Massachusetts, passed September 29, 1780
Broadside
1780
Ink on paper
10 x 3 7/8 in. (25 x 10 cm.)

Pocket scale
English, c. 1760
Brass, wood
1/2 x 5 5/8 x 1 in. (1 x 14 x 3 cm.)
1920.271
The Charles F. Gunther Collection

Continental currency
1775–83
Ink on paper

Esther De Berdt
Engraving from *The Women of the American Revolution*, vol. I, by Elizabeth F. Ellet (New York: Baker and Scribner, 1848)
Ink on paper
7 7/8 x 5 in. (20 x 13 cm.)

Petition of Elizabeth Ferguson to the Supreme Executive Council of Pennsylvania
Manuscript
June 26, 1778
Ink on paper
12 3/4 x 8 in. (32 x 20 cm.)

African-Americans

Poems on Various Subjects Religious and Moral
Pamphlet
by Phillis Wheatley (Albany, reprinted from the London edition: Barber and Southwick, 1793)
Ink on paper
7 1/2 x 5 3/8 in. (19 x 14 cm.)

Memoir and Poems of Phillis Wheatley, A Native African and a Slave, 2d edition
Book
by Phillis Wheatley (Boston: Light & Horton, 1835)
Ink on paper
6 x 3 1/2 in. (15 x 9 cm.)

The Colored Patriots of the American Revolution
Book
by William C. Nell (Boston: R. F. Wallcut, 1855)
Ink on paper
7 11/16 x 4 1/2 in. (20 x 11 cm.)

Battle of Bunker Hill, June 17, 1775
Painting
by Alonzo Chappel, 1859
Oil on canvas
15 5/8 x 11 3/4 in. (40 x 30 cm.)
x.34

Letter from David Lyman to Col. Henry Jackson requesting that his slave Fortune be prevented from reenlisting in Jackson's regiment
Manuscript
by David Lyman, June 5, 1779
Ink on paper
12 7/8 x 8 1/4 in. (33 x 21 cm.)

American Indians

Transcribed speech of Mingo leader Logan (Tah-gah-jute) to Lord Dunmore, the governor of Virginia
Manuscript
1774
Ink on paper
9 x 7 1/4 in. (23 x 18 cm.)

Half armlet
by Joseph Richardson, Sr., c. 1765
Silver
2 3/4 x 4 in. (7 x 10 cm.)
x.260
Helen Drake Collection

Joseph Tayadaneega called the Brant
Engraving, after the painting by George Romney
by J. R. Smith, 1779
Ink on paper
19 3/4 x 13 7/8 in. (50 x 35 cm.)
1957.406
Gift of J. R. Anderson

Military commission designating Tewaghtah-kothe as "captain of the Indians," issued by the United States Congress
Printed form, manuscript
June 5, 1779
Ink on paper, wax seal attached
6 3/8 x 11 5/8 in. (16 x 30 cm.)

Speeches of the Oneida chiefs to Israel Chapin, deputy agent of Indian affairs for the United States government
Manuscript
September 29, 1792
Ink on paper
12 1/2 x 7 3/4 in. (32 x 20 cm.)

Letter from George Rogers Clark
Manuscript
by George Rogers Clark, November 13, 1782
Ink on paper
7 3/4 x 6 1/4 in. (20 x 16 cm.)

Terms of surrender of Fort Sackville, agreed to by Henry Hamilton, lieutenant governor of Canada and commander of British forces at Vincennes, Indiana
Manuscript
February 24, 1779
Ink on paper
11 15/16 x 7 5/16 in. (30 x 19 cm.)

Seamen

Cutlass
by Richard Gridley, 1776–77
Steel, wood
29 1/2 in. (75 cm.)
1920.265
The Charles F. Gunther Collection

Quadrant of reflection
by Clark Elliott, New London, Connecticut, 1784
Ebony, brass, ivory
17 1/8 x 14 3/4 in. (43 x 37 cm.)
1941.2
Gift of Dr. Robert E. Graves

Bosun's whistles
Dates unknown
Metal
5 in. (13 cm.)
1920.1731
5 in. (13 cm.)
x.1471

Fids, thimble, and case
Dates unknown

Fid
Bone
17 3/4 in. (45 cm.)
1942.76
Gift of Mrs. Charles B. Pike

Fid
Bone
6 1/4 in. (16 cm.)
1942.77
Gift of Mrs. Charles B. Pike

Fid
Bone
4 1/2 in. (11 cm.)
1942.163.2
Gift of Mrs. Charles B. Pike

Thimble
Bone
3/4 in. (2 cm.)
x.1469

Fid case
Twine
7 in. (18 cm.)
1942.163.1
Gift of Mrs. Charles B. Pike

Dagger and sheath presented to John Paul Jones
French, 1779
Silver, ivory
9 in. (23 cm.)
1952.235ab
Gift of Mrs. Joseph M. Cudahy

Letter from William Warner to his "Honoured Parents"
Manuscript
by William Warner, May 16, 1777
Ink on paper
8 3/4 x 6 3/4 in. (22 x 17 cm.)

The Memorable Engagement of Captn. Pearson of the Serapis, with John Paul Jones of the Bonhomme Richard & His Squadron, Sep. 23, 1779
Hand-colored engraving, after the painting by Richard Paton
by Lerpiniere and Fittler, 1780
Ink on paper
19 1/4 x 23 3/4 in. (49 x 60 cm.)
1940.31
Gift of Charles B. Pike

Account of prize money paid to the crews of the *Bonhomme Richard* and the *Alliance*
Manuscript
February 23, 1780
Ink on paper
14 3/4 x 18 1/2 in. (37 x 47 cm.)

Sketch of American flags
Painting
Dutch, artist unknown, 1779
Watercolor
13 1/8 x 8 3/16 in. (33 x 21 cm.)
1920.321
The Charles F. Gunther Collection

Europeans in the American Cause

Major General Baron Steuben
Stipple engraving, after Benoit Louis Prevost, after Pierre Eugene Du Simitière
by B. B. Ellis, 1783
6 1/16 x 4 1/2 in. (15 x 11 cm.)
Gift of Vincent Bendix

Sword and scabbard
European, c. 1765
Steel, leather, brass, bone
26 3/4 in. (68 cm.)
1920.266ab
The Charles F. Gunther Collection

Regulations for the Order and Discipline of the Troops of the United States
Pamphlet
by Baron Friedrich von Steuben, 1782
Ink on paper
6 1/2 x 4 in. (17 x 10 cm.)

Thaddeus Kosciuszko
Engraving, after the painting by Joseph Grassi
by Gabriel Fiesinger, 1798
17 x 14 1/2 in. (43 x 22 cm.)

Letter by Thaddeus Kosciuszko recommending that Ignace Zaiaczek, a fellow countryman exiled from Poland for revolutionary activities, be welcomed in France for his service to the Republic
Manuscript
by Thaddeus Kosciuszko, January 31, 1799
Ink on paper
13 1/4 x 8 1/2 in. (34 x 22 cm.)

An accounting of the men and horses in Count Casimir Pulaski's regiment of light horse
Printed form, manuscript
Printed form, manuscript
Printed by John Dunlap, Philadelphia, Pennsylvania, October 10, 1779
Ink on paper
12 1/2 x 7 7/8 in. (32 x 20 cm.)

Artillery musket
French, c. 1777
Wood, brass, steel
55 in. (140 cm.)
x.1463

Medallion of Benjamin Franklin, after a drawing by Thomas Walpole
by Giovanni Battista Nini, French, 1777
Terra-cotta
4 3/4 in. diameter (12 cm.)
1937.36
Gift of Mrs. Moise Dreyfus

Miniature of the Comte de Rochambeau
by Alexandre Alaux, c. 1875
Tempera on ivory, brass frame
2 1/2 in. diameter (6 cm.)
1938.62
Gift of Mary L. Stevenson and Alexander F. Stevenson, Jr.

Gilbert du Motiér Lafayette
Hand-colored engraving
by Levacher, 1798
Ink on paper
14 1/4 x 8 3/4 in. (36 x 22 cm.)
Gift of Mary L. Stevenson and Alexander F. Stevenson, Jr.

George Washington and His Officers

George Washington
Painting, after the painting by James Peale, after the life portrait by Charles Wilson Peale
by Charles Peale Polk, 1795
Oil on canvas
36 1/2 x 28 1/2 in. (93 x 72 cm.)
1920.171
The Charles F. Gunther Collection

Sword knot
c. 1755
Silk and metal thread
20 in. (51 cm.)
1920.292ab
The Charles F. Gunther Collection

Baldric
c. 1770
Leather
24 in. (61 cm.)
1920.1720
The Charles F. Gunther Collection

Telescope
by J. A. Chapman, English, c. 1775
Wood, brass, glass
20 1/2 in. closed; 36 in. open (52 cm.; 91 cm.)
1920.291
The Charles F. Gunther Collection

Compass
c. 1775
Brass, iron, wood, glass
2 1/8 x 2 1/8 in. (5 x 5 cm.)
1920.293
The Charles F. Gunther Collection

English officer's hot-water plate, stamped on bottom: "26th Regt. - SPODE - 3504"
by Josiah Spode, English, c. 1776
Ceramic
9 1/2 in. diameter (24 cm.)
1941.193
Gift of Marie de Besche

Canteen
c. 1785
Wood, pewter, leather
5 5/8 in. diameter (14 cm.)
1920.701
The Charles F. Gunther Collection

Saddlebags
c. 1775
Leather
18 1/2 in. (47 cm.)
1920.1729
The Charles F. Gunther Collection

Dueling pistols
by Henry Knock, English, c. 1790
Steel, brass, wood
14 1/2 in. (37 cm.)
1920.82ab
The Charles F. Gunther Collection

Spurs
c. 1777
Iron, leather
5 in.; 3 in. heel width (13 cm.; 8 cm.)
1920.270ab
The Charles F. Gunther Collection

Account of the Battle of Brandywine
Manuscript with drawing
by George Weedon, September 11, 1777
Ink on paper
15 7/8 x 12 3/8 in. (40 x 31 cm.)

Victory and Peace

The Commissioners
Hand-colored etching
by M. Darly, 1778
Ink on paper
8 1/4 x 12 1/4 in. (21 x 31 cm.)
Gift of Charles B. Pike

Bowles's New Pocket Map of the United States of America
Map
by Carington Bowles (London, 1784)
Ink on paper
21 1/2 x 28 in. (54 x 71 cm.)

Flute
by Richard Potter, English, 1776
Mahogany, ivory, silver, brass
24 3/4 in. (62 cm.)
1920.274
The Charles F. Gunther Collection

Surrender of the British Army commanded by Lord Count Cornwallis to the Combined Armies of the United States of America and France . . . at Yorktown, Virginia, the 19th of October, 1781
Hand-colored etching
by Mondhare, c. 1782
Ink on paper
13 5/8 x 20 5/8 in. (34 x 52 cm.)
1928.22
Gift of Charles B. Pike

The Constitution and the Bill of Rights, 1787–91

The Papers of James Madison
Book
Henry D. Gilpin, ed. (New York: J. and H. G. Langley, 1841)
Ink on paper
8 x 5 1/2 in. (20 x 14 cm.)

The Federalist
Book
by James Madison, Alexander Hamilton, and John Jay (New York: J. and A. McLean, 1788)
Ink on paper
5 1/2 x 3 1/2 in. (14 x 9 cm.)

The Debates in the Several State Conventions on the Adoption of the Federal Constitution 2d ed., vol. 2
Book
by Jonathan Elliot (Washington: Taylor & Maury, 1854)
Ink on paper
8 x 5 1/2 in. (20 x 14 cm.)

James Madison, Esq.
Hand-colored stipple engraving, after the painting by Gilbert Stuart
by W. R. Jones, 1814
Ink on paper
9 3/8 x 7 1/8 in. (24 x 18 cm.)

Alexander Hamilton
Stipple engraving, after the painting by Ezra Ames
by W. S. Leney, 1810
Ink on paper
5 1/16 x 4 3/16 in. (13 x 11 cm.)

John Jay Esq., late Chief Justice of the United States
Stipple engraving, after the painting by Gilbert Stuart
by W. S. Leney, 1789
Ink on paper
8 13/16 x 5 3/8 in. (22 x 14 cm.)

Patrick Henry
Stipple engraving, after the painting by J. B. Longacre, after an anonymous miniature
by E. Wellmore, nineteenth century
Ink on paper
10 3/16 x 6 11/16 in. (26 x 17 cm.)

Elbridge Gerry
Stipple engraving, after a drawing by John Vanderlyn, from *Biography of the Signers to the Declaration of Independence*, vol. 8 (Philadelphia, 1827)
by J. B. Longacre, c. 1827
Ink on paper
10 7/16 x 8 6/8 in. (27 x 22 cm.)

Samuel Adams
Engraving, after a drawing by J. B. Longacre, after a painting by J. S. Copley
by G. F. Storm, mid-nineteenth century
Ink on paper
10 3/8 x 6 7/8 in. (26 x 17 cm.)

Pennsylvania Packet and Daily Advertiser
Newspaper
Published by John Dunlap and David C. Claypoole, Philadelphia, Pennsylvania, September 19, 1787, no. 2690
Ink on paper
16 x 23 in. (41 x 58 cm.)
Gift of the Rice Foundation in Memory of Daniel and Ada Rice

Journal of the First Session of the Senate of the United States of America
Book
(New York: Thomas Greenleaf, 1789)
Ink on paper
13 x 8 in. (33 x 20 cm.)
Gift of Mr. and Mrs. Edgar J. Uihlein

The Republic in Action

Letter from Isaac Backus to Lewis Lunford
Manuscript
by Isaac Backus, June 1, 1791
Ink on paper
7 1/2 x 12 1/2 in. (19 x 32 cm.)

Account book
by Jason Dunster, tax collector for Mason, New Hampshire, 1823
Ink on paper
5 1/8 x 8 in. (13 x 20 cm.)

Congressional Pugilists
Engraving
Artist unknown, 1798
Ink on paper
6 3/8 x 8 5/8 in. (16 x 22 cm.)

The Speeches . . . of Mr. Van Ness, Mr. Caines, the Attorney-General, Mr. Harrison, and General Hamilton, in the Great Cause of the People, against Harry Croswell, on an indictment for a Libel on Thomas Jefferson
Pamphlet
(New York: G. & R. Waite, 1804)
Ink on paper
7 1/2 x 5 in. (19 x 13 cm.)

Stephens's Philadelphia Directory for 1796
Book
(Philadelphia: Thomas Stephens, 1796)
Ink on paper
6 1/8 x 3 1/2 in. (16 x 9 cm.)

George Washington, Esq., President of the United States of America
Mezzotint
by Edward Savage, 1793
Ink on paper
18 x 3 7/8 in. (46 x 35 cm.)

Suit worn by George Washington at his second inauguration, 1793
Coat, waistcoat, and breeches reproduced from the original in the collection of the Chicago Historical Society (1920.304)
Silk velvet
45 in. length of coat (114 cm.)
1958.180abc
Gift of Hart, Schaffner & Marx

Suit worn by John Adams; coat, waistcoat, and breeches
c. 1780
Silk velvet, silk faille, cotton, linen, and wool lining fabrics
42 in. length of coat (107 cm.)
1946.15ab
Gift of Mrs. Randolph G. Owsley

Suit worn by John Adams; coat, waistcoat, and breeches
c. 1780
Silk voided uncut velvet, cotton, linen, and wool lining fabrics
40 in. length of coat (102 cm.)
1946.16abc
Gift of Mrs. Randolph G. Owsley

Republican Principles in Every Home

The President's Address to the People of the United States, Announcing his design of retiring from Public Life, at the Expiration of the present Constitutional Term of the Presidentship, first printing
by George Washington (Philadelphia, 1796)
Pamphlet
Ink on paper
7 1/2 x 5 1/2 in. (19 x 14 cm.)
Gift of the Guild of the Chicago Historical Society

Speech delivered by Thomas Jefferson, President of the United States, at his Inauguration
Broadside
by Thomas Jefferson, 1801
Ink on silk
21 5/8 x 11 1/8 in. (55 x 28 cm.)

Pitcher, transfer print decoration with the slogans: "Success to AMERICA whose MILITIA is better than Standing ARMIES," / "May its Citizens Emulate Soldiers and its Soldiers HEROES"
Liverpool, England, c. 1800
Ceramic
9 x 6 1/2 in. diameter (23 x 17 cm.)
1920.226
The Charles F. Gunther Collection

Pitcher, transfer print decoration with the slogans "PEACE PLENTY AND INDEPENDENCE" and "Spring"
Liverpool, England, c. 1800
Ceramic
7 1/2 x 6 in. diameter (19 x 15 cm.)
1920.222
The Charles F. Gunther Collection

Pitcher, transfer print with the slogan "Hail Columbia happy land. . . . The rights of man shall be our boast / And Jefferson our favorite toast."
Liverpool, England, c. 1800
Ceramic
7 1/4 x 7/12 in. diameter (18 x 19 cm.)
1920.223
The Charles F. Gunther Collection

Pitcher, transfer print with the slogans "Washington in Glory," "America in Tears," "PEACE / AND / INDEPENDENCE," "E. Pluribus Unum"
Liverpool, England, c. 1800
Ceramic
12 x 8 in. diameter (30 x 20 cm.)
1920.229
The Charles F. Gunther Collection

The Will of the Majority

The Gerry-Mander: or, Essex South District formed into a Monster!!
Broadside with woodcut
by Elkanah Tisdale, 1812
Ink on paper
18 x 7 5/8 in. (46 x 19 cm.)
Gift of J. M. Ryatt

To the Citizens of Anne Arundel County, Loyd Dorsey announces to his fellow citizens that he is a candidate for the Maryland General Assembly
Broadside
November 12, 1801
Ink on paper
10 1/2 x 6 1/2 in. (27 x 17 cm.)

Endorsement of Federalist candidates for political office in Rhode Island
Broadside
April 3, 1811
Ink on paper
13 1/4 x 8 1/2 in. (34 x 22 cm.)

New York Journal and Patriotic Register, a Republican paper
Newspaper
Wednesday, August 21, 1793
Ink on paper
19 1/4 x 11 3/4 in. (49 x 30 cm.)

Boston Gazette, a Federalist paper
Newspaper
Thursday, March 17, 1814
Ink on paper
19 3/4 x 13 in. (50 x 33 cm.)

Der Friedens Bothe (The messenger of peace), a German-language paper, "independent in politics"
Newspaper
Bucks County, Pennsylvania, March 14, 1816
Ink on paper
18 1/2 x 11 1/2 in. (47 x 29 cm.)

Proposals for Printing by Subscription, a Weekly News-Paper, Intituled "The Virginia Gazette, and Hobb's Hole Advertiser"
Broadside
January 1, 1787
Ink on paper
13 5/8 x 8 1/4 in. (35 x 21 cm.)

Women in the New Republic

Washington's reception on the Bridge at Trenton in 1789 on his way to be Inaugurated 1st Prest. of the U.S.
Engraving, after design by J. L. Morton
by T. Kelley, 1845
Ink on paper
4 7/8 x 7 1/4 in. (12 x 18 cm.)

"The Ladies Patriotic Song"
Sheet music
Boston, 1799
Ink on paper
12 7/8 x 18 1/2 in. (33 x 47 cm.)

Lansingburgh Academy
Broadside announcing the establishment of new Classical, Commercial, and Ladies' departments
Lansingburgh, New York, 1821
Ink on paper
12 x 7 in. (30 x 18 cm.)

The Lady's Magazine and Repository of Entertaining Knowledge, by a Literary Society, vol. I
Bound magazine
(Philadelphia: W. Gibbons, 1792)
Ink on paper
8 3/4 x 5 1/2 in. (22 x 14 cm.)

Maria Erwin's workbox
c. 1785
Painted tin
4 3/4 x 7 3/8 x 9 1/4 in. (12 x 19 x 24 cm.)
1974.35ab
Gift of Anne Williamson and Mrs. John Paul Welling

A New and Easy Introduction To the Art of Analytical Penmanship
Book
by James Carver (Philadelphia: W. Hall, Jr., & G. W. Pierie, 1809)
Ink on paper
8 1/4 x 6 1/2 in. (21 x 17 cm.)

Arithmetic notebook belonging to Elizabeth Braswell
Bound manuscript
1819
Ink on paper
12 1/2 x 8 in. (32 x 20 cm.)

The Young Lady's Accidence: Or, a Short and Easy Introduction to English Grammar, 14th edition
Book
by Caleb Bingham (Boston: E. Lincoln, 1803)
Ink on paper
5 1/4 x 3 1/4 in. (13 x 8 cm.)

Geography for Beginners
Book
by Emma Willard (Hartford: O. D. Cooke & Co., 1826)
Ink on paper
5 7/8 x 3 1/2 in. (15 x 9 cm.)

African Americans: Free and Unfree

Schedule of the 1790 United States census
Printed form, manuscript
October 24, 1791
Ink on paper
10 x 6 3/4 in. (25 x 17 cm.)

Slave-hiring badge issued for a "servant" in Charleston, South Carolina
by John Lafar, 1812
Copper
2 x 2 in. (5 x 5 cm.)
1920.5
The Charles F. Gunther Collection

Reward announced for Arch, a runaway slave
Broadside posted by Ignatious Davis in Frederick County, Maryland
September 7, 1791
Ink on paper
9 1/4 x 7 7/8 in. (23 x 20 cm.)

Manumission certificate emancipating forty-three-year-old Dinah from slavery
Manuscript
Signed by Robert Carter, January 2, 1792, Nomini Hall, Virginia
Ink on paper
7 3/4 x 4 1/8 in. (20 x 10 cm.)

An Act for the Gradual Abolition of Slavery
Broadside
New Jersey General Assembly, February 15, 1804
Ink on paper
10 x 8 3/4 in. (25 x 22 cm.)

Tape loom
c. 1790
Wood
13 x 6 1/2 x 18 1/2 in. (33 x 17 x 47 cm.)
1920.1304
The Charles F. Gunther Collection

Note from Hannah the weaver to her master Robert Carter
Manuscript
by Hannah [Harris], April 5, 1792, Westmoreland County, Virginia
Ink on paper
4 3/4 x 4 1/4 in. (12 x 11 cm.)

List of emigrants leaving Norfolk, Virginia, for Liberia, Africa, on board the brig *Nautilus*
Manuscript
January 20, 1821
Ink on paper
9 3/4 x 7 3/4 in. (25 x 20 cm.)

Promoting the Useful Arts

Letter from Thomas Jefferson to Robert Mills
Manuscript
by Thomas Jefferson, September 25, 1822
Ink on paper
7 5/16 x 7 1/4 in. (19 x 18 cm.)
1973.69
Gift of Adlai E. Stevenson III

Pitcher, transfer print decorations with the slogans: "E. Pluribus Unum," and "May success attend our Agriculture/Trade and Manufactures"
Liverpool, England, 1800
Ceramic
6 3/4 x 7 1/4 in. diameter (17 x 18 cm.)
1920.230
The Charles F. Gunther Collection

Notes on the State of Virginia, 2d American edition
Book
by Thomas Jefferson (Philadelphia: Matthew Carey, November 12, 1794)
Ink on paper
8 5/16 x 5 1/2 in. (21 x 14 cm.)

First patent granted by the United States government, issued to Samuel Hopkins for a new process to produce pearl and potash
Manuscript
July 31, 1790
Ink on parchment, attached seal
16 1/8 x 18 3/16 in. (41 x 46 cm.)

National Utility in Opposition to Political Controversy: Addressed to the Friends of American Manufactures . . . Letter from Benjamin Austin, Esq. to the Honorable Thomas Jefferson . . . Mr. Jefferson's Answer.
Broadside
(Boston: Rowe & Hooper, 1816)
Ink on paper
21 9/16 x 16 7/8 in. (55 x 43 cm.)

Letter from Eli Whitney to his brother Josiah
Manuscript
by Eli Whitney, February 13, 1798
Ink on paper
8 x 12 7/8 in. (20 x 33 cm.)

Eli Whitney
Stipple engraving, after the portrait by C. B. King
by David C. Hinman, c. 1847
Ink on paper
8 x 6 in. (20 x 15 cm.)

Bandanna, "A Geographical View of all the Post Towns in the United States of America"
Scottish, 1815
Cotton
19 x 24 1/2 in. (48 x 62 cm.)
1920.751
The Charles F. Gunther Collection

Advertisement for stagecoaches reproduced from *The New York Journal & Patriotic Register*
Newspaper
August 21, 1793
Ink on paper
4 1/4 x 2 1/4 in. (11 x 6 cm.)

Mail bag
c. 1800
Wool, leather
23 x 17 in. (58 x 43 cm.)
1923.97
Gift of Charles B. Pike, Eugene R. Pike, and William W. Pike

The Republic Moves West

An Ordinance for the Government of the Territory of the United States, North-West of the River Ohio, **1st printing**
Folio
July 13, 1787
Ink on paper
12 7/8 x 8 1/8 in. (33 x 21 cm.)
Gift of Mr. and Mrs. Theodore Tieken

Letter from Edward Coles to James Madison
Manuscript
by Edward Coles, July 20, 1819
Ink on paper
10 x 16 in. (25 x 41 cm.)

A Map of the United States and Canada, New Scotland, New Brunswick, and New Foundland
Map
(Paris: P.A.F. Tardieu, 1806)
Ink on paper
35 1/2 x 31 1/4 in. (90 x 79 cm.)

Travels in the Interior Parts of America
Book
by Captains Lewis and Clark, Dr. Sibley, and Mr. Dunbar (London, 1807)
Ink on paper
9 1/8 x 6 in. (23 x 15 cm.)

Land for Settlers

Letter from Uriah Chapman to his grandson, Chapman Forseth
Manuscript
by Uriah Chapman, December 19, 1803
Ink on paper
10 1/4 x 8 5/8 in. (26 x 22 cm.)

Plow
c. 1760
Wood, iron
80 in. length (203 cm.)
1934.90
Gift of A. Watson Armour II

Double oxen yoke
c. 1810
Wood, iron
40 in. length (102 cm.)
1941.187abc
Gift of Daniel P. Trude

Plat of the Seven Ranges of Townships being part of the Territory of the United States N.W. of the River Ohio which by a late act of Congress are directed to be sold
Engraving
by W. Barker (Philadelphia: Matthew Carey, 1796)
Ink on paper
24 1/2 x 14 in. (62 x 36 cm.)

Military land grant issued to John Transway
Printed form, manuscript
November 5, 1817
Ink on paper, with pen inscriptions
8 3/4 x 11 1/2 in. (22 x 29 cm.)

Sale of the Deserts of Scioto by the Anglo-Americans
Engraving
Artist unknown, 1799
Ink on paper
9 1/4 x 11 in. (23 x 28 cm.)

Announcement of a meeting of the Asylum Company officers
Broadside
1794
Ink on paper
16 x 9 7/8 in. (41 x 25 cm.)

The Emigrant's Guide to the United States of America
Book
by Robert Holditch (London: William Hone, 1818)
Ink on paper
9 x 5 1/2 in. (23 x 14 cm.)

Traveller's Directory through the United States, inscribed on flyleaf: "D. Armour," manuscript notations throughout by itinerant Methodist preacher
Book
by John Melish (Philadelphia, 1818)
Ink on paper
6 3/16 x 4 in. (16 x 10 cm.)

Box
c. 1800
Wood
7 x 14 5/8 x 7 in. (18 x 37 x 18 cm.)
1933.131
Gift of Miss Frances Stryker

Tea set (cup, saucer, and teapot)
English, c. 1820
Porcelain
1936.227ab,ef
Gift of Mrs. Mary Hobson Crenshaw

Doll
c. 1818
Wood
8 in. (20 cm.)
x.1476

Displacing the American Indians

Proclamation of protection for Kaskaskia Indians, signed by George Washington
Broadside
May 7, 1793
Ink on paper
23 1/2 x 19 7/8 in. (60 x 50 cm.)

Peace medal
by Joseph Richardson, Jr., 1793
Silver
5 1/4 x 3 1/8 in. (13 x 8 cm.)
1920.1295
The Charles F. Gunther Collection

Peace medal
by Joseph Richardson, Jr., 1793
Silver
7 3/16 x 5 in. (18 x 13 cm.)
1920.1294
The Charles F. Gunther Collection

Breastplate
by A. and J. Scrymgeour, 1820
Silver
8 1/4 in. diameter (21 cm.)
x.253

Sa-go-ye-wat-ha (Red Jacket)
Engraving, after the painting by R. W. Weir
by Mosely Danforth, date unknown
Ink on paper
5 x 3 1/2 in. (13 x 9 cm.)

Indian Treaty of Greenville, 1795
Painting
Artist unknown, 1795
Oil on canvas
21 7/8 x 27 in. (56 x 69 cm.)
1914.1
Gift of LaVerne Noyes

Treaty of Greenville, 1st printing
Folios
1795
Ink on paper
13 1/2 x 8 1/4 in. (34 x 21 cm.)

Ta-ma-kake-toke, Woman that Spoke First, A Chippeway Squaw
Lithograph, after painting by James Otto Lewis
by F. Barincou for George Lehman and Peter S. Duval, 1835
Ink on paper
18 x 12 in. (46 x 30 cm.)

Chippeway Squaw
Lithograph, after painting by James Otto Lewis
by F. Barincou for George Lehman and Peter S.
Duval, 1835
Ink on paper
18 x 12 in. (46 x 30 cm.)

*The Pipe Dance and the Tomahawk Dance of the
Chippeway Tribe*
Lithograph, after painting by James Otto Lewis
by F. Barincou for George Lehman and Peter S.
Duval, 1835
Ink on paper
11 1/16 x 18 in. (28 x 46 cm.)

Pipe tomahawk
c. 1770
Hand-forged steel; reproduction stem
6 3/4 in. length of head (17 cm.)
x.1202

Tens-qua-ta-wa, Shawnese Prophet
Lithograph, after painting by James Otto Lewis
by F. Barincou for George Lehman and Peter S.
Duval, 1835
Ink on paper
17 3/4 x 12 in. (45 x 30 cm.)

*A View of Col. Johnson's Engagement with the
Savages*
Colored wood engraving
by Nathaniel Dearborn, from *History of the Indian
Wars*, 1846
Ink on paper
6 x 13 1/4 in. (15 x 34 cm.)
1920.686
The Charles F. Gunther Collection

Creating an American Culture

Letter from John Adams to Joseph Ward
Manuscript
by John Adams, June 6, 1809
Ink on paper
8 7/8 x 7 1/4 in. (23 x 18 cm.)
Gift of Mrs. William T. Priestley and
Mrs. Morgan Reichner

Letter from Noah Webster to his publishers
Manuscript
by Noah Webster, January 3, 1806
Ink on paper
7 13/16 x 6 3/8 in. (20 x 16 cm.)
Gift of William B. Katz

Noah Webster
Engraving, after the portrait by Alonzo Chappel
Artist unknown, c. 1867
Ink on paper
7 1/2 x 5 1/2 in. (19 x 14 cm.)

*A Compendious Dictionary of the English
Language*
Book
by Noah Webster (Hartford: Sidney's Press, 1806)
Ink on paper
7 1/8 x 4 in. (18 x 10 cm.)

The American Spelling Book, **Thomas and
Andrews's 5th edition**
Book
by Noah Webster (Boston: Isaiah Thomas and
Ebenezer T. Andrews, 1793)
Ink on paper
6 3/4 x 3 1/2 in. (17 x 9 cm.)

*Memoirs of Andrew Sherburne: A Pensioner of the
Navy of the Revolution*
Book
by Andrew Sherburne (Utica: William Williams,
1828)
Ink on paper
7 1/4 x 4 1/4 in. (18 x 11 cm.)

*The Adventures of Ebenezer Fox in the Revolu-
tionary War*
Book
by Ebenezer Fox (Boston: Charles Fox, 1848)
Ink on paper
6 3/8 x 3 1/2 in. (16 x 9 cm.)

*The Female Review. Life of Deborah Sampson. the
female soldier in the War of the Revolution*, 2d
edition
Book
by Herman Mann (Boston: J. K. Wiggins & W. P.
Lunt, 1866)
Ink on paper
11 7/8 x 9 in. (30 x 23 cm.)

**Box with tea claimed to have been taken by
David Kennison at the Boston Tea Party**
Nineteenth century
Brass, glass, tea
3 1/4 x 5 x 3 1/2 in. (8 x 13 x 9 cm.)
x.108

**Affidavit signed by David Kennison attesting to
the authenticity of his "historic" tea**
Manuscript
November 17, 1848
Ink on paper
4 3/4 x 7 3/4 in. (12 x 20 cm.)

Washington Becomes a Legend

Mourning piece for George Washington
Stipple and line engraving after a design by John Coles, Jr.
by Enoch G. Gridley, c. 1800
Ink on paper
13 x 8 7/8 in. (33 x 23 cm.)

Commemorative pitcher, transfer print with the words: "Washington in Glory, America in Tears" and "Apotheosis"
Liverpool, England, c. 1800
Ceramic
10 1/4 x 11 1/2 in. diameter (26 x 30 cm.)
1940.14
Gift of Charles B. Pike

The Life of George Washington, **23d edition**
Book
by Mason Locke Weems (Philadelphia: M. Carey & Son, 1820)
Ink on paper
7 x 4 1/2 in. (18 x 11 cm.)

Snuff box with miniature of George Washington
c. 1800
Brass, shell, leather, with tempera miniature on ivory
1 1/8 x 3 1/8 in. diameter (3 x 8 cm.)
1939.37ab
Gift of Mrs. Richard T. Crane, Jr.

Memorial handkerchief, "The Effect of Principle / Behold the Man"
British, c. 1805
Linen, printed in blue ink
11 1/4 x 11 1/4 in. (29 x 29 cm.)
1930.15
Gift of Charles B. Pike

Memorial handkerchief, "The Love of Truth Mark the Boy"
British, c. 1805
Cotton
12 1/2 x 11 1/2 in. (32 x 30 cm.)
1963.218
Gift of William B. Katz

Statue of George Washington
Artist unknown, c. 1830
Painted wood
37 in. (94 cm.)
1948.54
Gift of the estate of Mrs. Charles B. Pike

The Domestic Arts Flourish

Valentine
by G. Mitchell, May 13, 1818
Paper cut-out
12 3/4 in. diameter (32 cm.)
1941.284
Gift of Ira C. Shellenberger

Sampler
by Eliza McCoy, age 10, 1800
Linen
17 x 9 1/4 in. (43 x 23 cm.)
Gift of Robert O. Lehmann

Sampler
by Mary Newhall, age 14, 1812
Linen
23 3/4 x 20 in. (60 x 50 cm.)
1971.336
Gift of Mr. and Mrs. Roy E. Tomlinson

Sampler
by Mary Bartlett, age 11, 1810
Linen
16 1/2 x 22 1/4 in. (42 x 57 cm.)
1924.8
Gift of Mrs. Lillie Robel

Sampler
by Phebe Hetfield, 1804
Linen
12 7/8 x 7 7/8 in. (33 x 20 cm.)
1965.31
Gift of Robert O. Lehmann

Sampler
by Rachel Bucknam, 1788
Linen
4 3/4 x 15 3/4 in. (12 x 40 cm.)
x.1233

Sampler
by Susanna Lane, age 11, 1776
Linen
22 x 22 in. (56 x 56 cm.)
x.1227

Sampler
by Julia E. Townsend, 1817
Linen
23 x 10 1/2 in. (58 x 27 cm.)
1919.76
Gift of Abbey Farwell Ferry

Sampler
by Catharine Elizabeth King, age 13, 1812
Linen
16 7/8 x 18 1/2 in. (43 x 47 cm.)
1965.20
Gift of Robert O. Lehmann

Sampler
by Anna Uran, age 11, 1798
Linen
28 x 11 in. (71 x 28 cm.)
x.654

Sampler
by Harriet Rich, age 11, 1822
Linen
23 x 16 1/4 in. (58 x 41 cm.)
1965.44
Gift of Robert O. Lehmann

Sampler
by Hannah Neill, no date
Linen
22 x 18 in. (56 x 46 cm.)
1964.185

Sampler
by Rhoda Norton, 1779
Linen
14 x 13 3/4 in. (36 x 35 cm.)
1962.34
Gift of Edythe Proctor

Keepsake box
c. 1818
Wood, with painted floral decorations
8 1/4 x 12 1/2 x 8 1/4 in. (21 x 32 x 21 cm.)
1922.51ab
Calmes/Wight/Johnson Collection

Lucy Calmes Wight
Painting
Artist unknown, c. 1830
Oil on canvas
25 x 21 in. (63 x 53 cm.)
1922.13
Calmes/Wight/Johnson Collection

Sampler
by Lucy Neville Calmes, age 9, 1811
Linen
21 1/4 x 15 in. (54 x 38 cm.)
1922.22
Calmes/Wight/Johnson Collection

Coverlet
by Phebe Machin, c. 1820
Wool, cotton
92 x 62 in. (234 x 157 cm.)
1960.444
Gift of Mrs. Elbert Crosby Pendleton

Coverlet
c. 1820
Wool, cotton
72 1/2 x 81 in. (184 x 206 cm.)
1961.67
Gift of Mrs. John H. Blair

Quilt
1797
Linen
78 x 70 1/2 in. (198 x 179 cm.)
x.1031
The Charles F. Guntner Collection

Coverlet
c. 1810
Wool, cotton
75 x 86 in. (190 x 218 cm.)
1945.186
Gift of Alma Vine Day

Walking wheel used to spin yarn from wool
Date unknown
Wood
57 3/4 x 43 in. diameter of wheel (147 x 109 cm.)
1966. 269abc
Gift of the Museum of Science and Industry

Sewing box
c. 1790
Wood, leather, paper, silver
3 x 7 7/8 in. (8 x 20 cm.)
1916.5a
Gift of Mrs. Ellen E. Longder Woodward

"Housewife," or traveling sewing kit
c. 1770
Silk, wool
16 1/2 x 4 in. (42 x 10 cm.)
1920.298b

Needlework box with pincushion
c. 1820
Leather
3 1/2 x 6 x 3 in. (9 x 15 x 8 cm.)
Gift of Mrs. Henrietta Johnson Thomas

Needlework and sewing accessories
1770–1820

Lacemaking pillow
c. 1800
Cloth, wood, paper
6 x 8 1/2 in. (15 x 22 cm.)
1920.478
The Charles F. Gunther Collection

Spool
c. 1820
Ivory
3 1/2 in. (9 cm.)
1931.162b
Gift of G. F. Washburne

Darning egg
c. 1820
Wood
3 1/8 in. (8 cm.)
x.1062

Thread waxer
Date unknown
Bone
3/8 x 7/8 in. (1 x 2 cm.)
1959.401.7
Gift of the Colonial Coverlet Guild of America

Knitting needles and case
c. 1770
Steel, tin
9 x 1/2 in. diameter (32 x 1 cm.)
1920.479abc
The Charles F. Gunther Collection

Sewing bird
c. 1820
Metal
5 x 3 1/2 x 1 1/2 in. diameter (13 x 9 x 4 cm.)
1973.32
Gift of Mrs. Frank L. Sulzberger

Spool spindle
c. 1770
Wood, brass
8 x 2 1/2 in. diameter (20 x 6 cm.)
1916.9
Gift of Mrs. Ellen E. Longder Woodward

A Republican Spirit in the Crafts

Diary of Jabez Briggs, a Massachusetts farmer and wheelwright
Manuscript
by Jabez Briggs, February through May 1791
Ink on paper
7 1/2 x 6 1/8 in. (19 x 15.5 cm.)

Wheelwright's mallet
c. 1800
Wood
16 5/8 in. (42 cm.)

Carved eagle originally affixed to the stern of a ship
Artist unknown, c. 1820
Wood
32 x 96 x 8 in. (81 x 244 x 20 cm.)
1948.60
Gift of the estate of Mrs. Frances Alger Pike

A View of New Orleans taken from the Plantation of Marigny, November 1803
Painting
by Boqueto de Woieseri, 1803
Oil on canvas
58 1/2 x 90 1/2 in. (149 x 213 cm.)
1932.18
Gift of Charles B. Pike

Federal mirror
c. 1810
Glass, gilt wood
29 in. diameter (74 cm.)
1962.46abc
Gift of Mrs. Joseph Davis McNulty

Empire sofa
Western Pennsylvania, c. 1830
Mahogany, wool
33 3/4 x 93 x 24 in. (86 x 236 x 61 cm.)
1967.6

Side chair
Attributed to Samuel McIntire; Salem,
Massachusetts, c. 1800
Mahogany, black horsehair
35 1/4 x 19 x 18 in. (90 x 48 x 46 cm.)
1933.7
Gift of Mrs. Emily Crane Chadbourne

Side chair
Attributed to Duncan Phyfe workshop; New York
City, c. 1830
Mahogany, silk, and satin
37 x 17 x 16 1/2 in. (86 x 43 x 42 cm.)
1967.441

Chippendale secretary
Massachusetts, c. 1770
Walnut
44 x 43 x 24 in. (112 x 109 x 61 cm.)
1913.61
Gift of Edward A. Hill

Serving dish
by Thomas Whartenby, Philadelphia, c. 1811
Silver
6 1/2 x 15 1/2 x 10 in. (17 x 39 x 25 cm.)
1969.146

Teapot
by Joseph Richardson, Jr., Philadelphia, 1786
Silver
10 1/4 in. (26 cm.)
1960.163
Gift of the Guild of the Chicago Historical
Society

*White's Great Cattle Show, and Grand Procession
of the Victuallers of Philadelphia*
Lithograph, hand-colored, after the painting by
Lewis Krimmel
by Frederick Bourquin, c. 1845
Ink on paper
14 1/4 x 23 3/8 in. (36 x 59 cm.)
1920.778
The Charles F. Gunther Collection

**Bowl, transfer print with the motto: "The Ship-
wright's Arms"**
English, c. 1825
Ceramic
8 1/4 in. (21 cm.)
1920.115
The Charles F. Gunther Collection

**Pitcher, transfer print with the mottos: "The
Merchant-Taylors Arms" and "Concordia Parae
Res Crescunt"**
Liverpool, England, 1802
Ceramic
11 1/2 x 10 1/2 in. diameter (29 x 26 cm.)
The Charles F. Gunther Collector

**Pitcher, transfer print with picture of a sailing
ship labeled "The William and Jane" and the
motto "Success to a Good Calker" "Joseph
Chaney"**
English, c. 1810
Ceramic
10 x 9 1/2 diameter (25 x 24 cm.)
1920.118
The Charles F. Gunther Collection

**Presentation pendant in the shape of a sextant,
with the inscriptions, "N.Y. Nautical Institution / No. 37" "Peter Price 1820"**
New York, 1820
Silver
3 3/4 x 3 7/8 in. (10 x 10 cm.)
1966.284
Gift of Mrs. Medard Welch

Symbols for a New Nation

A View of the Bombardment of Fort McHenry
Aquatint
by John Bower, c. 1815
Ink on paper
13 3/4 x 18 1/2 in. (35 x 47 cm.)
1936.5
Gift of Charles B. Pike

Fort McHenry, or the Star Spangled Banner
Sheet music
Published by G. E. Blake, 1814
Ink on paper
12 1/2 x 18 1/2 in. (32 x 47 cm.)

Field drum
by Porter Blanchard, Concord, New Hampshire,
c. 1815
Wood, leather
16 1/2 x 16 in. diameter (42 x 41 cm.)
Gift of William F. Ludwig, Jr., Ludwig Drum
Company

Brother Jonathan Administering a Salutary Cordial to John Bull
Engraving
by "Yankee Doodle Scratcher" (Amos Doolittle),
1813
Ink on paper
11 1/2 x 14 3/8 in. (29 x 36 cm.)
P.D.X.651

Yankee Doodle, or the American Satan
Etching
by Joseph Wright, c. 1778
Ink on paper
6 1/8 x 4 7/16 in. (16 x 11 cm.)

Five-dollar coin
1803
Gold
15/16 in. diameter (2 cm.)
Gift of Secor Cunningham

L'Amerique
Engraving
by Pierre Aveline, c. 1750
Ink on paper
7 1/8 x 9 1/8 in. (18 x 23 cm.)

America Guided by Wisdom
Engraving, after a drawing by John J. Barralet
by Benjamin Tanner, c. 1815
Ink on paper
17 3/4 x 24 in. (45 x 61 cm.)

Freebetter's New England Almanack
Book
(New London: T. Green, 1776)
Ink on paper
6 7/8 x 4 3/8 in. (17 x 11 cm.)

Acknowledgments

This book, like the museum exhibition on which it is based, was a collaborative effort. Both projects drew upon the talents of a large number of people and the enduring support of the Chicago Historical Society.

The exhibition *We the People: Creating a New Nation, 1765–1820*, which opened in September 1987 after four years of preparation, would not have been possible without the foresight of Ellsworth Brown, president and director of the Society. He had the vision of an American history wing in a midwestern urban history museum. Brown welcomed the challenge of bringing in "outside" scholars to serve as curators and to them he granted complete curatorial freedom.

Generous grants came from the National Endowment for the Humanities, the Prince Charitable Trust, the Rice Foundation, the Chicago Tribune, and the CityArts Program of the city of Chicago's Department of Cultural Affairs. The Illinois Humanities Council provided funds for the color reproductions. Marc Hilton, vice-president of development for the Society, was instrumental in raising funds in the private sector.

There would have been neither an exhibition nor a book without Mary Janzen. She served as project director for the exhibit as well as the book, applying her keen intelligence to planning, coordinating, and troubleshooting at every phase of both projects. She supervised photography for the book, which was carried out with unfailing good cheer and great skill by John Alderson and Jay Crawford. William Jennings, Jane Regan, and Walter Krutz also contributed to the photography.

Skillful editors at the Chicago Historical Society pushed the authors to meet the challenge of writing accessible prose for the elusive general reader. Russell Lewis was chief editor for the museum text, assisted by Meg Moss, Karen Goldbaum, Aleta Zak, and Margaret Welsh. Claudia Lamm Wood as project editor of the book, assisted by Rosemary Adams, held the authors to her high standards of clarity and precision. We are indebted to our typists Clare Ruffalo, Leslie Schuster, Judy Sponsler, and Jennifer Schima.

Kitty Hannaford compiled the Exhibition Checklist that appears at the end. As curatorial assistant for the exhibition, she assumed the complicated task of tracking down numerous details and undertook much of the research about Lucy Calmes Wight.

A small corps of museum curators, past and present, played an indispensable role in locating and interpreting objects from the Society's collections: Janice McNeill, librarian; Olivia Mahoney and Sharon Darling, decorative and industrial arts; Joseph Zywicki, paintings and material culture; Grant Dean, maps; Mary Frances Rhymer, Linda Ziemer, and Maureen O'Brien Will, prints and photographs; Teresa Krutz, registrar. Conservators Carol Turchan and Anna Kolata, with assistance from Dilys Blum, Robert Weinberg, Barry Bauman, Rick Strilkey, Bill Minter, and Gary Frost, lent their skills to the exhibition. Museum educators Carole Krucoff, Nancy Lace, and Genean Stec grappled with public interpretation.

To the curators of archives and manuscripts—Archie Motley, Linda Evans, and Ralph Pugh—we owe a special debt. The lives of ordinary people can indeed be recovered, but only through the enthusiastic efforts of such thorough scholars. Linda Evans conducted a relentless search among thousands of manuscripts and uncovered many of the gems that express the thoughts of ordinary people. Ralph Pugh was indefatigable and imaginative as principal researcher in solving such mysteries as the identity of James Pike and the authorship of the wheelwright's diary.

Raw materials do not an exhibit make. Barbara Charles and Bob Staples, both creative designers, served as visual editors and helped capture the spirit of the period with sensitivity and panache. Virginia Heaven brought enthusiasm and diligence to her role as coordinator of exhibit installation. Andrew Leo and Bill Van Nimwegen provided their talents as designers, and Paul Madalinski and Walter Reinhart as preparators.

We owe a special debt to many scholars in the academic and museum world. Our official consultants were Linda Kerber of the University of Iowa; Fath Davis Ruffins of the Smithsonian's National Museum of American History; John Kaminski and Richard Leffler of the Documentary History of the Ratification of the Constitution Project, University of Wisconsin; Helen Hornbeck Tanner of the Center for the History of the American Indian at the Newberry Library; and Garry Wills of Northwestern University. Our consultants for military history were Donald Kloster and Craddock Goins of the Smithsonian Institution, and Stephen Rosswurm of Lake Forest College. Consultants reviewed our proposals, read our scripts and labels, and met with us at several stages of our work. They saved us from many errors, challenged our interpretations, and pushed us in conceptualizing the project. All were invaluable; we are especially indebted to Linda Kerber, who shared her rich scholarship in women's history with us. Barbara Clark Smith read and offered comments on a draft of the Introduction.

For both the exhibition and the book, many other scholars answered our inquiries, authenticated objects, or helped us to understand subjects. They are: Aleine Austin, John Barden, Ira Berlin, Susan Branson, Joshua Brown, Bruno Cartosio, Michael Conzen, Charles Cullen, R. David Edmunds, Shelly Foote, John Hench, John Higham, Graham Hodges, Frederick Hoxie, John Jentz, Michael Kammen, Gary Kulik, Jesse Lemish, Jay Miller, Elaine Webber Pascu, William Pretzer, Elizabeth Reilly, Barbara Clark Smith, and Elizabeth Young. Needless to say, none of our cooperating scholars is responsible for any sins of commission or omission that remain.

For helping to turn an exhibition into a book, we are indebted to Tracy Baldwin for her creative design and to many at Temple University Press: to Stephen Brier and Susan Porter Benson, who conceived the idea; to Janet Francendese, senior acquisitions editor, who had faith in it; and to Debby Stuart for her superb editing.

Terry J. Fife and Alfred F. Young

Page numbers for illustrations are indicated in *italics.* If a subject is illustrated and discussed on the same page, the illustration is not separately indicated.

Index